VEILED
SENTIMENTS

Veiled Sentiments

HONOR AND POETRY
IN A BEDOUIN SOCIETY

LILA ABU–LUGHOD

University of California Press

Berkeley & Los Angeles
London

Portions of this work originally appeared in "Honor and the Sentiments of Loss in a Bedouin Society," *American Ethnologist* 12, no. 2 (1985): 245–61, reprinted here by kind permission of the American Anthropological Association.

Photographs: Lila Abu-Lughod/Anthro-Photo

University of California Press
Berkeley and Los Angeles, California
University of California Press, Ltd.
London, England
© 1986 by
The Regents of the University of California
Printed in the United States of America
5 6 7 8 9

First paperback printing 1988

Library of Congress Cataloging-in-Publication Data

Abu-Lughod, Lila.
  Veiled sentiments.

  Bibliography: p.
  Includes index.
  1. Bedouins—Egypt—Social life and customs.
2. Folk poetry, Arabic—Egypt—History and Criticism.
3. Bedouins—Egypt—Folklore. 4. Honor—Folklore.
5. Sex customs—Egypt. 6. Women—Egypt. I. Title.
DT72.B4A28 1986 306'.089927 86–6948
ISBN 0-520-05483-0 Cloth
ISBN 0-520-06327-9 Ppbk

To my parents

CONTENTS

Contents

Contents

ACKNOWLEDGMENTS

It is impossible to thank individually the many people who have contributed directly and indirectly, in ways large and small, to this project. I am grateful to them all but want to mention some in particular.

Financial support at various stages was provided by the National Institute of Mental Health, the Association of American University Women (Marion Talbot Fellowship), the Foreign Language and Area Studies Fellowships, and later the National Resource Fellowships. A small faculty research grant and travel funds from Williams College were helpful in the final stages of my work. Farhad Kazemi, director of the Hagop Kevorkian Center for Near Eastern Studies at New York University, generously offered me the facilities that enabled me to complete the manuscript during the summer of 1985.

For support, encouragement, and critical comments and suggestions, I want to thank numerous friends, colleagues, and teachers. Some pushed me, some sent me in fruitful directions, some read version after version of what I wrote, and some simply by being enthusiastic gave me the courage to keep struggling to make sense of my material. Particularly helpful were Wendy Brown, Vincent Crapanzano, Michael M. J. Fischer, Robert A. LeVine, Catherine Lutz, Karen Ericksen Paige, Sterett Pope, Dan Rosenberg, Nur Yalman, and John and Beatrice Whiting. It is hard to imagine how this book could have come into being without them. At various points Byron and Mary-Jo Good, Dale Eickelman, Ron Jenkins, Sally Falk Moore, and Amal Rassam helped me clarify my arguments. The advice, faith, and friendship of Vicky Burbank, Silvana

Castaneda, Mitzi Goheen, Laurie Hart, Gail Hershatter, Tim Mitchell, Nadine Peacock, Barb Smuts, and Carol Ockman gave me confidence. My editor, Sheila Levine, made the process of publishing a first book surprisingly enjoyable, and Anne Canright's superb editing transformed the manuscript, which I had printed with Randall Kromm's assistance.

Without the people who recited and helped me understand the poetry that this book explores, I could not have even written it. First, of course, I owe a debt to the many Bedouin friends and "family" who recited poetry. Then Fawzi Senussi, who combined a love of traditional Bedouin folk poetry with a tremendous gift for communication, gave me my first taste of these poems' richness by introducing me to the poetic vocabulary. Kevin McGrath worked on some of the translations and suggested the format for the presentation of poems. Without the inspired and dedicated help of Mohammed B. Alwan, however, I could never have begun to translate, interpret, or even truly appreciate the poems I collected. His poetic sensibility and deep knowledge of the Arabic language opened the way for me. I take this opportunity to offer him my profound thanks for his generous help.

Anyone who has worked in Egypt knows how important those who take one under their wings can be. I want to thank Dr. Ahmed Abou-Zeid for his enthusiastic support of my project, his advice, and his kind offer to affiliate me with the Department of Anthropology and Sociology at Alexandria University. Hind Khattab, of the Social Research Center at the American University in Cairo, was my guardian angel, taking me in when I was ill, comforting me when I was discouraged, encouraging me to pursue certain questions, and offering help with the myriad details of organizing and carrying out field research. Others at the Social Research Center, in particular Atif Nada, and in the Department of Anthropology and Sociology at the American University in Cairo also contributed greatly to the success of my research. Many of these friends and colleagues contributed as well to making my stays in Cairo enjoyable, and I thank them for that.

My most profound debt is to the people in the Bedouin community in which I lived, especially the Haj and his wives and children, whose patience I no doubt taxed but who bore me with humor and warmth. They gracefully overlooked my occasional irritable outbursts and my litany of complaints about the fleas and other annoyances of desert life, only to tease me gently when I was feeling better. They accepted me into their lives, cared for me, and taught me by sharing their deepest concerns and the dramas of their everyday world. My memories of the companionship of the long winter evenings huddled around kerosene lanterns and of the moonlit summer nights graced by gentle breezes when we shuffled indoors in our plastic sandals carrying sleeping children, goatskin bags, and the tea tray, after a long, uneventful day of talking, joking, and working or a wild day of minor crises or an exhausting if exhilarating day of wedding celebrations or visiting—all are vivid. The last page of my fieldnotes reads:

> The tents, the sheep, and the goats are all sights I will miss. I am sure I will forget so much of the texture of life, the feeling at the end of the day as we put away the food and pick things up in the semidark. As I sit in my room writing, I hear the muffled sounds of children running and shouting. R. calls out to her daughter. A car approaches the house. It is a quiet life I will miss. There is no loneliness, always someone to sit with. I feel so much part of something here. I don't remember ever feeling that before.

Indeed, they taught me not only about their way of life, some small part of which I have tried to convey in this book, but also about the joys of a sociable world in which people hug and talk and shout and laugh without fear of losing one another. I hope that too comes across.

There are a few more people whose influence on my life and work has been profound. Paul Riesman introduced me to anthropology and showed me what it could be. His ideas continue to inspire me and his encouragement to give me faith. If there is any sensitivity or insight in this study, I dedicate it to him. If anyone is responsible for this book being written at all, however, it is my parents. For their belief in me, their contributions, willing and often unwitting, to this particular project, and much more that I cannot begin to detail, I thank them.

A NOTE ON
TRANSCRIPTIONS

In a work focused on other matters, it is difficult to decide how much attention to devote to explicating peculiarities of the dialect spoken by Awlad 'Ali and their Cyrenaican cousins. Since the poems I deal with in this book are composed in the dialect rather than in classical Arabic, it seems useful to lay out a few basic rules of pronunciation to help orient the reader. I have chosen a system of transcription that is a compromise between a strictly phonetic one, which would be most helpful for reproducing the sounds of the poems, and one that gives enough clues to Arabists to enable them to recognize words, and hence meanings. It may be that in choosing this middle path I will frustrate both parties, but I hope that the guidelines presented below will clarify matters. Given my focus on the social use of poetry rather than on linguistics or even poetics, I consider this rough system adequate. For more technical linguistic material, the reader can consult an article in Arabic by 'Abd al-'Azīz Maṭar (1966) and two articles by J. R. Smart (1966, 1967), all of which contain several references to work done by other linguists.

My transcriptions conform, by and large, to the standard system for the transliteration of Arabic followed by the *International Journal of Middle East Studies*. I have made certain alterations to preserve peculiarities of the dialect. The system for vowels is close to that used by Smart (1967). What follows is a brief guide along with some general rules about the dialect.

I am grateful to the late Anne Royal for her help in developing the transcription system.

VOWELS

Key to the sound qualities

Short vowels:

a   as in *but* or the "a" in *abut*
e   as in *bait* but shortened
i   as in *bit*
u   as in *book*

Long vowels:

ā   as in *bat*, sometimes *bob*
ē   similar to the sound in *bait*, but lengthened
    (This is the equivalent of the diphthong *ay*
    in classical Arabic.)
ī   as in *beet*
ō   as in *boat*
    (This is the equivalent of the diphthong *aw*
    in classical Arabic.)
ū   as in *boot*

Notes on vowels

1. Unstressed short vowels tend to be centralized, especially when they occur in the middle of words. Thus *a, i,* and *u* often sound quite similar.

2. The morphemic *h* increases the length of long vowels, but it does not affect the pronunciation of short vowels at all. I thus transcribe it in the former case and not in the latter.

3. The *a* is pronounced either as the vowel in *but* or the first vowel in *abut,* depending on the surrounding consonants. For the sake of simplicity I have not marked the distinction in the transcribed texts, since it is phonetic rather than phonemic.

4. The long front vowel *ā,* when pronounced as in *bat,* is extremely nasalized. I have chosen not to mark it in the text, unlike

Smart who sometimes transliterates this sound as *ie*. He quotes Mitchell's description of the sound as "a falling diphthong moving from half close front to mid front and occurring only in prominent syllables" (Smart 1967, 256).

5. This dialect has no glottal stop (*hamza*) except as an initial sound, which, since English speakers automatically pronounce an initial vowel with a glottal stop, I have not indicated in the transcriptions.

SEMIVOWELS

y   corresponds to the semivowel   ي
w   corresponds to the semivowel   و

I use the first consistently as the prefix of the third masculine singular imperfect of the verb, and the second for the conjunction *and* (و), even though the actual pronunciation of both semivowels varies from word to word. I also use them to mark the two classical Arabic diphthongs *ay* and *aw*, when they are pronounced as such. As Smart (1967, 256) notes, Awlad 'Ali occasionally and inconsistently use diphthongs.

CONSONANTS

The simplest way to describe the transliteration system for consonants is to list the written Arabic equivalents, marking with an asterisk pronunciations peculiar to the dialect. In parentheses following some of these letters are their standard transliterations, which I use only when I have taken the word not from the spoken language of the Western Desert but from texts in modern standard Arabic.

In addition to *w* and *y*, treated above, the consonants are transliterated as follows:

ب	b	ص	ṣ
ت	t	ض	d̲h̲*(ḍ)
ث	th	ط	ṭ
ج	j*	ظ	ẓ*
ح	ḥ	ع	‘
خ	kh	غ	gh
د	d	ف	f
ذ	dh	ق	g*(q)
ر	r	ك	k
ز	z	ل	l
س	s	م	m
ش	sh	ن	n
		ه	h

Notes on sound quality

    j   soft like the French *j*

   d̲h̲   the letter ض is usually pronounced as a velarized *dh* rather than a velarized *d* as in classical Arabic

    ẓ   a velarized *dh*, almost identical to d̲h̲ (ض)

    g   hard as in *good*

Notes on consonants

   1. Especially in the poems, the three letters ذ, ض, and ظ (dh, ḍ, and ẓ in classical Arabic) are pronounced almost identically. To help readers who know classical Arabic, however, I transcribe them as distinct letters, but I use d̲h̲ rather than ḍ for the letter ض to remain closer to Awlad ‘Ali pronunciation.

   2. The most prominent peculiarity of the dialect is in the pronunciation of initial syllables. Awlad ‘Ali generally drop the first vowel in a word. For instance, they say *bhar* rather than *baḥr* (sea). They compensate by preceding the initial consonant with what might be thought of as a glottal stop or with an *i*. Behnke (1980) indicates this by preceding the consonant with an *i*, as in the word *imraabiṬ* (for *mrābiṭ*). I worry that this will confuse the reader

familiar with classical Arabic who might mistake the initial *i* for a phoneme, so I have chosen not to mark it in the transcriptions.

3. However, Awlad ʿAli tend to drop the phonemic initial *a* of classical and many other eastern Arabic dialects. Thus they pronounce the word *abū* (father) as *bū*. I have transcribed such words as I heard them.

THE DEFINITE ARTICLE

In Arabic, when the definite article *al* is attached to consonants requiring the use of the front of the tongue, it is assimilated, doubling the consonantal sound. The consonants involved, among Awlad ʿAli, are: t, th, j, d, dh, r, z, s, sh, ṣ, ḏẖ, ṭ, ẓ, l, n. I have marked these as they are pronounced. In addition, the initial *a* is influenced by the final vowel of the word that precedes it, and there is elision. I only roughly indicate how the initial *a* is influenced. I join the definite article to its noun by a hyphen.

PLACE NAMES AND COMMON PROPER NAMES

I have followed standard English spellings for common proper names like Mohammad ʿAli and well-known places like Alamein, as well as for common Arabic words found in English dictionaries, such as *haj*.

TRANSLITERATIONS

For transliterations from Arabic written sources, I have followed the system of the *International Journal of Middle East Studies*.

VEILED
SENTIMENTS

1

GUEST AND DAUGHTER

The Community

One takes the road that leads west, leaving behind the stately buildings and palm-lined boulevards of Alexandria, passing rows of identical sand-colored buildings with balconies crowded with children, men in undershirts, women shouting across to neighbors, and clotheslines covered with multi-colored garments that dry instantly in the bright Egyptian sun. One must then cross a tiny bridge, which can accommodate only one lane of traffic. Awaiting their turn alongside horse-drawn carts and passenger cars are long lines of trucks and group taxis (those ubiquitous white Peugeot station wagons nicknamed "flying coffins" by cynical foreigners who too often see their abandoned carcasses of mangled steel by the sides of major roads). Only the pedestrians cross in a steady stream.

Once across the bridge, malodorous fumes and tall reeds herald the marshy shores of Lake Mariut. Fishermen by the side of the road hold high their catches, hoping for a sale. One continues on, leaving the lake behind, and comes to the beginning of the desert. This is not the impressive stark sand desert found far inland, nor the white sandy beach along the Mediterranean coast, nor even the steppe dotted with shrubs of spurge flax that lies twenty kilometers south of the coast. Rather, it is a flat, dusty place of packed

---

1

earth, a limestone plateau dotted with factories and open-air storage areas for the new trucks and automobiles unloaded on the docks of Alexandria.

As one travels westward, these signs of the encroaching metropolis thin out, replaced by scattered one-story houses of stone or whitewashed cement. These crude structures, often painted yellow, light blue, or pink, embellished with simple hand-painted designs and surrounded by scrubby dwarf fig trees, are sure signs that one has entered the Western Desert, which stretches five hundred kilometers to the Libyan border and is the home of the Bedouin tribes known collectively as Awlad 'Ali.[1] These houses have, for the most part, taken the place of the Bedouins' traditional tents of woven wool. Even summer tents, sewn from old burlap sacks, are not always left pitched near the houses, especially in this eastern edge of the desert where sedentarization has proceeded the furthest. A glimpse of a woman working confirms that Bedouins live in these homes: one notes the distinctive glint of silver on her wrists, a vibrant full-length dress gathered at the waist by a red cummerbund, a head covered in black.

The first time I took this road, all this was pointed out to me. I strained to see it, to commit it to memory, and I wondered if it would ever seem familiar. Once I had settled down in a community of Awlad 'Ali, my reaction was different. Each time I traveled this way, my heart raced as we passed the marshes and factories and came across the open spaces with their pastel houses. I knew that at the government checkpoint not far from the major town, when we turned off the road stretching through the desert south to Cairo, we would begin to pass the tents and houses of some of "our" relatives—which was how I came to conceive of the kin of the family with whom I lived. I always looked to see if I could spot my favorite aunt, hoping to be able to report the sighting to those ahead. They loved news from the world beyond.

Each time, I noted the change of season in the fields we passed. In winter, thanks to peripatetic rains, green barley shoots thrived in

some patches and barely came up in others. The spring carpets of
wildflowers disappeared during the summer months, leaving nothing but desiccated earth. An occasional camel grazed desultorily;
small herds of sheep or goats foraged, nibbling on clumps of grasses
in rock crevices. Crouching alongside the road might be a turbaned
old man waiting patiently for a taxi to come by. An old woman
might bounce along on her donkey. More rarely, a woman, her face
swathed in the black headcloth that doubles as a veil, might walk
briskly, a large bundle on her head, an infant on her back, and a
couple of children straggling behind. I always turned to see if I could
recognize them, again to report to those ahead.

Returning from the crowded and noisy streets of Cairo or Alexandria, I often felt relieved to see the open spaces, to note the
silence. The only sounds were shouts in the distance, a braying
donkey, a barking dog. As we approached the area where I lived
for the whole period of field research, there was a bit more vegeta-
tion: palm trees, olive orchards, rows of spindly evergreens planted
by the government to retard soil erosion, a guava orchard (maintained with great difficulty). Then came a barren area. A few
houses and tents, widely spaced, stood out on the rocky ground.
Some were made of stone and mud, blending into the landscape;
some were painted pastels. One modern compound was made of
white blocks. This was where I lived.

Turning off the road onto a track etched by a succession of cars
bringing visitors and residents to the house, I strained to see who
might be around. One never could predict. Usually the first to
spot the car were the children, always on the lookout for activity.
Their initial timidity would vanish as soon as they recognized the
passenger. Some would run back to announce my arrival; others
would run toward the car. By the time I arrived at the doorway,
the women would have come to meet me, unless male guests
were sitting out front. If men were there, I would greet them
politely and hurry into the house. Just inside, out of sight of the
men, I might find the women and girls, arms around each other,

crowding the entrance. After putting away my things and distributing sweets I had brought, I would settle down to have a snack, drink tea, and catch up on what had happened in my absence.

I lived in this household between October 1978 and May 1980.[2] Its composition shifted numerous times over the course of this period, but the core members were the head of the household, a charismatic, wealthy, and somewhat unconventional tribal mediator close to fifty years old, whom people referred to as the Haj (an honorific recognizing his performance of the holy pilgrimage to Mecca); his senior wife, who was also his paternal first cousin, a warm, plump, and intelligent woman who seemed older than her thirty-seven years; and many of his eighteen (by the time I left) children. Sometimes his second wife, whom he had unofficially divorced a year before my arrival, and all her children lived there; she spent the rest of the time in the old house in which they had all lived with his mother and his brother's family until I joined them.[3] Not all her children accompanied her on these moves. Her nineteen-year-old son, the eldest of the Haj's children, lived in our household most of the time. During the second year I was there, the Haj's third wife joined us, bringing her three children. She and the Haj had argued months before my arrival, and he had sent her back to her family, intending to divorce her. When he discovered that she had been pregnant and had given birth to twins, he was persuaded to take her back. Later in the year the Haj's younger brother took a second wife, whom he brought to live in our household. Although he sometimes spent nights at his old house (with his first wife and his six children), he spent more time at ours. In addition, overnight guests—nephews and nieces, cousins and aunts, and even a woman peddler who attended the nearby market regularly—came and went.

This household was one of about fifteen in what its residents considered their community. There were fifty-three adults in these households, and about twice as many children, including all unmarried adolescents. The smallest household comprised a couple and their infant; the largest had twenty-five people living in four

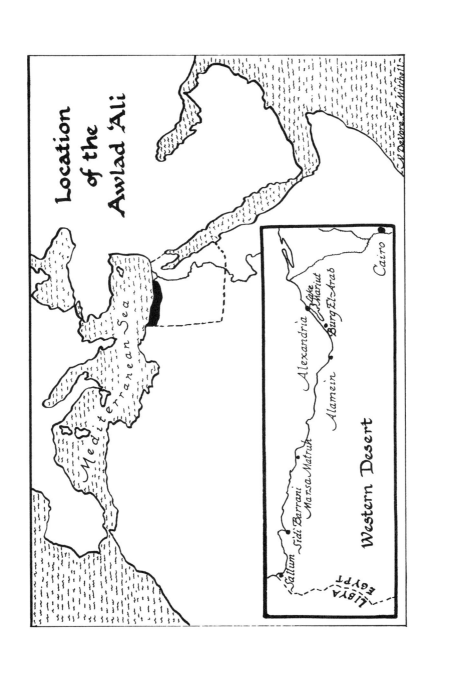

Location
of the
Awlad 'Ali

E. N. Delore & T. Mitchell

Mediterranean Sea

Western Desert

Sallum
Sidi Barrani
Marsa Matruh
Alamein
Alexandria
Lake
Mariut
Burg El-Arab
Cairo

LIBYA
EGYPT

rooms in two houses, who, by virtue of sharing an economic base and food, were considered one household. The Bedouins describe households by the phrase "They eat from one bowl."

Bedouins view residential communities as social units defined by ties of agnation.[4] The term Awlad 'Ali use for a residential community is *naji'*, the same term they originally applied to the tent camps in which they used to live. Most camps take their name from the lineage or cluster of agnates forming the core of the camp, even though most also include other families that have attached themselves to the group—some are distant kin, some affines, some maternal kin, others are unrelated clients. Everyone referred to the community in which I lived as the camp of the family (*'ēt*, spelled *'ait* by North Africanists) of the Haj's great-grandfather, which, strictly speaking, included only the five core households headed by the sons of two brothers. However, the *'ēt* was usually understood in its extended sense as including two numerically weak and poor collateral lineages related genealogically four generations back, as well as a number of client families. Bonds of agnation among the core families were reinforced by patrilateral parallel-cousin marriages in the adult generation and in the upcoming one. Because people in so many of the community's households were joined by kinship ties, they visited constantly and often spent nights at each other's households. This was particularly true of the children, who were free to sleep either with their mothers, grandmothers, aunts, or (if boys) their cousins or uncles.

In the past, spatial arrangements within a camp accurately reflected social relations. Tents were pitched side by side in a straight line, all facing the same direction, with the tent ropes of adjacent households of kin crossing. At the center were the core households of the community, usually those of the senior kinsmen and their families, with more distant kin and clients occupying the periphery. Now permanent structures make the fit between social and spatial distribution less tight. Modern camps are a motley array of houses and tents. Nevertheless, houses of the core members of each community cluster together, and those who come from outside either set up tents near the households to which they are most closely attached or move into or build new houses nearby.

It would be a mistake to assume from this description that the cluster of houses was isolated, as is often the case in the less populated desert areas farther west. This community, lying between a town and village in the more densely settled eastern district called Mariut, was surrounded by other houses. Despite spatial proximity and an almost haphazard arrangement of houses, the social barriers between the households of separate communities (defined by tribal affiliation) were unmistakable, and the invisible boundaries well known. Our community had amicable, neighborly relations with some other communities; with others, there was little contact except through the men who prayed together on Fridays at the mosque attached to a nearby saint's tomb.

The degree of contact individuals had with those outside the community varied tremendously. The Haj had traveled as far as Qatar, to visit a friend he had met while falcon hunting in the Western Desert. Some of the men had been to the cities of Alexandria and Cairo. Most had been to Marsa Matruh, the largest city in the Western Desert, and even to Libya in the days before the border was closed. Nearly all of the men at least occasionally attended the major sheep market to the west and did business in the non-Bedouin market town to the east. Many went daily to the nearby town or the village between which their hamlet lay. The women were more restricted in their movements. All but the oldest women traveled only to visit their families, to attend weddings and funerals, and to see the doctors at the clinics in the nearby town and village. Older women were more mobile, often attending local markets if their health permitted.

The particular group of people with whom I lived was more traditional than some in the area, especially those in town, but it was also more involved in the major transformations in Bedouin life of the last few decades than poorer and more isolated groups living farther west. The members of this community considered town life corrupting and most of its inhabitants immoral, and they had no interest in moving there. The core families' long-standing wealth, which suffered a brief setback in the 1950s but was regained through the Haj's shrewd economic direction, had shielded them from government interference and freed them from having to cooperate in government settlement schemes. This economic viability allowed the core families to support clients and poor relations, thus keeping them within the group. It also enabled the community to set its own moral standards and maintain a separate identity.

All the trends in the shifting Bedouin economy (to be described in chapter 2) were represented in the diverse activities by which the members of this community supported themselves. The core families had large sheep herds, which they viewed as their main enterprise, and they had small camel herds for prestige. They had planted olive and almond trees and regularly pressed olive oil for their own consumption. They owned bits of agricultural land from which they hoped to make some profit. Every year they sowed barley. The first year of my stay, there was little rain and no harvest; the second year there was a small crop. The Haj, unlike his brothers, had contacts in Cairo and Alexandria for whom he acted as a middleman in real estate ventures on the coast, and in turn he was persuaded to invest with his partners in urban property. All of the brothers had engaged in smuggling in an earlier period. The various client families attached to these core families worked as shepherds and did odd jobs, including building, harvesting, painting, gardening, and so forth, for their patrons. They also raised rabbits, pigeons, and a few goats.

What changes in lifestyle they had made were voluntary adaptations to shifting conditions. Although they had taken advantage of government assistance in tree planting, they had built their own houses, and when the government claimed all Western Desert lands, they had arranged for the purchase of their traditional land. They had last migrated to desert pastures seven years before my arrival, but for a host of practical and emotional reasons they had stopped going; each year, however, the idea was raised anew. They had no electricity, although the Haj had purchased a generator that sat broken most of the time I was there. One house had tapped into a pipeline that brought water nearby, but most of the households sent their adolescent girls with donkeys carrying jerrycans to fetch water from the main taps. In the spring, after the rains, people got some of their water from a well shared by several neighboring communities. They had requested that a government school be built nearby, which many of their children attended.

This sketch must serve as an introduction to a community that the reader will come to know in depth. The problem this book explores became apparent to me in the course of living with this group of people, and in part as a function of the interactions I had with them. Therefore, the reader will need some sense of the fieldwork experience before the theoretical issues are presented.

Fieldwork

An honest account of the circumstances of fieldwork, not merely a perfunctory note stating the dates the anthropologist was in the host country, is, as Maybury-Lewis points out in his introduction (1967), both essential for the evaluation of the facts and interpretations presented in an ethnographic report and sometimes embarrassing. Especially for young anthropologists, perhaps insecure about their professional competence, the cloak of secrecy shrouding the fieldwork experiences of successful predecessors inspires fantasies. It is easy to imagine, for example, that these great figures were not plagued by doubts about their abilities, the adequacy of the material they collected, or their hosts' feelings toward them. Rather, they must have begun with the ideas set forth in their final products, polished, crisp, and profound. But on a day when people are busy and you are alone in a desolate landscape, suffering from fever and being eaten alive by fleas or annoyed by a child poking fun at you, the question of whether *this* is the experience that carries such dignified labels as "research" or the more scientistic "data collection" nags. And yet, the nature and quality of what anthropologists learn is profoundly affected by the unique shape of their fieldwork; this should be spelled out.

I do not believe that the encounter between anthropologists and their hosts should be the sole object of inquiry. Only a rare sensitivity and perceptiveness can redeem the solipsism of this project.[5] However, to ignore the encounter not only denies the power of such factors as personality, social location in the community, intimacy of contact, and luck (not to mention theoretical orientation and self-conscious methodology) to shape fieldwork and its product but also perpetuates the conventional fictions of objectivity and omniscience that mark the ethnographic genre.[6]

Taking an intermediate position, I will present only a few of the elements in my fieldwork situation that were most salient in setting the parameters of what I could do and discover. Out of this experience, shaped by how others in the community perceived me and what I felt comfortable with in my relations with them, arose the issues treated in this book. Thus the exercise is necessary to introduce the proper subject of study, which is the relationship between Awlad 'Ali sentiments and experiences and the two contradictory discourses that express and inform them: a genre of oral lyric poetry of love and vulnerability on the one hand, and the ideology of honor in ordinary conversation and everyday behavior on the other.

I arrived in Cairo at the beginning of October 1978 and ensconced myself at an unpretentious pension frequented by generations of Arabists, Egyptologists, and scholars of modest means. The hotel boasted a view of the Nile, such illustrious neighbors as the great old hotels—the Semiramis, Shepheard's, and the Hilton—and easy walking distance to the American University. In the many years since I had last stayed there as a young girl traveling with my family, nothing much had changed—the lumpy beds, the plumbing, and the gentle hotel personnel bore the inevitable marks of old age. Outside, however, the city seemed to be in the throes of change. The progressive dilapidation of old buildings had in some cases led to their collapse, and in other parts of the city construction of massive new luxury hotels was underway.

I familiarized myself with the city, more crowded and noisy than ever, and awaited my father's arrival. Here the reader might pause. I suspect that few, if any, fathers of anthropologists accompany them to the field to make their initial contacts. But my father had insisted that he had something to do in Egypt and might just as well plan his trip to coincide with mine. I had accepted his offer only reluctantly, glad to have the company but also a bit embarrassed by the idea. Only after living with the Bedouins for a long time did I begin to comprehend some of what had underlain my father's quiet but firm insistence. As an Arab, although by no means a Bedouin, he knew his own culture and society well enough to know that a young, unmarried woman traveling alone on uncertain business was an anomaly. She would be suspect and would have a hard time persuading people of her respectability. I of course knew of the negative image of Western women, an image fed by rumor, films, and, to be sure, the frequent insensitivity of Western women to local standards of morality and social communication patterns.[7] But I had assumed I would be able to overcome people's suspicions, first by playing up the Arab half of my identity and not identifying with Westerners, and second by behaving properly. I was confident of my sensitivity to cultural expectations because of my background. Not only had I lived in Egypt for four years as a child, but, more significant, I had also spent many summers with relatives in Jordan. As part of that household I had had to conform to some extent to the codes of conduct appropriate to Arab girls, my many cousins providing models for this behavior. I felt I had internalized much that would help me find my way with the Bedouins and not offend them.

What I had not considered was that respectability was reckoned not just in terms of behavior in interpersonal interactions but also in the relationship to the larger social world. I had failed to anticipate that people as conservative as the Bedouins, for whom belonging to tribe and family are paramount and the education of girls novel, would assume that a woman alone must have so alienated her family, especially her male kin, that they no longer cared about her. Worse yet, perhaps she had done something so immoral that they had ostracized her. Any girl valued by her family, especially an unmarried girl whose virginity and reputation were critical to a good match, would not be left unprotected to travel alone at the mercy of anyone who wished to take advantage of her. By accompanying me, my father hoped to lay any such suspicions to rest.

After making contacts in Cairo, we set off for Alexandria. There we spoke with social researchers conducting a study of the Mariut Extension, the site of a land reclamation and resettlement scheme in the Western Desert. The director of field research generously offered us accommodation, transport to the Bedouin town closest to their research, and a promise to introduce us to his Bedouin contact. I still remember driving out to the sun-baked town, which, at midday, was quiet and nearly deserted. We drove around in search of this informant, finally tracking him to his small house. My father and the research director had a long conversation with him while I sat quietly in the back of the vehicle, shy, barely understanding what was being said, and feeling distinctly unlike an anthropologist.

My father had explained that his daughter, who had been raised in the United States, wished to improve her Arabic and to learn about their society and would need to find a good family with whom to live. After some deliberation, the man guided us to a hamlet consisting of a number of houses and tents. As we approached we could see people scurrying to shake out straw mats from the tents. We were greeted by several men. My father went with the men into one of the houses, and I, along with a couple of the female researchers from the Mariut project, was invited into a nearby tent. We sat surrounded by a large group of curious women and children. We asked them questions and they asked questions of us. Again, I felt peripheral. I understood little of what the Bedouin women were saying and had to rely on the Egyptian university students to translate from the fast-paced dialect. They too had some difficulty understanding. We did not stay long but soon piled into the van over the protests of our hosts, who wished us to stay for a meal. The project director explained that they wanted to slaughter a sheep for us, as they would for any honored guest. The Haj, head of the community, had not been there; my father had spoken instead with his brothers and had left him a letter explaining the situation and placing me under his protection. When I returned the next day, the Haj welcomed me and said that he would be happy to have me live with them.

This introduction to the community profoundly affected my position and the nature of the work I could do. First, it identified me, despite my poor linguistic skills and my apparent foreignness, as a Muslim and an Arab. My Muslim credentials were shaky, as I did not pray and my mother was known to be an American. But most assumed that I shared with them a fundamental identity as a Muslim, and my father's speech was no doubt so sprinkled with religious phrases that they believed in his piety, which in turn rubbed off on me. Many times during my stay I was confronted with the critical importance of the shared Muslim identity in the community's acceptance of me. As always, the old women and the young children bluntly stated what most adults were too polite to say. The hostility they felt toward Europeans (*naṣāra*, or Christians) came out in the children's violent objections to my listening to English radio broadcasts, an old woman's horror at the thought of drinking out of a teacup a European woman visitor had just used, and comments made about an American friend who came out to visit me (whom they liked very much) that she was good "for someone of her religion" (*'ala dīnhā*).

It was also clear that I came from a good family and good stock, so the Haj's family could accept me as a member of their household without compromising their social standing. My father's beautiful Arabic and the fact that he was not an Egyptian but a "Jordanian" (as he had been introduced) were topics of much discussion. The Bedouins believe that all non-Egyptian Arabs are Bedouins, speaking a decent dialect and living a lifestyle similar to their own. So they considered my father a fellow tribesman and a person with noble roots (*aṣl*), the importance of which will be explored in the next two chapters. I often heard them defend their acceptance of me on these grounds.

Most of all, by accompanying me my father had shown those with whom I would be living and on whose good opinion and generosity my life and work would depend that I was a daughter of a good family whose male kin were concerned about her and wanted to protect her, even when pursuit of education forced her into potentially compromising positions. The Haj and his relatives took seriously their obligation to my father, who had given them the sacred trust of protecting me. Although the Haj understood that I was there to find out about their customs and traditions (*'ādāt wtaqālīd*) and in our initial chat assured me that I must feel free to go anywhere that my study required as long as I informed him of my whereabouts, I soon discovered that my freedom was in fact restricted. Through the subtle cues of tactful but stubborn adults, I came to understand that I was to feel free to go anywhere within the camp but that to step beyond the bounds of the community, particularly alone, was not appropriate.

The restrictions on my movements had several motives. As the Haj explained to me in one exasperated moment, they feared for my safety. They would be responsible if anything happened to me, and they did not relish the idea of becoming embroiled in vengeance matters. Also, by living with them I was automatically identified as a member of their family. Perceived by all as one of the women in the Haj's kin group, my actions reflected on them and affected their reputations. They had to make sure I did nothing that could compromise them by insuring that, as far as possible, I conformed to the same standards of propriety their women did, meaning that I was restricted in where I could go, by whom I could be seen, and with whom I could speak. But I also realized later that another reason they discouraged me from visiting those outside the community was that I would thus involve them in social obligations they had not chosen. If I visited another tribal group, I would be greeted as a member of the Haj's group. People usually offer a feast for first-time guests, and I would thus incur a social debt for them.

The other consequence of my introduction to the community as my father's daughter was that I was assigned and took on the role of an adoptive daughter. My protection/restriction was an entailment of this relationship, but so was my participation in the household, my identification with the kin group, and the process by which I learned about the culture, a sort of socialization to the role. Although I never completely lost my status as a guest in their household, my role as daughter gradually superseded it. The choice pieces of meat they initially set aside for me were later offered to other guests instead. I became part of the backstage when we had company, found myself contributing more to household work than I wished, and had my own chores. Men occasionally shouted commands at me and felt free to get me up late at night along with the women and girls to help serve tea to visitors.

I should not give the impression that this role was forced on me. I was a willing collaborator. In a society where kinship defines most relationships, it was important to have a role as a fictive kinsperson in order to participate. I knew what was expected of an obedient daughter and found it hard to resist meeting those expectations. Not everything I did to help in the household was because of my status as daughter. I was grateful to the people in my household for graciously including me in their lives and counting me as a member of the family. Although I was not that much of an extra burden, I felt uncomfortable being idle when the women and girls worked so hard. With time I developed close relationships with the Haj's first wife, Gatīfa, and his daughters. It was to assist them that I worked, especially during difficult periods such as when Gatīfa was ill and was trying, before her co-wife joined her, to run the household with only the help of one adolescent daughter. During her difficult pregnancy, I spent much of my time with her, massaging her and worrying about her health, trying to take over what little of her work I was competent to do. During these periods, as I filled water containers, collected straw for the oven, carried trays of bread, or peeled endless zucchinis for dinner, I would worry that I was not filling my notebook with information and that time was passing. If I was occasionally resentful, mostly I felt that the personal responsibilities I had toward the individuals who cared for me and treated me not as a researcher but as a member of a household came first.

Two other aspects of my identity affected the nature of my social relationships with the Bedouins, and thus the type of research I was able to carry out. First, I could not have been a daughter without being female. As a woman I often found myself confronted with difficulties not faced by male researchers, but I also enjoyed advantages of access and unexpected pleasures of intimacy in the women's world. In my first few weeks I tried to move back and forth between the men's and women's worlds. Gradually I realized that I would have to declare my loyalties firmly in order to be accepted in either. With the exception of the Haj, whom I got to know very well through almost daily conversations and occasional long car rides to Cairo, I found visits with the men boring because of the limited range of topics we could politely cover. So I opted for the women's world, refusing more and more to leave their company when the men called. This choice met with silent approbation from the women and girls, and so I was incorporated into their world, involved in their activities, and made privy to their secrets. Because relations in the women's world are more informal than in the men's, I was able to get beyond polite conversation more quickly.

The other factor was my unmarried status, the problems of which have been noted by two Arab women trained as anthropologists in the West who returned to do fieldwork in their societies of origin (Altorki 1973; Abu-Zahra 1978). Being unmarried not only cast me in the role of daughter, but since I was far older than the unmarried Bedouin girls, it also placed me in an ambiguous position. I wished to be part of the women's world, but I did not have one of the most important defining characteristics of women: children. The gap between the two categories is symbolized by clothing, and when I decided to convert to wearing clothing like theirs I was in a quandary. Married women wear black veils and red belts (see chapter 4), whereas unmarried girls wear kerchiefs on their heads and around their waists. I compromised, wearing some women's clothing and some girls' and then tying my kerchief in a non-Bedouin way. In the end, they put me in an intermediate category. The only real problem this status caused was that it prevented me from asking certain questions about sexuality—I was assumed to be ignorant, and I had no intention of disabusing people of this view, as I wanted to protect my reputation. But women seemed to talk openly, joking bawdily even in front of children, and so I did not feel that the topic was completely closed.

In the first months, even as I appreciated the warm acceptance I received, I chafed at the restrictions of my role and position in the community. It was difficult being so dependent. Also, although I enjoyed living in the Haj's household and felt infinitely more comfortable around the people I knew best, I was worried by the idea of what anthropologists were supposed to do. I thought I should be going door to door, meeting everyone in the vicinity, and conducting surveys. I did not think it appropriate to confine my contacts to one kin group or community. And yet to defy my hosts would have been insulting and would have seriously jeopardized my relations with them. They, after all, had undertaken to protect and care for me. My obligation as a dependent was to respect their wishes, and my role as a daughter, like that of Jean Briggs among the Eskimos (Briggs 1970), made defiance especially inappropriate.

My relations with people in the community changed over time, at certain junctures shifting radically, as when a new woman moved into our household, catapulting me into the inner circle of those who already belonged; but for the most part change was gradual. Where I had at first strained to understand what was being said, felt awkward, and done more observing than interacting, as I came to know more people and as my language abilities improved I began to participate more. In the first few months I went to Cairo as frequently as every two or three weeks to shower, eat, buy medicine, get mail, and speak English. By the end I felt enough at home that I went for a period of nearly three months with only a day in Cairo to attend to some urgent business.

What bothered me most after the first few months was that my relationship with the people I lived with did not seem symmetrical. I do not mean this in the usual sense of a power or wealth differential in the anthropologist's favor; I was, after all, a dependent and daughter with nothing to offer but my company. Rather, I was asking them to be honest, so that I could learn what their lives were like, but at the same time I was unwilling to reveal much about myself. I was presenting them with a persona: I felt compelled to lie to them about many aspects of my life in the United States simply because they could not have helped judging it and me in their own terms, by which my reputation would have suffered. So I doctored my descriptions and changed the subject when they asked about me, but I felt uncomfortable doing so. How ethical was it to present myself falsely, to pretend that I shared their values and lived as they did even when I was not with them? They knew nothing of my former life, my friends, family, university, apartment—in short, much of what I considered my identity. Unlike other anthropologists, who not only can present themselves as different but can use the difference as a way of stimulating discussion, I had to dissociate myself as much as possible from Americans. With my Arab identity, I dared not say, "Where I come from, they do . . ." What bits they heard were sufficient to make them doubt my father's wisdom in choosing to live and bring up his children among non-Muslims.

Eventually, this sense of inauthenticity subsided. As I participated more fully in the community and loosened my ties to my other life, and as we came to share a common history and set of experiences on which we could build relationships, I *became* the person that I was with them. That was sufficient for honest interchanges. Although there always remained an element of asymmetry in that I was writing about them and was observing perhaps a bit more closely than they were, for the most part I felt that we came together as individuals responding to situations in which we participated equally. This experience may correspond to what some other analysts of the fieldwork experience call the development of intersubjectivity (Rabinow 1977, 155).

There were moments when I became aware of a transition in my relations with people, even though the process of change went unnoticed. The intensity of my feeling of belonging and the extent to which this life had become natural struck me one day about fifteen months into fieldwork. I was awakened in the morning by one of the Haj's daughters, who ran into my room with the exciting news that our neighbor had returned from the pilgrimage. We had feared him dead or imprisoned because he had been caught without a passport during the seizure of Mecca's Haram Mosque and had not been heard from. She urged me to hurry and ready myself to attend the feast welcoming him home. I dressed in my best clothes.

As we set off, I realized how proud I was that I finally had the proper items: a new dress my hosts had given me at the last wedding, made of a colorful synthetic, the latest in Bedouin fashion; a red belt; and a black shawl to wear on my head. I knew that my new sweater (worn *under* my dress), brightly colored and interwoven with metallic threads, would be much admired, as would my gaudy new bead necklace, a gift from my friend the seamstress. I was able to see myself as I would be seen by others, and I took pleasure in knowing that I was finally acceptably attired for a festive occasion. I was also prepared to cover my face with my shawl as we passed in sight of the men's tent en route to the women's section. By this time I would have felt uncomfortable had I not been able to veil.

On entering the tent crowded with women, I knew exactly which cluster to join—the group of "our" relatives. They welcomed me naturally and proceeded to gossip conspiratorially with me about the others present. This sense of "us versus them," so central to their social interactions, had become central to me, too, and I felt pleased that I belonged to an "us." Later, when there was a shortage of help in preparing the tea for the guests, I assisted, assuming the proper role of a close neighbor.

I left the festivities with a few of the women from our community and spent the rest of the day going from household to household, visiting, catching up, listening to different sides of the story of the latest camp crisis, an argument between an aunt and niece. In the late afternoon a few of the adolescent girls came to find me, urging me to come with them while they collected firewood from a nearby olive orchard that was being pruned. It was a beautiful day, and I welcomed the chance to be outside, so I hurried off with them. They showed me where their cousins had just killed a large snake and explained more about the family argument I had just been hearing about. We hauled branches and twigs and loaded them onto donkey carts for a while, and then, as the sun sank, we started for home. A donkey cart driven by two young men from our camp passed us. My companions—two women, three girls, and a toddler, all from my household—flagged them down, begging for a ride. But the young men were in a hurry and tried to wave us aside, no longer treating me as an honored guest to be pampered. We gave chase, though, and jumped onto the moving cart, laughing wildly and exchanging joking insults with the young men.

That evening as we sat around the kerosene lantern, talking about the celebration we had attended, swapping bits of information we had gathered, and feeling happy because we had eaten meat, I became aware of how comfortable I felt, knowing everyone being discussed, offering my own tidbits and interpretations, and bearing easily the weight of the child who had fallen asleep on my lap as I sat cross-legged on the ground. It was only that night, when I dated the page in my journal, that I realized it was only a few days until Christmas. My American life seemed very far away.

Even though my feelings toward them had changed, I do not think it was until a certain funeral that I became fully human (because social) to many in the camp. People's fears that I did not care about them in the same way they cared about me came out in their half-joking accusations that I would forget them as soon as I left and that I would never return to visit. The Haj's mother was not domineering, but she was a key figure in the camp, the ultimate moral authority. I knew that although she liked me, she wondered what I was really doing there, and she was always a bit reserved. Her brother's funeral finally changed her attitude toward me. When we got word that he had died, I insisted on going with the women in our household to pay condolences. I found the whole scene very moving, with the wailing and "crying."[8] When I squatted before the old woman to embrace her and give her my sympathies, I found myself crying. Her grief pained me, and because she had been ill for a while, I feared for her health. With each new arrival the ritualized mourning laments would begin again, and I could not hold back my tears. This funeral had awakened my own grief over the death of my grandmother and a cousin, neither of whom I had mourned properly.

I later heard from others how touched the old woman had been that I had come immediately, like her kinswomen and daughters-in-law, to mourn with her. Others told me that it had meant a great deal to her to know that I genuinely cared and could feel with her the grief over the loss of her only blood brother. From that time on, she treated me differently, even weeping as she sang me a few poignant songs about separation just before I left the field.

The sorts of constraints and advantages my particular position in the community created for my ethnographic project should be apparent from what I have described. However, if my hosts' assumption that I was part of their moral community, not a foreigner with immunity, placed restrictions on me, it also allowed me to participate in a unique way. By being a daughter, I was forced to learn the standards for women's behavior from the inside, as it were—it was a process of socialization as much as observation. The only drawback was that, like Altorki (1973), I found that people expected me to know things that I did not in fact know, and my hesitation to betray my ignorance, especially in matters of religion, did prevent me from pursuing some topics that I otherwise might have. Nevertheless, living in a social world defined by the same boundaries as those experienced by members of the community allowed me to grasp more immediately just how the social world worked and how its members understood it.

It suited my temperament and my interests to be confined to a small group whose members I could come to know intimately. As I became more familiar with the people I lived with, I felt less and less interested in meeting strangers. I found the superficial conversations possible with them tedious, and I quickly tired of answering questions about what they grow in *amrīka*. I had become interested in the complexities of interpersonal relations in Bedouin society and was seeking the concepts by which Awlad 'Ali understood their social world and acted within it. This kind of knowledge could only come from knowing people intimately, and over time.

The lacunae that result from a close study of daily life are not minor. I sometimes despaired that I was not compiling histories of the relations between tribal groups or tracing patterns of territorial control. But what I sacrificed in breadth was, I believe, amply compensated for by a depth of knowledge of individuals, on which the analysis to follow draws. And counting out-married kinswomen, affines, and people about whom I heard a great deal but never met, I am convinced that my knowledge of the society is based on a "sample" larger than the fifteen households that formed the core community.

Whether this community could be considered representative of Awlad 'Ali is perhaps a meaningless question. Insofar as other Bedouins were considered within the same social and moral universe (unlike Egyptians)—and those I met on visits to other communities seemed to differ little except in the quality and quantity of traditional and modern goods they possessed—I would say that this community was representative. However, unique "cultures" develop in any close community, including individual families, and in this sense my community probably differed from all others. I do not think this makes my observations less valid.

My concentration on the women's world might also be considered a limitation. In many ways, however, my access to both worlds was more balanced than a man's would have been. Except in rare instances, male researchers in sex-segregated societies have far less access to women than I had to men. Not only was my host an extremely articulate and generous informant about himself and his culture, but his younger brother, sons and nephews, and the client-status men were all frequent visitors in the women's world with whom I could speak relatively freely. Furthermore, the structure of information flow between the men's and women's worlds was not symmetrical. Because of the pattern of hierarchy, men spoke to one another in the presence of women, but the reverse was not true.[9] In addition, young and low-status men informed mothers, aunts, grandmothers, and (for the latter) wives about men's affairs, whereas no one brought news to the adult men. A conspiracy of silence excluded men from the women's world.[10]

My research was perhaps most profoundly affected by the non-directive approach I took. The result of the confluence of principle, personal predilection, and circumstance, my unwillingness to pursue questions aggressively or conduct structured interviews limited the extent to which I could study some matters systematically. It also enabled me to form my inquiry around matters that the Bedouins themselves found most interesting and central. My position of powerlessness in the community prevented me from coercing people into discussions in which they had no interest. Nor had I any desire to do so. I appreciated their perception of me as different from those researchers they had previously encountered. I heard stories of the "exams" these researchers had given them (questionnaires) and the hilariously wild tales the Bedouins had fed them. But because I had wished to live with them they assumed it must be on ordinary social terms. I was reluctant to violate these terms, and thus I rarely took notes or tape-recorded when they spoke (except later when I began collecting poetry) but rather wrote notes from memory at night or at odd moments during the day, and I tried to ask questions when people were already discussing a particular subject or event instead of out of the blue. In this manner I was able to elicit freely the Bedouins' conceptions of their social world, and I was led to the discovery of poetry's importance in social life. Had I rigidly structured my research in advance, I would have been blind to both.

Poetry and Sentiment

A fog of despair shrouds
the eye, just when it starts to clear . . .

yiksīhā dhbāb il-yās
il-ʿēn wēn mā rāg jūhā . . .

This poem was recited to me by the robust, middle-aged wife of a powerful tribal leader. We were sitting together at a ceremony of reconciliation (ṣuluḥ) involving two extremely close tribal segments that had split after a death resulting from a squabble between cousins. The atmosphere was tense. The women, sitting in a tent overlooking the plain where several large white ceremonial tents had been pitched for the men, anxiously watched the men's comings and goings. At one point several of the women disappeared into the nearby house and began a haunting chant. When I looked puzzled, the woman who had taken me as her responsibility in this group of strangers explained that they were reminded of and crying over their deceased relative. As the hours passed and it became clear that the meeting had gone smoothly, the women relaxed a bit. Some of those not closely related to the reconciling segments tried to entertain me by reciting poems, including the one above.

When I returned home after that long day, the women of my camp quizzed me on every detail of whom and what I'd seen, speculating and arguing as I gave my account. When I read this poem and described the woman who had recited it, they figured out who she was and explained the meaning of the poem. They did so not by telling me what the words meant but by recounting to me how she had lost her only son two and a half years earlier. He had been shot through the mouth in an altercation between some Bedouin men and a group of Egyptian soldiers riding on a train through a Bedouin area. It was not until much later that I was able to translate the poem and to grasp its significance as an expression of the sadness she had felt at losing him, an expression triggered by the painful remembrance of the murdered young man on the occasion of his relatives' reconciliation and perhaps recited in empathy with the mourning women.

Listening and observing everyday life and social interactions both in public and in the intimacy of the domestic world, I had noticed that people often sang or punctuated their conversations with short poems. Everyone showed great interest in these poems and often seemed moved when they heard them. At first I ignored them, since I had no interest in poetry. I had come to study the patterning and meaning of interpersonal relations, in particular between men and women, so I merely jotted in my fieldnotes that people seemed to love reciting some sad-sounding short poems. After a few incidents, however, I began to wonder what these poems meant and why they were so valued by the Bedouins. I began to pay attention to them.

The first poem I recorded was by an old woman in another camp I visited. She and some of the other women there knew women in my own community. She told me to write something in my note-book, slowly reciting and repeating her poem to make sure I had it right. She then told me to recite it to a certain woman in my camp. Before I left, I asked for the old woman's name, and she gave me one. When I returned home, I dutifully repeated what to me were then nonsense syllables. The women were puzzled when I gave the name of the woman in the other camp. They all agreed on another name, and I later realized she had given me a false name. For a week, in every household I went to in my community, women asked me to recite the poem this woman had sent. They were fascinated, and I was mystified about why she had disguised her identity.

My first realization of the sensitive nature of the poems came a bit later. A shepherd's wife was helping out in our busy house-hold by baking bread at our makeshift oven. After a minor disap-pointment, she broke into one of these poems. I insisted that she repeat it so I could write it down. That evening as I talked with the Haj about what I had seen and heard that day, asking him questions and getting explanations, I read him the poem. His kindly and pedagogical manner suddenly changed. Agitated, he demanded to know who had recited it. I hesitated, suspecting that I had unwittingly betrayed something important, but when I fi-nally confessed that it was the wife of one of his shepherds he was palpably relieved. He explained that the poem had to do with despair in love; she sang it because she had lost one husband and her present husband was old and about to die. I then understood that he had feared that one of his wives had recited the poem. When I reported my confession to Gaṭīfa, the Haj's senior wife, she scolded me for my indiscretion and told me never to reveal any women's poems to men.

People's reactions to these poems were my first clues to the importance of poetry as a vehicle for personal expression and con-fidential communication. I began to write or tape-record poems whenever individuals recited them spontaneously in conversation or sang them. It turned out that the plaintive songs I heard women, and sometimes men, sing were the same genre as the short poems they recited. The Bedouins' keen interest in the poems and their approval of my recognition of their importance assured me that I had chanced on something critical. Yet most women were not able to explain poems to me. When I asked what a poem meant, they either simply repeated the words or described the type of situation that might elicit that poem. I rarely had a chance to discuss the poems with men, for reasons that will become clear in later chapters. For quite a while I recorded them phonetically, understanding little because the vocabulary was obscure, the images condensed, and the referents ambiguous. Eventually, with the help of both a few individuals in the community and a patient and highly articulate, educated young Libyan in Cairo, I began to interpret them.

I found that these poems, called *ghinnāwas*[11] (literally, little songs), were lyric poems, like Japanese haiku in form[12] but more like the American blues in content and emotional tone. They usually described a sentiment and were perceived by others as personal statements about interpersonal situations. The ethnographic literature on Awlad 'Ali had not prepared me for the vital part oral literature played in their daily lives. Of the anthropologists who had worked with Awlad 'Ali and their Cyrenaican cousins, only Peters (1965) made any mention of songs or poetry, and he did not elaborate on their importance. What published material I was later able to locate on Awlad 'Ali poetry offered no information about the social contexts in which poetry was recited.[13]

Yet the cultural centrality of poetry and song, which are fully integrated into everyday life in other Arab societies, is apparent from some of the best early ethnographic studies. Unmatched in the modern literature are the records of such thorough ethnographers as Granqvist (1931, 1935) and Musil (1928) who, over fifty years ago, studied Palestinian villagers and Rwala Bedouins, respectively. Granqvist's texts are replete with poems and songs associated with every major and minor life event of the villagers she so vividly portrays. Musil also collected rich poetic material from the Rwala Bedouins. For the most part, however, despite the frequency with which scholars of Arab culture comment on the high value Arabs place on poetry, few have tried to situate this poetry in its living social context. Those who do deal with literary matters are rarely ethnographers; they neither record poems as they occur in the course of daily life, nor do they analyze them with reference to their social uses, devoting most of their attention instead to classical literary poetry. Some, such as Zwettler (1976, 1978), are beginning to consider classical forms in the light of what we know about oral literature, without, however, being able to consider one of the major issues of oral tradition—namely, the social context of *performed* poetry.[14]

Because most of the poetry I collected was spontaneously recited in specific social contexts, I could not but recognize it as a form of discourse well integrated into Bedouin social life rather than an obscure art form set apart from daily life and of concern only to specialists.[15] The question, however, for all those who study discourses, from poetry to prayer, proverb to myth, is how they relate to social life. Two recent anthropological studies of Arab tribal poetry (Meeker 1979; Caton 1984)[16] define the relationship between poetry and society in ways that go beyond both the old notion of folklore as a receptacle and source of cultural wisdom and values and the Western aesthetic notion of the arts as the expression of individual genius. Michael Meeker, in a brilliant and complex analysis of Rwala Bedouin poetry and society based on ethnographies from the early part of this century, defines the link thus:

> Bedouin words, far more than Bedouin actions, were the center of an effort to work out the various possibilities and impossibilities of uncertain political relationships. These words reveal systematic strategies for putting together a kind of political order in spite of uncertain political relationships. From the forms of a Bedouin voice, one can begin to understand with some precision the shape of Bedouin experience. (1979, 27)

Two points should be noted here. First, Meeker ties literature to what, in his view, are the central concerns of Rwala life, namely, uncertain political relations and the struggle among mounted men with weapons. Second, like Lévi-Strauss, who at least sometimes, as in "The Story of Asdiwal" (1967), argues that myth is a means for resolving philosophical/social dilemmas at the heart of a society, Meeker sees poetry as a primarily intellectual means of dealing with these central concerns.

Steven Caton, although sharing Meeker's intuition that poetry is tied to political conflict, argues persuasively for a more pragmatic relationship between Yemeni tribal poetry and Yemeni social life. Drawing on the insights of Kenneth Burke and focusing on the use of poetic exchanges in dispute mediations, he argues that "poetry is an act embedded in socio-historical reality, an aggressive instrument like swords or rifles but brandished in a *verbal* war of political rhetoric" (1984, 8).

These understandings of the function of poetry differ markedly, but they share an interesting set of assumptions that bear scrutiny precisely because they reflect widespread biases, biases my work calls into question. Both Meeker and Caton treat the problem of conflict and social order as the central concern of the Yemeni and Rwala tribesmen, and both examine only certain genres of poetry: men's formal rhyming verse. Although there is ample evidence that these tribesmen are obsessed with conflict and political alliances, I suggest that the primacy these authors attribute to this aspect of social life derives equally from their own immersion in the anthropological literature on the Middle East, a great deal of which is devoted to debates about the segmentary lineage model. That anthropologists, including Evans-Pritchard, the man most responsible for this debate about segmentary lineage organization, should have been interested in political organization in the era of colonial rule is hardly surprising.[17] I would rather raise a more general issue: the relationship between men and politics.

Although the existence of universal associations of men with politics and of women with the domestic sphere—explored in feminist scholarship (de Beauvoir 1953; Elshtain 1981; Rosaldo and Lamphere 1974)—can certainly be challenged, this configuration does describe a fact of social life in modern Western society. While I would not accuse Meeker, Caton, Evans-Pritchard, Peters, or any others of inappropriately projecting their own interests onto a situation, it strikes me that a felicitous correspondence between the views of Arab tribesmen and those of European men has led each to reinforce particular interests of the other and to slight other aspects of experience and concern. These aspects, such as the personal and interpersonal as opposed to the abstract and group-oriented, the domestic, private, and informal as opposed to the public, ceremonial, and formal, and the affiliative as opposed to the agonistic, are by no means the concern only of women (Western or Bedouin). But they are more difficult to ignore if one includes women's experiences in the study of a society. In fact, women in Bedouin society are deeply concerned with strictly political matters concerning the tribe and group conflict, affairs such as the tribal reconciliation described above in which their husbands, fathers, and sons are directly involved. They share the martial ethos of Bedouin society. But just as Bedouin women are fiercely loyal to the tribe and dedicated to autonomy, so Bedouin men are more than merely political actors. They too have families, desires, and aspirations and suffer personal tragedies in love and friendship. I argue that we should broaden our vision of Middle Eastern tribal societies to encompass these dimensions of experience in the analysis of social life. It will quickly become clear how inseparable these aspects of life are.

In all these societies there are numerous poetic genres: some, elaborately structured and heroic in subject matter, are recited or chanted only on ceremonial occasions or in specific public contexts;[18] others, simpler in structure and concerning personal matters and feelings, are more appropriate to informal social situations. The former are generally the exclusive domain of men, and the latter tend to be officially devalued by male elders as the unimportant productions of women and youths.[19] Perhaps as a consequence, the love poems and songs of tribal societies of the

Middle East, despite widespread reference to their prevalence, are virtually unstudied.[20]

Meeker and Caton follow this pattern, dealing exclusively with the former type, perhaps because of their interest in the political.[21] For Meeker, the choice was deliberate. Of the rich corpus of poems available in Musil's collection, he chose to analyze only the poems and narratives of war found in one chapter, ignoring the many love poems and ditties included in another chapter. This choice is indirectly rationalized by Meeker's argument (1979, 26, 94–97) that the Rwala were little concerned with the domestic life of the camp, in contrast to sedentary or semisedentary Middle Eastern peoples. In discussing the domestic life of the camp, Meeker, following Charles Doughty, notes only the *mejlis,* or men's gathering in the chief's tent. Caton, who spent a considerable period doing field research in Yemen, had less choice. He moved almost exclusively in the world of men in this sex-segregated society, tape-recording poems recited by men at formal public occasions, where he was welcomed as a guest among other guests, and interviewing tribal poets. His access to the domestic world of home and intimate gatherings of close friends and relatives was limited.

The fact that I moved within the intimate world of the Awlad 'Ali, having as a primary research interest neither poetry nor politics but social life, particularly the life of sentiment, certainly has some bearing on the genre of poetry I encountered and found central and on the relationship I ultimately draw between Bedouin poetry and society.[22] The *ghinnāwa* can be considered the poetry of personal life: individuals recite such poetry in specific social contexts, for the most part private, articulating in it sentiments about their personal situations and closest relationships.

The most striking thing about the poems recited by Awlad 'Ali men and women I knew was the radical difference between the sentiments expressed in them and those expressed about the same situations in ordinary social interactions and conversations. The Bedouins' propensity to joke about or deny concern in personal matters and to express anger in difficult situations had struck me as defensive. But the constellation of sentiments expressed in their poignant lyric poems, for the most part having to do with vulnerability and deep attachment to others, were ones I could readily appreciate and ones that they too seemed to find moving.

This discrepancy suggested the problems this study explores. How is the fact that individuals express such utterly different sentiments in poetic and in nonpoetic discourse to be understood? Is one discourse a more authentic expression of personal experience than the other? Robert LeVine, in his assessment of the anthropological study of the self, states that "interpersonal communication is the medium through which we discover how individuals experience their lives and how cultural beliefs shape that experience" (1982a, 293). He notes the difficulties posed by such communication taking place in multiple arenas and media and the possible inconsistency of the messages conveyed. The messages of poetry in Arab Bedouin society are deeply meaningful and culturally central; they are thus critical to an understanding of Awlad 'Ali experience.

The central question that emerges from a consideration of Awlad 'Ali *ghinnāwa*s, then, concerns the relationship between the Bedouin poetic discourse and the discourse of ordinary social life.[23] To begin to explore this relationship, we must look beyond both the immediate context of the recitation situation and the broader context of the life events of the reciters and attempt to understand the basic cultural notions the Awlad 'Ali hold about society, social relations, and the individual—in short, the ideology of social life.[24] To this end, I outline in chapters 2, 3, and 4 the basic elements of this ideology, presenting the concepts the Bedouins use to make sense of their world and the dominant ideas that orient their actions and interactions.

Because the ideology of kinship, in particular the concept of "blood" in its two aspects of ancestry and agnation, structures the Awlad 'Ali vision of their social world, defines individual social identity and collective cultural identity, and shapes individual attitudes and sentiments toward others, I discuss it first. The organization of political life takes form around this ideology. But perhaps more pressing as everyday concerns of social living for the Bedouins, who hold autonomy dear and pride themselves on their egalitarianism, at least in political life, are matters of hierarchy and of power and status. Here the key terms of honor and modesty come in. Most would agree that values associated with the notion of honor, however defined, are at the heart of the social ideologies of various circum-Mediterranean societies.[25] Most also recognize the link between honor and stratification.[26] But defining the terms of the honor code, determining the arena of its significance, explaining the link between honor and sexual modesty, and understanding why this code is so central have proven less tractable tasks. These must be undertaken in the ethnographic context of particular communities.

In chapters 3 and 4 I explore the logic of the ideology of honor and the relationship of modesty to honor in Awlad 'Ali society. I show how this ideology serves to rationalize social inequality and the control some have over the lives of others in a system that idealizes the equality of agnates and the autonomy of individuals. It does so primarily through reference to morality, which guarantees that individuals will be motivated to act in ways that perpetuate the political and social system. In Awlad 'Ali thought, greater moral worth is the basis of one's authority or social precedence, with moral worth measured by the extent to which an individual embodies the ideals of personhood, ideals suggested by the code of honor and revolving around the values of autonomy. But if honor derives from virtues associated with autonomy, then there are many, most notably women, who because of their physical, social, and economic dependency are handicapped in their efforts to realize these ideals. Although they share the general ethos and display some of the virtues of autonomy under certain conditions, their path to honor in this system is different. To have moral worth, these people must show modesty (*hasham*), which must be understood as voluntary deference to those in the system who more closely embody its ideals. Why sexual modesty, especially for women, is a critical aspect of this deference to social superiors, in particular senior male agnates, is elucidated in chapter 4, where I explore Bedouin ideas about gender and the place of sexuality in a system based on the bonds of agnation. The soundness of this interpretation of sexual modesty is demonstrated by its capacity to make sense of honor killings and the pattern of women's veiling.

How this moral system associated with the ideology of honor affects individuals in what they say and do and even in the most intimate realm of what they say they feel is the subject of the second part of the book. But once we are talking about personal life we are back to poetry, because people express sentiments and responses to personal situations both through ordinary conversation and through poetry. So, after a brief introduction in chapter 5 to the poetic genre of Awlad 'Ali expression and to the contextual analysis of this poetry, I turn in chapters 6 and 7 to an exploration of Bedouin responses to various life situations, particularly crises of loss and love. Here the consistent disjunction of the sentiments individuals express in poetic statements, on the one hand, and nonpoetic statements, on the other, leads us to conclude that the sentiments they express have cultural meanings. In fact, I use the term *sentiment* rather than *emotion* or *affect* specifically to signal the literary or conventional nature of these responses. Although the embeddedness of all emotional responses in cultural contexts that differentially value certain sentiments has been the subject of much recent work by psychological and interpretive anthropologists (see Geertz 1973a; Lutz 1982; Riesman 1977, 1983; Rosaldo 1980, 1983, 1984), I want to push this further. I intend to show that sentiments can actually symbolize values and that expression of these sentiments by individuals contributes to representations of the self, representations that are tied to morality, which in turn is ultimately tied to politics in its broadest sense. The sentiments of ordinary discourse are congruent with the ideology of honor and modesty. The sentiments generally expressed in poetry suggest a self that is vulnerable and weak, a self moved by deep feelings of love and longing. These are not at first glance the sentiments of proud and autonomous individuals, nor are they the sentiments of chaste individuals.

What are individuals symbolizing about themselves through expression of these non-virtuous sentiments? What is it about poetry that allows it to be used to express sentiments contrary to those appropriate to the ideals of honor without jeopardizing the reputations of those who recite it? What are individuals communicating about themselves and the society they live in through poems that express sentiments suggesting defiance of the moral system? Recognizing that both sets of responses are conventional, what is the significance of having two cultural discourses for the articulation of individual sentiments? To the extent that what people say, either in ordinary discourse or in the conventional and stylized discourse of poetry, can serve as a window into their experience, what does the discrepancy between the two modes of discourse tell us about the power of the ideology of honor and modesty to shape experience? Finally, what does the extraordinary cultural valuation of the poetic discourse tell us about the relationship between the ideology of honor and not only individual experience but also the organization of Bedouin social and political life as a whole? We turn to these questions in the final chapter, where what began as a puzzle about the meaning of a single poetic genre becomes a reflection on the fundamental issues of the politics of the discourses of sentiment, the nature of ideology, and the relationship between ideology and human experience.

Part One

THE IDEOLOGY OF
BEDOUIN SOCIAL LIFE

2

IDENTITY
IN RELATIONSHIP

This world full of people whose lives I came to share was not at all what I had envisioned. Several romantic images had informed my subconscious expectations. Knowing that Awlad 'Ali inhabited a coastal strip along the northern edge of the Libyan Desert,[1] I had imagined tents along a white-sand beach, the turquoise Mediterranean glimmering in the background. In my mind glowed a vivid passage from *Justine*, the first volume of Lawrence Durrell's "Alexandria Quartet":

> We had tea together and then, on a sudden impulse took our bathing things and drove out through the rusty slag-heaps of Mex towards the sand-beaches off Bourg El Arab, glittering in the mauve-lemon light of the fast-fading afternoon. Here the open sea boomed upon the carpets of fresh sand the colour of oxidized mercury; its deep melodious percussion was the background to such conversation as we had. We walked ankle deep in the spurge of those shallow dimpled pools, choked here and there with sponges torn up by the roots and flung ashore. We passed no one on the road I remember save a gaunt Bedouin youth carrying on his head a wire crate full of wild birds caught with lime-twigs. Dazed quail. (1957, 34)

I discovered, however, that despite its proximity, the sea played little part in the Bedouins' lives, and what appreciation of natural beauty they expressed was for the desert where, until sedentarization, their winter migrations had taken them. The members of my community all spoke with nostalgia about the inland desert, "up country" (*fōg*), although they had last migrated seven years before I arrived. They described the flora and fauna, the grasses so delectable to the gazelle, the umbellifer that whets the appetite, the herb that, boiled with tea, cures sundry maladies, the wild hares that must be hunted at night, and the game birds that suddenly take flight from deep within a shrub. They praised the good "dry" foods of desert life[2] and disparaged as unhealthy the fresh vegetable stews that are now an important part of their diet. They recalled with pleasure the milk products, so plentiful in springtime when rains have created desert pastures,[3] and savored memories of the taste of milk given by ewes who have fed on aromatic wormwood (*shīḥ*).

And yet, despite their appreciation of the desert's natural gifts, the Bedouins think of the territory in which they live primarily in terms of the people and groups who inhabit it. Theirs is an intensely social world in which people's activities and relationships are riveting, and solitude so abhorred that no one sleeps alone; those who spend time alone are thought to be vulnerable to attack by the evil spirits (*'afārīt*) who thrive wherever there are no people.

I had also expected tent-dwelling pastoral nomads who lived quietly with their herds but found instead that these same people who touted the joys of the desert lived in houses (even if they continued to pitch their tents next to them and spent most of their days in the tents), wore shiny wristwatches and plastic shoes, listened to radios and cassette players, and traveled in Toyota pickup trucks.[4] Unlike me, they did not regard these as alarming signs that they were losing their identity as a cultural group, that they were no longer Bedouins, because they define themselves not primarily by a way of life, however much they value pastoral nomadism and the rigors of the desert, but by some key principles of social organization: genealogy and a tribal order based on the closeness of agnates (paternal relatives) and tied to a code of morality, that of honor and modesty. Their social universe is ordered by these ideological principles, which define individuals' identities and the quality of their relationships to others. These principles are gathered up in Awlad 'Ali notions of "blood" (*dam*), a multi-faceted concept with dense meanings and tremendous cultural force, two aspects of which will be explored below.

Aṣl: *The Blood of Ancestry*

Blood both links people to the past and binds them in the present. As a link to the past, through genealogy, blood is essential to the definition of cultural identity. Nobility of origin or ancestry (*aṣl*) is a point of great concern to Awlad 'Ali. The clans or tribes known as Awlad 'Ali migrated into Egypt from Libya. Most accounts concur in viewing them, like the other Sa'ādi tribes of Cyrenaica, as descendants of the Beni Suleim and Beni Hilal, the Arab invaders from the Najd who swept through North Africa during the eleventh century. Some sources put their migration into Egypt at the end of the seventeenth century, although others favor the end of the eighteenth.[5] Along with the Mrābṭīn, other ambiguously related tribal groups with whom they share the Western Desert, they have remained marginal to the agrarian society of the Nile Valley, the economic and demographic core of Egypt.[6] By all estimates, the Bedouins of the Western Desert constitute far less than 1 percent of the total population of Egypt, a percentage that has probably been decreasing over the past century.[7]

The fortunes of Awlad 'Ali have always been tied to more than rainfall and the state of pasture, despite the fact that their traditional economy was based primarily on herds of camels, sheep, and goats, supplemented by rain-fed cereal cultivation in the littoral and some trade. Their movements and livelihood were determined not only by internal competition with other tribal groups who shared their way of life but also by external political and economic events affecting Libya and Egypt. They have been in contact with Europeans, Libyans, and Egyptians through trade, smuggling, and invasions, both peaceful and violent. Yet, despite centuries of contact with other groups and the efforts of successive central authorities in the Nile Valley—from Mohammad 'Ali through the British to Nasser and the current regime—to control and later to assimilate them, the Awlad 'Ali Bedouins maintain a distinct cultural identity.

In the nineteenth century, the free movement of Awlad 'Ali, their control over caravan routes, and their lack of respect for the law were a bane to Mohammad 'Ali. Finally, in exchange for their help in patrolling the borders, quelling internal rebellions, and assisting in foreign campaigns, he rewarded them with usufruct rights to the land in the Western Desert and with exemption from taxation and military conscription. By the time the British governed, the Awlad 'Ali were still far from subjugated or settled, although many had been induced to take up agriculture by the high value of cash crops, and the beginnings of competition from the railroad had loosened their hold on trade and driven them to concentrate on sheep rather than camels.[8] The British, insecure about the nomads' close ties to Libya and their smuggling activities, periodically and unsuccessfully sought to revoke their privileges to carry firearms and to claim exemption from military conscription. During World War II the Bedouins suffered the loss of herds, wells, and possessions when the battles between the British and Germans were fought on their soil.[9]

Only after the revolution and Nasser's rise to power in 1952 did government goals shift from political control to assimilation. The motives underlying the government's interest in integrating the Bedouins into the Egyptian polity, economy, and national culture were both ideological and material. As the anthropologist Ahmed Abou-Zeid explained in 1959, "Rightly or wrongly, it is generally assumed in Egypt that nomadism and semi-nomadism represent a phase of deterioration which is no longer compatible with the actualities of modern life and therefore should be abolished" (1959, 553). The government initiated projects to settle the nomads: it reclaimed land for agriculture; subsidized olive, fig, and almond orchards; subsidized fodder through the cooperatives; and made laws giving individuals who built a house the right to keep the land on which it was erected. The government also worked to improve pasture and herds, to encourage local industries, and to provide medical and educational services. In concert with Bedouin initiatives, primarily in commercial ventures, these projects radically altered the basic economy and work patterns of the Awlad 'Ali and contributed to sedentarization.[10] Nevertheless, Abou-Zeid's sanguine prediction about what impact government development projects would have on Awlad 'Ali rings hollow some twenty-five years later:

> The crowning achievement of these projects will be the reduction of the cultural and social contrast which exists at present between the Western Desert, with its nomadic and semi-nomadic inhabitants, and the rest of the country. This contrast is manifested in the different patterns of social relationships, the different values and modes of thought, and the different structure prevailing in the desert and the Nile Valley. (1959, 558)

Despite many changes in Awlad 'Ali society and economy, the goal of assimilation has not been achieved. On the contrary, much of the Bedouin identity and sense of self is articulated through distinction from or in opposition to non-Bedouins, be they *flūḥ* (peasants), *maṣriyyīn* (Egyptians, Cairenes), or *naṣāra* (Christians).[11] There are signs of integration into the state: most Bedouin men are aware of events in the world political arena, some hold opinions on the relative merits of the superpowers, and most have some knowledge of Egypt's internal political situation as well as its international involvements. But their passions are aroused only by tribal affairs—intra-Bedouin disputes, reconciliations, alliances, and hostilities. They may hear Egyptian programs on the radio, but their excitement is reserved for one program called "Iskandariyya-Maṭrūḥ" (Alexandria-Matruh). Once a week young and old, men and women, crowd around small radios and listen with rapt attention and visible enjoyment to this program, which features traditional Bedouin songs, poems, and greetings for various parties, all identified by name and tribal affiliation.

The Bedouins' sense of collective identity is crystallized in opposition to the Egyptians or peasants, who are lumped together as "the people of the Nile Valley" (*hal wādi n-nīl*). In the Bedouins' view, the differences extend beyond the linguistic and sartorial to the fundamentals of origin, defined by genealogy, social organization, modes of interpersonal interaction, and a sort of moral nature.[12] How accurate the Bedouins' characterization of the Egyptians might be is not at issue. For Awlad 'Ali, the Egyptians with whom they share a country defined by political borders they consider arbitrary constitute a vivid "other," providing a convenient foil for self-definition; by looking at how the Bedouins distinguish themselves from the Egyptians, we can isolate the nodes of Bedouin identity.

Blood, in the sense of genealogy, is the basis of Awlad 'Ali identity. No matter where or how they live, those who can link themselves genealogically to any of the tribes of the Western Desert are *'arab* (Arabs), not Egyptians.[13] Awlad 'Ali more frequently refer to themselves as *'arab* than as *badū* (Bedouins). As in many cultures, the word they use to designate themselves also connotes the general term *people*—for instance anyone returning from a visit to kin is queried, "How are your Arabs?" But the term has a more specific meaning when used to distinguish the Bedouins from their Egyptian neighbors. In that context, it implies the Bedouin claim to origins in the Arabian Peninsula and to genealogical links to the pure Arab tribes who were the first followers of the Prophet Muhammad. It also suggests their affinity to all the

Arabic-speaking Muslims of the Middle East and North Africa who, because of common origin, they presume to be just like themselves.

Blood is the authenticator of origin or pedigree and as such is critical to Bedouin identity and their differentiation from Egyptians, who are said to lack roots or nobility of origin (*aṣl* or *mabdā*). Some Bedouins stated this idea by characterizing the Egyptians as mixed-blooded or impure; others attributed to the Egyptians Pharaonic origins, as the following story told to me by one Bedouin man suggests:

> When Moses escaped from Egypt, the Pharaoh and all of the real men, the warriors, set off after him. They left behind only the women, children, and servants/slaves [*khadama*]. These were the weak men who washed women's feet and cared for the children. When Moses crossed the Red Sea, the Pharaoh's men drowned chasing him. This left only the servants. They are the grandfathers [ancestors] of the Egyptians. That is why they are like that now. The men are women and the women are men. He carries the children and does not take a seat until he sees that she has.

The centrality of blood, in the sense of a bloodline, pedigree, or link to illustrious forebears, is apparent from these remarks. Underlying this concern is the belief that a person's nature and worth are closely tied to the worthiness of his or her stock. By crediting the Egyptians with no line to the past or, more insulting, a line to an inferior, pre-Islamic past of servitude, this man was making a statement about their present worthlessness. The ignominy of origin is a metaphor for present shortcomings.

Nobility of origin is believed to confer moral qualities and character. Bedouins value a constellation of qualities that could be captured by the umbrella phrase "the honor code." Although the entailments of this code will be detailed in the next two chapters, a few of the Bedouins' criticisms of Egyptians will introduce the themes. Men variously described Egyptians as lacking in moral excellence (*fadhīla*), honor (*sharaf*), sincerity and honesty (*ṣadag*), and generosity (*kurama*), at the same time claiming these as Bedouin traits. One example they gave of Egyptians' lack of honor was their insistence on using contracts in transactions—for the Arab, they explained, a person's word is sufficient.

The most highly prized Arab virtue is generosity, expressed primarily through the hospitality for which they are renowned. As one Bedouin man put it, "We like to do [our duty to guests], not have done to." To honor guests, ideally a sheep is slaughtered. If this is not feasible, a smaller animal may be substituted. Failing that, at least some food must be put out. No guest or even passerby can leave without being invited to drink tea. Of the Egyptians one man said, "It is rare for them to invite you to their homes. You are lucky if they invite you for a cup of coffee or tea, and that after you have invited them to your home, slaughtered a sheep for them, and given them everything it was in your power to give." Some Bedouins also accuse the Egyptians of being opportunistic, of not knowing the meaning of friendship.

Fearlessness and courage are qualities considered natural in Bedouin men and women as concomitants of their nobility of origin. Although the days of tribal warfare are over, Bedouin men maintain the values of warriors, carrying arms and resorting to violence if challenged or insulted. Women support these values. All describe Egyptians as easily frightened and cowardly and lacking in the belligerence that, as we shall see, is so important in the ideology of honor.

Perhaps even more indicative of *aṣl* are moral qualities associated with relations between men and women. The Egyptians' lax enforcement of sexual segregation and the intimacy husbands and wives display in public are interpreted as signs of Egyptian men's weakness and the women's immorality. (The connection between these will be elucidated in the following two chapters.) The pivotal role of sexual segregation in Awlad 'Ali definitions of their own culture was brought home to me on a visit to a settled Bedouin family living in Bhēra, an agricultural province. Genealogically Awlad 'Ali, this family of landowners lived on a large and productive agricultural estate, they dressed in that peculiar mix of peasant and urban garb common to the rural elite, and they spoke an Egyptian rather than a Libyan dialect. When I challenged them, the women adamantly defended their Arab identity. One argued, "We are not like the peasants. Their women go out and talk to men. We never leave the house, we don't drink tea with men, and we don't greet the guests."

That the Bedouins attribute the ease of social intercourse between men and women and men's show of affection toward women to men's weakness is clear in the story of the Pharaonic origins of the Egyptians recounted above. The point was made that the servants left behind were those who "washed women's feet and cared for the children." To this day, the man who told me that story said, Egyptian men were weak and doted on their wives. The antiquity of this view of Egyptians is attested to by Lord Cromer's comment in 1908 that "the Bedouins despise the fellaheen [peasants], whom they consider an unmanly race" (1908, 198). Many Bedouin men and women echoed this man's sentiments:

> Among the Arabs the man rules the woman, not like the Egyptians whose women can come and go as they please. When an Egyptian family goes out, the man carries the baby and the wife walks in front of him. Among the Arabs, a woman must get permission to go visiting. Among the Arabs, if there are guests in the home, a wife can come to greet them only if they are kinsmen. She does not stay in the room. If they are nonkin, she does not enter at all.

Further evidence of the reversal of proper power relations is the alleged public affection Egyptian husbands show their wives. Stories of men cooking for bedridden wives, bringing them flowers, or doing them other favors provoked strong reactions in Bedouin women and men alike. The women's disapproval was tempered by an occasional wistful comment such as "the Egyptians spoil their women—they love their wives," but Bedouin men were less equivocal. They considered such behavior simply unmanly and a testament to female rule (which is not to deny that many of them felt affection for their wives and treated them with respect).

The other side of the coin to men's weakness is women's immodesty. Once two women giving me advice about what to do when I got married earnestly confided, "You should not let the groom have sex with you on the first night." I argued that we knew for a fact that a certain bridal couple had consummated their marriage the first night. They countered, "Oh, she is a peasant. They don't care. They have no shame [*mā yithashshamūsh*]."[14] They laughed uproariously as they recalled another peasant woman who had announced to her women guests the morning after her wedding that her husband had made love to her twice, and added, "She had no shame at all!" Bedouin brides vehemently deny that sexual intercourse has taken place, even when it is obvious to all that it has. One woman put it this way:

> The Egyptians are not like us. They have no shame. Why, the So-and-So's [an Egyptian family we knew] have a photograph from their wedding hanging on the wall in their living room where everyone can see it. In it, he has his arm around her. And they sit together and call each other pet names. An Arab woman would be embarrassed/modest [*tahashsham*] in front of an older brother, her mother-in-law, people.

Many of the ideas the Bedouins have about Egyptians are based on hearsay and the imposition of their own cultural interpretations on reported behavior. Very few of those living in the desert have much opportunity to see Egyptians at home. But, as the following incident shows, when they do have such opportunities, their ideas are confirmed. During the holidays celebrating the Prophet's birthday, an Egyptian army officer, a friend and business partner of the Haj, decided to bring his family for a weekend visit to the Western Desert, and they spent a day and a night with us before going on to a beach resort. Their visit occasioned a great deal of commotion, including the purchase and preparation of special foods, a massive cleanup, and the household's rearrangement to vacate rooms for their comfortable accommodation. The visit strained everyone's nerves and energy, but it provided an intriguing close-up look at the Egyptians.

Everyone knew about the Egyptians' lax sex segregation, so they were not surprised that the women and girls ate with the men and spent time as a group in the men's guest room. However, the evening's events were unexpected. After dinner, the man, his wife, their daughters, and his wife's sister all retired to their rooms, only to emerge in nightclothes and bathrobes and go to the men's guest room, where they sat chatting with their host and his brothers. This immodesty of dress sent shock waves through the community. Next came the scandalized realization that husband and wife intended to sleep in the same room. Although Bedouin husbands and wives sleep together under normal circumstances, they would not do so when visiting; each would sleep with members of his or her own sex. In fact, it is considered rude for a host or hostess not to sleep with his or her guests. The public admission of active sexuality implied by the couple's wish to sleep together was considered the height of immodesty. Yet everyone was polite, the values of friendship and hospitality outweighing the deeply offended sense of propriety. Perhaps more important, the Bedouins excused their guests' behavior because they recognized that the Egyptians were another sort of people, whose lack of pedigree made it difficult (although not impossible) for them to behave with honor.

Garāba: *The Blood of Relationship*

The concept of blood is central to Bedouin identity in a second sense: through its ideological primacy in the present, as a means of determining social place and the links between people. Above all,

Awlad 'Ali conceive of themselves in terms of tribes, notoriously ambiguous segmented units defined by consanguinity or ties to a common patrilineal ancestor.[15]

This tribal social organization is another point on which the Awlad 'Ali proudly differentiate themselves from their Egyptian neighbors, whom they disparage as a "people" (*sha'b*)—meaning that the Egyptians are not organized tribally, do not know their roots, and identify with a geographic area or, worse, with a national government. The importance of blood in social identity is apparent in the identification of Bedouins by family, lineage, and tribe. One of the first questions asked a newcomer is "Where are you from?" The answer to this question is not a geographical area (that would be the response to another question, "Where is your homeland [*wuṭn*]?") but rather a tribal affiliation. Because Awlad 'Ali apply the term *tribe* (*gabīla*) to many levels of organization, people belong to numerous named tribes simultaneously.[16] The tribe a person chooses to identify with at any given moment depends largely on the rhetorical statement the speaker wishes to make about his or her relationship to the inquirer. To assert unity and closeness, a person will point to the shared level of tribal affiliation (a common ancestor), establishing himself or herself as a paternal kinsperson of the appropriate generation.

The tribal terms in which Bedouins conceive of social bonds lend a distinctive cast to their social life. Most of the anthropological literature on Bedouins has focused on how kinship provides an idiom for political relations. I am less concerned with whether the Bedouins really organize politically in terms of segmentary lineages (Peters 1967) or with how the theory of segmentary opposition, the genealogical ordering of political life, and kinship and affinity relate to Bedouin economy and ecology (Peters 1960, 1965, 1967, 1980; Behnke 1980) or even to the historical problem of uncertain political relations (Meeker 1979) than with how kinship ideology shapes individual identity and the perceptions and management of everyday social relations. This is not to deny either the importance of kinship as the language of sociopolitical organization or the dialectic between the political and interpersonal spheres, as later arguments will show. It is merely to shift the focus to kinship as the idiom for Awlad 'Ali feelings about, and actions toward, persons in their social world, in order to show how deeply this ideology penetrates everyday life and sentiment.[17]

The social world of the Awlad 'Ali is bifurcated into kin versus strangers/outsiders (*garīb* versus *gharīb*), a distinction that shapes both sentiment and behavior. Bedouin kinship ideology is based on two fundamental propositions. First, all those related by blood share a substance that identifies them, in both senses of the word: giving each person a social identity and causing individuals to identify with everyone else who shares the same blood. Agnates share blood and flesh (*dam wlham*), although the fact that a relationship through maternal ascendants is characterized as one of *dmāya* (the diminutive of "blood") suggests that the Bedouins do recognize distant maternal links as a weak form of kinship. Second, because of this identification with each other, individuals who share blood feel close.

The term for kinship is *garāba*, from the root meaning "to be close." The Bedouin vision of social relations is dominated by this ideology of natural, positive, and unbreakable bonds of blood between consanguines, particularly agnates, including putative or distant agnates, those related through common patrilineal descent as manifested by a shared eponymous ancestor. Tribal bonds, or relations between paternal kin, are called *'aṣabiyya*, which one man expressively characterized as "son-of-a-bitch bonds you can never break."[18] The Bedouins look down on the Egyptians, alleging that they know no one but their immediate kin.

Agnation has indisputable ideological priority in kin reckoning. Descent, inheritance, and tribal sociopolitical organization are conceptualized as patrilineal, extending the strong relationship between father and son (and father and daughter) back in time and outside the immediate family. The significance of agnation is reflected in how rights are distributed among members of a family.

*Kinsmen preparing tea in
a desert camp*

For one thing, children take their father's tribal affiliation, although their mother's affiliation affects their status (Abou-Zeid 1966, 257). In case of a divorce, the mother has no right to keep her children, although she may temporarily take unweaned children with her and she may set up a separate household with adult sons. The superior claim of agnates to children was expressed in a comment I heard one woman (a paternal first cousin of her husband) make to her co-wife in the midst of a heated argument. She asserted, "Your son is ours, and even if we decide to sacrifice him [like a sheep], you have no right to say a word." The hyperbole produced by flared passions does not invalidate the essential message—that paternal kin have jural rights to all children born to wives of agnates.

The Bedouins consider this not just a right but also a natural bond based on sentiment, as is clear from the following story I heard about a neighbor of ours. This woman was divorced by her husband after he had brought her to her natal home for a visit and never returned for her. Her young son, considered too young to part from his mother, was with her. After a year, the boy's paternal grandfather came to the house to take his grandson back. According to reports, he asked his five-year-old grandson, "Would you like to come with me?" Although the boy had never seen him before, he ran to pack a few clothes, put his hand in his grandfather's, and left with hardly a glance back. His mother was heartbroken. Men who heard the story nodded their heads and did not seem surprised; "Blood" was all they said by way of explanation. Although women, too, perceive social relations and identity primarily in terms of agnation, their experiences lead them to a slightly different position. Many of their closest relationships, to their children and to coresident women in their marital communities, are not those of agnation. Most of the women who heard the story were moved and reacted differently, wondering if the grandfather had used magic (*katablu*) to lure the boy into abandoning his mother.

Much has been written on the close (if often troubled) relations between men, especially brothers, in patrilineal, patrilocal societies.

Yet the position of women and attitudes about the bonds created by marriage give the clearest index of the ideological dominance of agnation in social identity and relationships in Bedouin society. A woman retains her tribal affiliation throughout her life and should side with her own kin in their disputes with her husband's kin; I heard many stories of women who left for their natal homes, abandoning children, under such conditions. In her marital camp people refer to her by her tribal affiliation, and she may refer to herself as an outsider even after twenty years of marriage.

The extent to which women remain a part of their own patrigroup is clear from the following incident. In one camp, when a paternal aunt of the core agnates died, her nieces and nephews all agreed that it would have been better if she had come to spend her last days with them and died and been buried in her father's camp. Even after forty years of married life away from the camp, they considered it her true home. Of the five people who washed her corpse, only one was from her husband's family; the others were her sisters and her brothers' wives. Although a woman can never be incorporated into her husband's lineage, if she has adult sons she becomes secure and comfortable in her marital community. Once her husband dies and she becomes head of the household, her close association with her sons makes her seem the core of the agnatic cluster. There are many such matriarchs.

Not only do women derive their identities from their patriline, but they also retain their ties to their kin, even after marriage, for both affective and strategic reasons. A woman remains dependent on the moral, legal, and often economic support of her father, brothers, or other kinsmen. Only they can guarantee her marital rights. A woman cut off from her family is vulnerable to abuse from her husband and society (Mohsen 1967, 157), but a married woman with the backing of her kin is well protected. When mistreated or wronged, she argues that she need not put up with such treatment because "behind me are men." When angry, she packs a few of her possessions in a bundle and heads off toward her family's camp. And in case of divorce, she can return home, where she is entitled to support. But because she is identified with her kin, her behavior affects their honor and reputation, just as theirs affects hers. Her kin, not her husband, are ultimately responsible for her and are entitled to sanction all her wrongdoings, including adultery.

Although strategically useful, these kin ties are conceived of as based on sentiment. The sense of closeness, identification, common interests, and loyalty is expressed in the way women talk about their kin and in their attitudes toward visits home and even toward visits by their kin. Women are preoccupied with news of their kin. They rush home (if their husbands permit) whenever an event is celebrated or mourned: if they hear of an illness, a wedding, a circumcision, a return from the pilgrimage, a release from prison, or a funeral, they visit, and they are dejected and frustrated if for some reason they cannot. When a young wife left our camp "angry" without any apparent reason, some of the men suspected magic, but the women thought it more plausible that she just missed her relatives and wished to see her brother, who had just been released from prison. Her husband had been too busy to take her home for a visit, and she had been crying for days.

Visits home are anticipated with excitement, suffused with warmth, and remembered nostalgically. Women always return from such visits reporting how happy, pampered, and well fed they were. They bring back gifts, dresses, jewelry, soap, perfume, and candies. Their hair is freshly braided and hennaed, smelling sweetly of expensive cloves—kinswomen's grooming favors. And when a brother or other kinsman visits a woman's marital home, although sexual segregation may sometimes prevent her from sitting with him, she will certainly offer the choicest provisions and devote herself to the preparations personally, rather than delegating her responsibilities to grown daughters or younger co-wives. The tone of their greetings, however brief, invariably betrays affection.

Marriage presents serious problems for the consistency of an ideological system in which agnation is given priority over any other basis for affiliation. The Awlad 'Ali commitment to this system is expressed in their contempt for the perceived Egyptian propensity to reside in nuclear family units, a shameful sign of the valuation of marital ties over agnatic ones. One man said, "Arabs say that mother, father, and brother are the most dear. Even if an Arab loves his wife more than anything, he cannot let anyone know this. He tries never to let this show."

The way to resolve this problem of marriage is to fuse it with identity and closeness of shared blood. Patrilateral parallel-cousin marriage may be preferred because it is the only type consistent with Bedouin ideas about the importance of agnation (see chapter 4). As in other parts of the Middle East, this type of marriage is the cultural ideal, although it is only one of many types of marriage practiced. Because of the prevalence of multiple kinship ties between individuals (Peters 1980, 133–34) and because the term *paternal cousin* extends to all members of a tribe (however widely defined), a range of marriages can be interpreted as conforming to this preferential type and will be justified in terms of this preference even when arranged for other reasons. Thus, even if cousins are more directly related through some maternal link, their relationship will be described in terms of the paternal one.[19] The actual frequency of cousin marriages varies depending on a number of circumstances that are too complex to explore here but that have been much debated in the theoretical literature (see Bourdieu 1977, 32–33). The actual incidence in any particular community is, however, less important than the ideological preference. In the community in which I did my fieldwork, the incidence happened to be quite high. Four of the five core household heads had married their paternal first cousins (FBD); of those who took second wives, three married more distant cousins, women from another section of their tribe. In this generation, the eldest daughter and eldest son of two brothers had married, and the brothers planned to marry other sons and daughters to each other in the near future.

What differentiates marriage to paternal kin from other types of marriage, and how are the differences evaluated? For most, the advantages do not have to do with sexual excitement. Indeed, some older men complained that the "marital" (sexual) side of such marriages was limited. As one polygynously married man put it, "My other wives are better with me personally," although he went on to explain that he nevertheless preferred his cousin-wife, for reasons to be enumerated below. Certain young men complained that the trouble with marrying a cousin was that she was like a sister.[20] An unmarried man mused, "You won't feel like talking and flirting. And she knows everything about you, where you go, who you see." He implied that she would therefore not be in awe of her husband, reducing the power differential. Girls occasionally voiced a wish to see something new by marrying an outsider, since then they would leave the camp. They did not talk (at least to me) about the sexual aspect of marriage.

The advantages of such marriages are that they presumably build on the prior bonds of paternal kinship to take on the closeness, trust, identification, and loyalty appropriate to such bonds. In polygynous unions, the wife who is a paternal kinswoman is usually better treated than her co-wives. The young man who complained that there was no mystery with a cousin-wife also claimed that he would not beat her as much as he would an outsider. And the older man who confessed the lack of sexual excitement with his cousin-wife considered this wife to be first in his affections and in charge of his household. His other wives had tried in vain to displace his cousin in his affections, something he claimed was impossible because,

> after all, she is my father's brother's daughter. I know that if I am gone, she will take care of the house, entertain my guests graciously, and protect my property and all of my children. Haven't you noticed how even though she loves her own children more, she cares for the children of my other wives, even protecting them from their mothers'

harshness? After all, the children are closer to her, they are her kin, her tribe. Also, if something is on my mind, it will be on her mind too. Outsiders don't care. They don't care who might enter the house while I am gone, what gets spilled, ruined, or stolen. They don't care about your name or reputation. But a father's brother's daughter cares about you and your things because they are hers.

Another man, even though he was no longer sleeping with his postmenopausal wife, treated her as head of the domestic household, entrusted her with all his money and valuables, and took only her with him on important visits. He explained, "I take my father's brother's daughter with me when I go to visit outsiders because I trust her." Nearly all the young children born to his other wives slept with her, ate with her, and spent more time with her than with their own mothers. They called her *hannī,* or grandmother, the person for whom children feel the deepest affection.

Women see innumerable advantages in this marriage arrangement. As wives, they are more secure and powerful if they marry paternal kin because they remain among those whose duty it is to protect them. They are not as dependent on husbands, since their right to support derives from their claim to the common patrimony. They also feel comfortable in the community, living among kinfolk with whom they share interests, loved ones, and often a lifetime of experience. Even if the match does not work out, they need not leave their children. Marriages between coresident cousins are often more affectionate because they build on childhood experiences of closeness, in a society in which relations between unrelated members of the opposite sex are highly circumscribed and often either distant or hostile (see chapter 4).

In contrast, wives who are not patrikin to their husbands are often treated differently from wives who are paternal cousins or, even more, mothers and sisters of the core agnates. In the camp in which I lived, the men tended to overlook or skimp on gifts to these outside women at festive occasions such as weddings when men buy clothing and jewelry for the camp's women. In defense, the outsider wives tended to form alliances with one another, but this process was not haphazard either: agnation created special bonds even between in-marrying wives. Two women from the same tribe who had married men in my camp spent a great deal of time together, helped each other with work, and supported each other in arguments. If one was angry with a certain person or family, the other would also refuse to speak to them. Thus, whatever the material consequences,[21] marrying agnates protects women from having to be vulnerable to people who do not have their interests at heart and keeps them close to sources of support, and it saves men from having to bring into their households women whose primary loyalties and interests lie elsewhere.

As we have seen, consanguinity provides the only culturally approved basis for forming close social relationships in Awlad 'Ali society. However, agnation, although primary, is not the only factor informing social identity and social relationships. Awlad 'Ali individuals unite on a variety of other bases, usually trying to couch these in the idiom of kinship.

Maternal Ties and a Common Life

Besides agnation, the two most important bonds between individuals are maternal kinship and coresidence (*'ishra*). On the surface, these two bases for forming relationships might seem to lie outside the dominant principle of agnation, but the Bedouins do not perceive them so. Using different conceptual means, they reconcile each with the ideology of lineage organization, subordinating both to the principle of paternal kinship.

Their task with regard to maternal bonds is made simpler by the fact that the distinction between maternal and paternal kin is not always clear-cut. Patrilateral parallel-cousin marriage fuses maternal and paternal ties. As Peters (1967, 272) also points out, the density of overlapping ties created by intermarriage within the lineage and by continual exchanges of women between the same two lineages over several generations also clouds the question of whether behavior and sentiment conform to the jural rules. But at least in conversation, and when applying kin terms, the Bedouins tend to give priority to the ties between agnates in cases where multiple connections can be drawn. Thus, in the camp I lived in, the children of the two brothers who had married two sisters who were their paternal first cousins always called their uncles and aunts by the term for paternal, not maternal, uncle and aunt (*sīd, 'amma,* not *khāl, khāla*).

In general, individuals and their maternal kin share bonds of great fondness and a sense of closeness, but maternal descent hardly defines social identity, because it cannot be carried further than one generation, and it does not provide a strong sense of identification with others. The only hints of belief in shared substance are proverbs proclaiming the children's resemblance to their maternal uncles. The honor of the matriline can touch a woman's children in refining their status vis-à-vis the children of her co-wives. The factors that reinforce social relationships based on agnation, such as shared jural responsibility, common property, or coresidence, rarely support maternal bonds. But the tie symbolized in the word *dmāya* (the diminutive of "blood") carries with it sentiments of loyalty and amity and obligations of reciprocal attendance and gift giving at ritual occasions.

This closeness to maternal kin does not conflict with the principle of agnation. In fact, a careful look at the relationship between a woman's kin and her children will reveal that the maternal bond derives indirectly from agnation itself. First, because adults, not children, initiate relationships, the bond to a woman's child is an extension of the bond between the woman herself and her paternal kinfolk. As one man explained, "A woman is always part of her tribe, even when she marries outside of it," so her kin care about her children because they care about her. They certainly shower affection on both when they come for visits. Indirect evidence of

Mother and son

the way Bedouins conceive of such relationships can be found in the kinship terms for nephew and niece, which are built on siblingship: all nephews and nieces, however distant and whatever generation, are called "sister's son" or "brother's son" (*ibnakhiyyi* or *ibnakhīti*). From the point of view of those who initiate relationships, the bonds to nephews and nieces are consistent with the bonds of agnation, since these are merely the children of paternal kin.

In Bedouin society, relationships between mothers and children are, with few exceptions, extremely close and affectionate throughout life. Based on initial dependency and later concern, the mother-child bond is taken for granted, and it presents the only undisputed and undisguised exception to the rule equating closeness with agnation. Once children are older, after having lived with and come to identify with paternal kin, they feel affection or some sort of link to maternal kin as an extension of their affection for their mothers. If they love their mother, they will love those with whom she identifies and is identified. Thus, from the child's perspective, maternal kin are neither confused with nor in competition with paternal kin; they are merely thought of as the mother's agnates. If anything, the competition is between mother and father, as highlighted in the playful questioning of one father who, as his wife sat nearby, tickled his two-year-old daughter and asked over and over, "Whose daughter are you? Are you your father's daughter or your mother's?"

The other type of close relationship in Bedouin society is that between nonkin who live together, or, as one man described it, *garāba min l-galb* (kinship from the heart). By a logical reversal, Awlad 'Ali justify the development of close bonds between individuals who are neither maternal kin nor from the same tribe or who, although from the same tribe, are genealogically distant. Since close genealogical kin ideally live near each other, coresidence and paternal kinship are strongly associated. By a subtle shift, those who live together develop relationships similar to those between paternal kin. In talking about such relationships, Awlad 'Ali tend to stress the link of paternal kinship, however distant—if it exists at all. Where there is no genealogical link, the nature of the relationship is downplayed, and kinlike bonds are created through actions.

The bond of living together or sharing a life is called *'ishra*. Although marked by impermanence,[22] it suggests the kinlike bonds of enduring sentiments of closeness, as well as a more or less temporary identification and the concomitant obligations of support and unity. The bond is symbolized by the notion of sharing food, which in Bedouin culture (like many others) signifies the absence of enmity. The expression used to describe a relationship based on proximity or a shared life, *'ēsh wmliḥ* (cereal and salt), applies to husbands and wives, past and present neighbors, and patron and client families alike.

With sedentarization, the variety and permanence of neighbors has changed. Within the settled hamlets, neighbors become quasi-kin: they visit and assist each other at feasts marking circumcisions, weddings, and funerals and at births and illnesses, and they respect the mourning periods of neighboring families. They stand together politically in confrontations with other groups, especially those living nearby. They also spend a good deal of time together.

Many camps and hamlets, especially the wealthier ones, include a number of families or individuals who have attached themselves to the group, or to particular men, as clients. In the camp I lived in there were five such households, all so closely tied to the core families that I initially mistook them for kin. Some were indeed distant kin, a status that was stressed, but most were not, and their tribal identity was played down except in crisis situations. Yet, like kin, most had spent their whole lives in the community. For example, one family consisted of a young man, his wife and two children, and his old blind father. The old man had been a shepherd to the fathers of the core agnates, as had his father before him. The women and children called the old man by the kinship term for close paternal uncle (*sīd*), since older people in the community are rarely referred to without a kinship term. The young man was a constant visitor in the core households, entertaining guests when the patrons were absent or assisting in serving meals when they were present, helping with work, and so forth. He played a social role similar to that of the core agnates' nephews, to whom he was in fact very close.

Another client family had lived with the group for over thirty years. The head of the household had initially joined the camp as a shepherd, and he eventually entered into a partnership with one of his patrons. While I was there, his patron's brother decided to marry the old man's attractive young daughter. It was interesting to see how her attitude and those of the other camp women differed from that of a bride who married into the camp from outside at the same time. The outsider bride was uneasy, and people were tense around her. This was not true of the client's daughter—the bonds of 'ishra already tied her to all the others in the camp. When I remarked on the difference, people explained, "She was born in the camp. There is no strangeness [ghurba]. Everyone is relaxed."

Merely living together confers rights and obligations comparable to those of kinship, as is evident in the following two examples. A woman who was both sister to the men in the core community and a neighbor (having married a man of a different lineage who lived nearby) was indignant at not having been invited to accompany her kinsmen to her brother's engagement feast (siyāg) or to the bride's ritual visit home after the wedding (zawra), where meat is plentiful and the groom's kinswomen need not work. As part of her appeal for justice, she argued, "I'm their sister! Why, even as a neighbor I should have gone!" Another woman, scolding someone for not assisting her pregnant kinswoman, told of a woman whose neighbor—"not even a relative!"—had baked her bread, brought her water from the well, and even washed her clothes for her.

It is not enough to argue simply that because kin usually live together, those who live together are conceived of as kin. The question is, why does living together create such strong bonds? Because the relationships that develop are upheld not by jural responsibilities but by strong sentiment, I think the key lies in

Bedouin attitudes toward "familiarity." The term *mwallif ʿale* (to be used to or familiar with) is most often used to describe a child's feelings of extreme attachment to caretakers other than its mother (usually a grandmother, older sister, or father's wife), as evidenced by the child's violent protest when forced to part from the caretaker, miserable crying, and refusal to eat or be comforted. The term was also used in conjunction with the idea of a homeland; people explained that they felt uneasy and "didn't know how to sit or stay" in territories they were not used to. Thus the idea of attachment to the familiar emerges. Living together makes strangers familiar and hence more like kin, who are automatically familiar by virtue of being family.

Identification and Sharing

Shared blood signifies close social relations only because it, in the Awlad ʿAli conception, identifies kin with one another. Kin share concerns and honor; ideally they also share residence, property, and livelihood.[23] They express this sense of commonality through visiting, ritual exchanges, and sharing work, emotional responses, and secrets. In times of trouble their fierce loyalty sometimes leads them to take up arms together and, in the case of homicides, is institutionalized in the corporate responsibility for blood indemnity (*diyya*).

This strong identification with patrikin manifests itself in several ways. First, in many contexts individuals act as if what touches their kin touches them; an insult to one person is interpreted as an insult to the whole kinship group, just as an insult to a kinsperson is interpreted as an affront to the self. A woman, threatening to leave her husband for slurring her father's name in the heat of a marital dispute, appealed to anyone who would listen, "Would you stay if anyone said that about your father?" Likewise, one family member's shameful acts bring dishonor on the rest of the family, just as everyone benefits from the glories of a prominent agnate or patrilineal ancestor. The rationale for both vengeance for homicides and honor killings (in practice extremely rare) is that an affront to one individual or a shameful act by one person affects the whole group, not just the individual.[24]

Second, people are perceived, at least by outsiders, as nearly interchangeable representatives of their kin groups. When a host honors a guest, the assumption is that he honors the person's whole kin group, which explains why sheep are sometimes slaughtered for women guests or individuals who are not especially important personally. Members of my adopted family eagerly asked how I was treated whenever I visited people outside our camp, because they took it as an index of the esteem in which *they* were held. Only one member of an agnatic cluster need actually attend ceremonies of outside groups to fulfill the obligation of the whole group. In arranging marriages, the individuals are less important than the kin groups involved. Men would arrive at our camp and request "one of your girls" in marriage, apparently caring little which one, since they had chosen the family to *nāsib* (create an affinal relationship with). Some of these men were refused because of grudges against their kin groups. Even close personal ties with the men of our camp, in one case due to maternal kinship, were overshadowed by the suitors' tribal affiliations and the state of intertribal relations.

People often describe the existence of bonds between people, whether based on paternal or maternal kinship or just a common life, by using the phrase "we go to them and they come to us" (*nimshūlhum wyjūnā*). This expression conveys nicely the way bonds between individuals are expressed and maintained. "Coming and going" refers to reciprocity in both everyday visiting and ritualized visiting on particular occasions (*munāsabāt*), usually those marking life crises or transitions. Since these occasions are unofficially ranked in order of importance, failure to attend some is interpreted as a sign that the relationship has been terminated and the bond broken.

The impetus for such visits is identification (the sense that what happens to kin is happening to the self) and the desire to be with those who share one's feelings. Visits also provide occasions for strengthening identification between those who already have bonds. This is most obvious in the least ritualized visits, those undertaken in times of trouble or illness. During my first two months in the field, my host was mysteriously absent for a stretch. Guests kept appearing at our household, and many stayed. At the time, I did not know enough to realize that this constant flow of visitors was unusual; I merely thought that the Bedouins were indeed very sociable people. When my host returned, there was a celebration, sheep were slaughtered, and guests were plentiful and lively. I later understood that he had been detained for questioning by government authorities; everyone had been worried that he had been arrested, and they had gathered out of concern, to be with those closest to him and thus most affected. After his safe return, well-wishers came by to share their relief. Visits to the ill follow a similar protocol. Failure to visit a person who is ill is taken as an insult and a breach in relations precisely because it is a departure from what would be a "natural" concern for the well-being of those you love.

The worst form of trouble, of course, is death. Not to go to a camp in which a person has died, if you have any link either to that person or to his or her relatives or coresidents, is to sever the tie. I will describe funeral rituals in greater detail in chapter 6, but a brief look at one aspect of women's mourning behavior will clarify the participatory quality of ritual visits. Women who come to deliver condolences (*y'azzun*) approach the house or camp wailing (*y'aytun*), and then each squats before those family members to whom they are closest and "cries" (*yatabākun*) with them. This ritualized crying is more than simple weeping; it is a heartrending chant bemoaning the woman's own loss of her closest deceased family member, usually a father. When I asked about this unusual behavior, one woman explained, "Do you think you cry over the dead person? No, you cry for yourself, for those who have died in your life." The woman closest to the person whose

Women going to pay a visit

death is being mourned then answers with a chant in which she bemoans her loss. Women speak of going to "cry with" somebody, suggesting that they perceive it as sharing an experience. What they share is grief, not just by sympathizing, but also by actually reexperiencing, in the company of the person currently grieving, their own grief over the death of a loved one. Not only may such shared emotional experiences enhance the sense of identification that underpins social bonds, but participation in rituals that express sentiments might also generate feelings like those the person directly affected is experiencing, thus creating an identification between people where it did not spontaneously exist. The same process might apply to happy occasions celebrating weddings, circumcisions, return from the pilgrimage to Mecca, or release from prison.

Going and coming is accompanied by the exchange of gifts, animals for slaughter, money, and services.[25] I would argue that these exchanges are considered not debts, as Peters (1951, 166–67) maintains, but acknowledgments, in a material idiom, of the existence of bonds. Although gifts and countergifts are essential to social relationships, they do not establish relationships; rather, they reflect their existence and signify their continuation. If gift giving occasionally takes on a burdensome quality, it is because individual experience and contingencies of personality and history can never be fully determined by the cultural ideals of social organization.

Sharing is the common theme that runs through these ways of expressing and maintaining bonds. Visits are prompted by the sense of identification felt with individuals to whom one is close, and they provide occasions for participating in emotionally charged events that increase the basis of what is shared. By giving gifts of both material goods and services people share what they have. As we shall explore in the second half of this book, sharing thoughts and feelings, especially ones that do not conform to the ideals of honor and modesty, is also a significant index of social closeness.

Identity in a Changing World

The profound changes that currently affect the Awlad 'Ali interact in complex ways with the ideology of blood outlined above. Kinship is still the dominant ideological principle of social organization, and despite the different look of the land, settlement patterns are marked by continuity. Although clusters of houses and tents like those described in the first chapter are today more common than the traditional scattered encampments of between two and ten tents, both are called by the same name (*naji'*, pl. *nawāji'*) and are seen as similar. The dwellings may be permanent, but the communities, which take the name of the group's dominant lineage or family, remain socially rather than territorially defined units.

The new economic situation created by the Bedouin involvement in a cash economy—through smuggling, legitimate business, land sales, and agriculture—has radically altered both the volume and distribution of wealth. Because an economy based on herds and simple cereal cultivation depends on rainfall, assets are precarious in a region that averages two to four inches of rain per year and has drought periods every seven years or so. Herds can be wiped out in a season. Rain might or might not fall on a sown plot. Although there have always been rich and poor among the Bedouins, fortunes often reversed unpredictably, and a concentration of wealth in the hands of any one person or family was never secure. Now social stratification has become more marked and fixed: the wealthy have the capital to invest in lucrative ventures and the poor do not.

Perhaps even more important for consolidating social and political power has been the gradual expansion of the types of resources that can be privately owned, which has enabled some people to make others dependent and thus to control them. Whereas formerly, economic, political, and social status were not tied—as status and leadership were based largely on genealogy and achieved reputation, and dependency implied less economic helplessness—today they are becoming increasingly coterminous.

However, disintegration of the tribal system is hardly imminent. Kinship ties still crosscut wealth differentials, and the vertical links of tribal organization overshadow the horizontal links of incipient class formation. Although individual ownership and private control of resources are beginning to undermine the economic bases of the tribal system, the tribe remains ideologically compelling. Ironically, the cooperative societies the government introduced to break down the lineage system instead served to strengthen lineage loyalties, because the new resources made available were distributed following lineage lines by the traditional lineage heads who had assumed leadership in the new system (Bujra 1973, 156).

The new levels of wealth have even allowed the realization of traditional ideals of lineage solidarity unattainable in the traditional economy. For instance, greater access to wealth and opportunity has reduced some of the pressure on lineages to fission, enabling extended families to remain coresident units. Stein notes that in the new situation "the individual members of the extended families have each specialized to certain sources of income which in aggregate guarantees the subsistence and provides social security for the extended family as a whole" (1981, 42). This division of labor has revitalized the ideal of lineage solidarity and the extended family. It may also have lessened pressures to keep up alliances with lineages in other territories, thus involuting the orientation toward agnation. Another ideal that can be more readily realized with the new wealth is large family size—wealthy men marry more wives and can support more children.

The ideals of manly autonomy and tribal independence persist in resistance to government attempts to impose restrictions and curtail the Bedouins' freedom to live their own lives and run their own affairs. Although after military rule ended in the late 1950s administration of the Western Desert province was outwardly like that of any other, with a few modifications to accommodate tribal organization (Mohsen 1975, 74), in practice the province simply cannot be run the same way. For example, Bedouins vote on the basis of tribal affiliations in electing their representatives to the national parliament. And young men still try to avoid conscription into the Egyptian army by escaping to Libya or into the desert with the herds. Most disputes are settled by customary law. In the case of serious crimes such as homicides, which cannot be kept from the authorities, the judgments of the state courts are not considered valid. Furthermore, since the Bedouins look to achieve a culprit's quick release so they can settle matters according to customary law, they are often uncooperative in the courts. Wittingly or unwittingly, most people live outside the law, smuggling, crossing closed borders, carrying unlicensed firearms, avoiding conscription, not registering births, not having identity papers, evading taxes, and taking justice into their own hands. Arrests and jailings carry no stigma for the Bedouins; rather, they occasion self-righteous curses of the government agents responsible.

Nevertheless, more subtle processes linked to the persistence of old ideals and values in new circumstances have begun to transform the Bedouins' everyday existence. Women have been particularly affected. In the camp and household, the worlds of men and women have become more separate. Although sexual segregation seems always to have characterized Bedouin social life to some extent, it has ossified with the move from tents to houses. In the tents, a blanket suspended in the middle of the tent separated male and female domains when men other than close kin were present. The blankets—unlike walls—were both temporary and permeable, allowing the flow of conversation and information. Now, with each room housing one woman and her children, it has become customary to build a separate men's room (*marbū'a* or *manẓara*) for receiving guests.

The shift from subsistence to market reliance has altered the extent to which men's traditional control over productive resources allows them to control women. Women may never have owned or even controlled resources, but women were needed to extract a livelihood from them, and men and women contributed complementary skills to the subsistence economy. This balance has been undermined. In the traditional division of labor, men cared for the sheep, sowed and harvested the grain, and engaged in limited trade. Women were responsible for the household, which involved not just cooking and childcare but also grinding grain, milking and processing milk, getting water (often from distant wells), gathering brush for the cooking fires (arduous because of the primitive adze the women use and the long distances they must travel with heavy loads), and weaving tents and blankets. Peters (1965, 137–38) makes much of the interdependence of the men's and women's spheres and the rights conferred on women by control over their special tasks in the traditional economy of the Cyrenaican Bedouins. However, as women's work has become peripheralized, these rights may have diminished. Housing and furnishings are now bought with cash, food requires less processing, water is close by, and much cooking is done with kerosene, available through purchase. Women's work is confined to an increasingly separate and economically devalued domestic sphere. Women have also become profoundly dependent on men, as subsistence is now based on cash rather than on the exploitation of herds and fields, which required the labor of men and women and entitled both to a livelihood.

The code of modesty and rules of veiling have a long history, but in the new context of permanent, settled communities they determine to a much greater extent what women do. The likelihood that neighbors will be nonkin or strangers and that they will live in close proximity is greater than it was in the isolated desert camps, where members were usually tied by kinship bonds of one sort or another. In addition, the settlements often have visitors from the wider range of contacts the men develop outside the kin group in the course of their travels and commercial ventures. Because the sexual codes (see chapter 4) require that women avoid male nonkin and strangers, they must now be more vigilant in keeping out of sight, spending more time veiled and confined to the women's section. This has curbed their freedom of movement.

With sedentarization and new economic options, these codes have restricted women's social networks and widened the gap between men's and women's experiences. Women rarely venture far from their camps except to visit natal kin. Their contacts are limited to kin, husband's kin, and neighbors. In the past, seasonal migrations brought new neighbors; in settled communities, the set of neighbors tends to become fixed, and opportunities to meet new people and make new friends diminish. In contrast, men have become more oriented to the world outside the camp. Mechanized transport has only increased men's mobility, and although men still conduct much of their business with kinsmen whom the women also know, they have more contact with outsiders whom the women do not meet. Thus, men and women from the same community live in different social worlds. A household's men and women now spend less time together, know fewer people in common, and have divergent experiences in daily life. This gap will widen as education becomes more universal, since boys are increasingly enrolled in school but old values keep girls at home.[26] Soon men will be literate and women not.

The changes in the relations between men and women and in their relative status and opportunities are neither the result of disaffection with the old system nor an emulation of the mores of imported cultures. They are certainly not the result of government policy. The Bedouins do not experience any jarring sense of discontinuity, although they acknowledge several ways things were different, say, forty years ago. Their sense of continuity may stem from the stability of the underlying principles of their life, which in new contexts created by sedentarization and market economics produce different configurations.

On close inspection, some of the most conspicuous changes prove superficial. Rather than heralding the demise of Bedouin culture and society, they merely demonstrate the Bedouins' openness to useful innovations and their capacity to absorb new elements into old structures. To take an example, the automobile and pickup truck now popular throughout the Western Desert are status objects in much the same way horses were in the past. Accordingly, the purchase of a new car occasions a sheep sacrifice

Herd owners bring supplies in their truck to hired camel-herders

and a trip to the holyman to get a protective amulet to hang on
the rearview mirror. Men are identified by and with their cars.
They want to be photographed with them. In young girls' rhyming ditties, young men are referred to not by name but by the
color and make of the cars they drive, as in the following two
songs:

> Welcome driver of the jeep
> I'd make you tea with milk if not shameful

> yā sawāg ij-jēb tafaḏẖḏẖal
> ndīrūlak shāy biḥalīb lū mā ʿēb

> Toyotas when they first appeared
> brought life's light then disappeared

> Tayūtāt awwal mā jaddun
> jābū nūr l-ʿēn wraddū

Like their animal antecedents, cars are used not just for transport
but also for ritual. A bride used to be carried from her natal home
to the groom's home in a litter mounted on a camel, accompanied
by men and women riding on horses, donkeys, or whatever could
be mustered, all singing, dancing, and firing rifles. Now, although
the size of the bridal procession is equally important, its composition has changed; Toyotas, Datsuns, and Peugeots race, the men
leaning out of the speeding vehicles firing rifles, the women sitting
in the back seats singing traditional songs. Just as the procession
used to circle the bridal tent before setting down the new bride, so
now the cars careen around the new house or a nearby saint's tomb.

It is clear that the fundamental organizing principles of social and
political life, the ideology and the values, have endured. If the most
fashionable weddings are now celebrated with a blaring *mīkrōfūn*
(loudspeaker system) and flashing lights visible for miles against
the cloudless night skies, and if the bride is brought in a car with
her trousseau following in a pickup truck, weddings are nevertheless held on traditionally auspicious days of the week and celebrated

with traditional song and poetry, sheep sacrifices, and feasting. The defloration still takes place in the afternoon, with the proof of virginity triumphantly displayed. Marriages are still linked to the history of marriage alliances between tribal sections, arranged by families, the bride-price negotiated by kinsmen. At marriage the groom does not gain economic independence from his father but brings his wife into the extended household. If women have traded their embroidered leather boots and somber baggy gowns for pink plastic shoes and bright synthetic fabrics, they have not relinquished the black veils they use to demonstrate their modesty and recognize the distance and respect between men and women (see chapter 4).

The most profound changes in the lives of the Awlad 'Ali are a result of new circumstances that have undermined the operation of traditional principles. This is clearest in the towns. The identification of kin with one another is based conceptually on common substance but is intensified by common property and coresidence. Studies of Bedouins who have settled in the city of Marsa Matruh show that residence patterns determined by accident and factors outside their control have significantly weakened the bonds between kin in favor of those between neighbors ('Abd al-Ḥamīd 1969, 129). The introduction of education and wage labor may eventually marginalize the pastoral way of life and loosen the hold of the family and tribe as educated Bedouins abandon the life of the desert, the politics of the tribe, and the values of honor and modesty at the center of the Bedouin world. This has not yet come to pass. Although they are becoming settled, the Awlad 'Ali Bedouins are a long way from being peasants. By no means detribalized, they strain under the yoke of political control and prefer to guard what autonomy they have by minimizing dealings with government authorities. In contact with non–Bedouins and the object of numerous government plans, they are still far from being assimilated. As we shall see in the next two chapters, the ideology of honor and modesty so closely associated with nobility of origin has a powerful hold on every Awlad 'Ali individual.

3

HONOR AND THE VIRTUES
OF AUTONOMY

Autonomy and Hierarchy

"Blood," the central concept in the definition of both Bedouin
cultural identity and individual identity is, as I argued in the last
chapter, seen as closely tied to moral nature. And Awlad 'Ali
believe that morality is what most distinguishes them from and
makes them superior to other peoples. At the heart of their moral
system are the values of honor and modesty. What these values
are and how they shape individual actions, interpretations of
others' actions, and even the life of sentiment must be explored.

This system of morality is especially important to understand
because it is the basis for the hierarchical social divisions that exist
in the Bedouin social system. Although this social system is often
touted as highly egalitarian, and is indeed more egalitarian than
many, the realities of power differences are inescapable, especially
within the family and lineage. What is intriguing is how, through
several ideological means, Awlad 'Ali reconcile their basic value of
equality with the hierarchical system by which they live. First, they
view as ultimately moral the bases of greater status, control over
resources, and such control as people can exercise over others.
Individuals must achieve social status by living up to the cultural

---

ideals entailed by the code of honor, in which the supreme value is autonomy. The weak and dependent, who cannot realize many of the ideals of the honor code, can still achieve respect and honor through an alternative code, the modesty code. Second, Awlad 'Ali mediate the contradiction between the ideals of equality and the realities of hierarchy by considering relations of inequality not antagonistic but complementary. They invest independence with responsibility and a set of obligations and dependency with the dignity of choice.

Autonomy or freedom is the standard by which status is measured and social hierarchy determined. It is the consistent element shaping the Bedouin ideology of social life, in which equality is nothing other than equality of autonomy—that is, equality of freedom from domination by or dependency on others. This principle is clear in Bedouin political organization, the segmentary lineage model. Although anthropologists disagree about many other aspects of this system, there is consensus that the system has as its central feature the maximization of unit autonomy (Eickelman 1981; Lancaster 1981; Meeker 1979). Each tribal segment is theoretically equal to every other through opposition. No leader is given authority over the whole confederation of tribal segments, and there are no offices or titles, although there is informal leadership at various levels of segmentation. The value of political autonomy to Awlad 'Ali is even borne out by their continuing resistance, described in chapter 2, to the imposition of state authority, first by the colonial powers and later by the Egyptian government.

The relationship between autonomy and hierarchy is manifested in the broadest social division in the Western Desert, between the Sa'ādi tribes, the true Awlad 'Ali, and their traditional client tribes, the Mrābṭīn. The Sa'ādi are known as the "free" (*ḥurr*) tribes, and the word *mrābiṭ* means "tied"—in this case, tied by obligations of clientage. In the past the Mrābṭīn paid tribute to their Awlad 'Ali patrons, had no tribal territorial rights, and depended on their patrons for the right to use land, wells, and pastures. Although the Mrābṭīn are now independent, able to own land, and no longer paying tribute, the distinction of freedom remains a source of social differentiation because of the moral implications of their ancestry.

Despite the rhetoric regarding the jural equivalence and equality of agnates, tremendous inequalities of status and authority exist within the lineage or tribe as well. These amount to differences in degree of autonomy and are linked, like the distinction between the Sa'ādi and Mrābṭīn, to control of resources. The primary distinction is between elders and juniors, involving primarily a differential authority to make decisions. Lineage elders control resources such as tribally owned wells and land. (Livestock is individually owned and is a separate matter.) Senior men make decisions and arrange marriages for junior men. In fact, this relationship is modeled on the extended family, where the father and his brothers (paternal uncles) have authority over sons and nephews. By extension, all older men, as important figures in their own lineages, are deferred to by younger men, who are less important. Junior members serve senior men and sit quietly on the fringes, listening but rarely speaking at gatherings.

Within the family itself, the inequality of patriarch and dependents—in the nuclear family, the man and his wife and children (who are known collectively as his *washūn*)—is similarly an inequality in relative independence. The family, as I will discuss in the next section, is the prototype of hierarchical relationships. The patriarch controls resources; his dependents are weaker, younger, and control no resources independently. But other relationships within the family are also unequal, for instance that between older and younger siblings, older siblings having precedence. The relationship of inequality between the sexes is usually a function of the familial relationships obtaining between them. Fathers have authority over daughters, as over sons. Older brothers have authority over younger sisters, although, as children, older sisters care for younger brothers and can order them around.

Familial relationships alone do not determine relationships of inequality between the sexes, however. Women are always dependents, as the most common term of reference for women, *wliyya* (under the protection), indicates. The hierarchical relationship between male and female in general is somewhat independent of particular roles (see chapter 4). For example, advantages of age and responsibility for younger siblings are erased in the case of older sisters and younger brothers. As adults, even younger brothers are responsible for their older sisters and have authority over them. Similarly, the relationship between mother and son, in which initially the mother is all-powerful, controlling access to food and other resources and having the authority to tell sons what to do, equalizes with time. Husband and wife, although both adults and ideally from tribes and lineages of equal standing, are also never equal. There may be severe limits on the husband's ability to impose his will on his wife, yet she remains dependent and subordinate.

The Family Model of Hierarchy

Among Awlad 'Ali, the fundamental contradiction between the ideals of independence and autonomy and the realities of unequal status is mediated by a conceptual device: all relations of inequality are conceived in the idiom of relations of inequality within the family. Since an idiom functions to suggest a possibly obscure relationship through analogy to a well-known relationship, this analogy with the family rhetorically or metaphorically transfers the qualities believed to inhere in family relations to those between persons outside the family.[1]

The familial idiom downplays the potential conflict in relations of inequality by suggesting something other than simple domination versus subordination. It replaces opposition with complementarity, with the forceful notions of unity and identity, emphasizing the bonds between family members: love and identity. Even more important, the familial idiom suggests that the powerful have obligations and responsibilities to protect and care for the weak. The weaker members, epitomized by the helpless infant, and by extension all children, are dependent on the strong. This responsibility of the strong is, in the familial idiom, motivated not only by a sense of duty but also by concern and affection. Thus, inherent in the division between weak and strong is a unity of affection and mutual concern. The key terms of this rationale legitimizing inequality are dependency and responsibility, embedded within a moral order.

Two specific family relationships provide the models for this metaphorical extension: father/son and elder brother/younger brother. In the case of the relationship between the Sa'ādis and the Mrābṭīn, the model is that of brotherhood. Each Mrābiṭ tribe was tied to a particular Sa'ādi tribe or segment in a relationship of *khuwwa* (brotherhood). In return for paying tribute to his Sa'ādi "brother," the Mrābiṭ was entitled to his protection. Because only Sa'ādis bore arms or fought, this arrangement allowed the Mrābṭīn to go about their business as herders and farmers without fear of harassment by other tribes. Sa'ādi tribal patrons were also responsible for representing their Mrābiṭ clients in disputes. By likening the relationship to that of brothers, the exploitative connotations of Sa'ādi dominance were de-emphasized and the protectiveness and mutuality of the relationship highlighted. At the same time, this model suggests the fixed relations between the two groups. Just as with elder and younger brothers, there can never be any reversal of the hierarchical relationship between the two through succession.

The father/son family relationship provides the model for other relations of inequality, including that between lineage elders and juniors and that between patrons and clients. Lineage elders are all known by one of two terms for "father's brother," unless they are of the next older generation, in which case they are referred to as "grandfather" (*jadd*). The linguistic distinction sometimes made in the case of elders is between actual father's brother (*sīd*) and other paternal relatives (*'amm*). Like fathers, although to a lesser degree, these people are responsible for providing their descendants with access to lineage resources and the wherewithal to marry. Lineage juniors contribute their labor, as this maintains and increases the patrimony which they will some day inherit. Like sons, lineage juniors will eventually succeed their elders and rise to positions of responsibility.

Although client tribes are no longer bound to free tribes, in the Western Desert individuals or households still attach themselves to wealthy patron families as clients. Patron/client relations, which are like family relations in many ways, share elements of both the father/son and elder brother/younger brother relationships. Like father and son, the patron is responsible for his clients who in turn are dependent on him for the basic necessities of life and provide him with both political support and labor. Yet, like brothers, clients cannot succeed their patrons, despite an increasing involvement in the economic and social affairs of the patron family through which they derive their financial support and in which they share, to the extent that they are able, through partnerships.

The individual client, often a younger man of a poor lineage who has no resources, may be accompanied by his dependents or, more often, he marries and establishes a family once he has become a client. His wife, although primarily in charge of running his household, also performs some services for the women of the patron's household, and she too is considered a client. The men usually herd sheep for the patron and do odd jobs as required, including building houses and corrals, planting and harvesting barley, and so forth. They stand by their patrons as dependents and supporters in political confrontations. They appear at every large gathering and, along with the sons and nephews, serve guests. Adult male clients take responsibility for greeting guests and watching the patron's house and may even sleep in the men's guest room when their patrons are absent.

Patrons provide a means of support for clients, giving them a house, a room in a house, or sometimes a tent; money for food; clothing at special occasions; and usually the means (bridewealth) to marry. They often enter into partnerships with their clients, for

A client family harvesting barley

example, providing sheep for the clients to care for, receiving in return a fraction of the herd. Alternatively, a patron might buy one or
two cows, which the client cares for and feeds, and get in exchange
the milk as well as part of the profit when the cows are sold.

A distinctive moral quality of reciprocal obligation and affection characterizes these relationships of inequality, whether within
the family or merely conceptualized in the familial idiom. Thus,
Bedouins assert, these are relations not of domination and subordination but of protection and dependency. The analogy with
families also suggests that the differential control over property
and people is not arbitrary or the result of force but is based on
the greater competence and abilities of adults and the "natural"
dependency of the helpless child who needs care. This construct,
of course, masks the arbitrary control over resources that allows
one group to be autonomous and forces the other into a position
of dependency, creating a differentiation that the Bedouins then
use to validate their various social statuses.

Honor: The Moral Basis of Hierarchy

Those who would have social precedence have more than just a
responsibility to care for dependents. In Bedouin ideology, the
tension between the ideals of equality and independence on the
one hand and the reality of status differentials on the other is
mediated through the notion that authority derives neither from
the use of force nor from ascribed position, but from moral
worthiness. Hierarchy is legitimated through beliefs about the dis-
parate possession of certain virtues or moral attributes. Furthermore, Bedouins act as though authority must be earned. Because
authority is achieved, it can also be lost. This is where the analogy
to kinship breaks down. In the family, the roles of provider and
dependent and the prerogatives and duties associated with each are
more or less fixed or ascribed; certainly the positions of family

members are unchangeable. But in social life at large there is more flexibility and room for achievement.

Individuals must earn the respect on which their positions rest through the embodiment of their society's moral ideals. Although the regularities of status distinction expressed in principles of the precedence of genealogy, greater age and wealth, and gender might seem to contradict any notion of achievement, Awlad 'Ali view these principles as being generally associated with, and hence rough indices of, the moral virtues described below. Insofar as persons demonstrate these virtues, they are entitled to the respect that validates, if not establishes, the social precedence and authority generally associated with these principles. But, as I will illustrate, the principles themselves are not sufficient to determine status. In other words, greater age or wealth, better genealogy or ancestry, or even gender does not necessarily guarantee greater authority or social precedence.

The ideals or moral virtues of Bedouin society together constitute what I refer to as the Bedouin code of honor. The honor code is, despite (or perhaps because of) the tremendous amount of anthropological attention devoted to it in studies of both Christian and Muslim circum-Mediterranean cultures, strangely difficult to define.[2] Friedrich (1977, 284) provides the most attractive way of thinking about it: "Honor is a code for both interpretation and action: in other words, with both cognitive and pragmatic components." In its first aspect it is "a system of symbols, values, and definitions in terms of which phenomena are conceptualized and interpreted." In the second, honor guides and motivates acts "organized in terms of categories, rules, and processes that are, to a significant degree, specific to a given culture. . . ." Friedrich then goes on to outline the structure of Iliadic honor as a "network" of propositions about honor and "honor-linked values" that he considers specific to Homeric Greek culture.

The values of the Bedouin honor complex are not those of the Iliad, nor those of the complex as found in Spain, Sicily, Algeria, or any other Mediterranean society. The critical term in the

Awlad 'Ali honor code is *aṣl* (ancestry/origin/nobility), a term expressive of a range of ideas. As I discussed in chapter 2, it is the basis for the proud differentiation of Bedouin from non-Bedouin. Drawing on the genealogical notion of roots, or the pure and illustrious bloodline, it also implies the moral character believed to be passed on through this line. Thus *aṣl* is the primary metaphor for virtue or honor.

What is the Awlad 'Ali network of honor-linked values? And how do these values legitimate greater social standing? First, there are the values of generosity, honesty, sincerity, loyalty to friends, and keeping one's word, all implied in the term usually translated as honor (*sharaf*). Even more important, however, is the complex of values associated with independence. Being free (*ḥurr*) implies several qualities, including the strength to stand alone and freedom from domination. This freedom with regard to other people is won through tough assertiveness, fearlessness, and pride, whereas with regard to needs and passions, it is won through self-control. Failings or weaknesses in any of these areas disqualify one for positions of responsibility and respect and put one in a position of dependency or vulnerability to domination by others.

Applied in numerous contexts to distinguish both individual Bedouins and families and lineages, the qualities associated with *aṣl* are apparent in the way the differences between Sa'ādis and Mrābṭīn are characterized. Technically, only the Sa'ādi tribes are known as the Awlad 'Ali, or sons of 'Ali. Their ability to trace their genealogical connection to a single eponymous ancestor is a matter of pride, as is the corresponding ability to find a relationship of kinship between any two individuals, lineages, segments, or tribes. By contrast, the Mrābṭīn are considered an unrelated conglomeration of tribes with no overarching genealogical unity. This absence of genealogy implies lesser moral worth.[3] Sa'ādis describe Mrābṭīn as lacking in the virtues of honor, such as generosity (Mrābṭīn are said to be stingy), ability to fight and resolve disputes, and efficaciousness in the world (Mrābṭīn are described as "all talk," or as "a pot that boils and boils"). In fact, even

Mrābṭīn view themselves as inferior to the Saʿādi. One Mrābiṭ explained to me, "We are weak, humble. It is not a matter of money, because some Mrābṭīn are wealthy. But a Siʿdāwi [sing.] has 'standing,' pride, boldness, and goodness. He has a 'face in front of people' [respect, reputation]."

Sometimes Mrābiṭ individuals are recognized as noble, as displaying the moral qualities associated with *aṣl;* but people explained that in such cases, if one probed, one always discovered the existence of some Saʿādi blood in the family line—a Saʿādi maternal uncle or grandfather, perhaps—which indicates how closely the Bedouins associate blood and character.

The ideals of Bedouin manhood highlight the importance of freedom to *aṣl.* One man explained, "A real man stands alone and fears nothing. He is like a falcon [*shahīn*]. A falcon flies alone. If there are two in the same territory, one must kill the other." Freedom and fearlessness are coupled in another word for falcon, "free bird" (*ṭēr ḥurr*). The courage of the warrior ethic applies not just to matters of war or fighting, as described in the contrast between Bedouin and Egyptian and between Saʿādi and Mrābiṭ, but to the interactions of everyday life. The "real man" is not afraid of being alone at night, despite the risk of confrontation with wild animals and spirits (*ʿafārīt*) in the open desert where there are no lights and few humans. Fear of anyone or anything implies that it has control over one.

A powerful person is described in terms of *gadr* (power), from the root meaning capability or ability. Capability as such is realized in a number of arenas and has much to do with confrontation with others. *Gadr* is the particular ability to resist others through equal or greater strength; it depends both on personal courage and assertiveness and on wealth, since generosity and hospitality are means of making others dependent. The quality of challenge and the competition for dominance involved in *gadr* come out clearly in an amusing incident I witnessed. An older man was sitting with his younger brother. His youngest daughter, a charming and much-loved toddler, wandered in and went to cuddle with her father. Her uncle teased her, threatening to kill her (using the same word used to talk about slaughtering sheep). Her father coached her to throw back the challenge, asking rhetorically, "*Yagdar?*" which implied both "Is he capable?" and "Does he dare?" This interchange was repeated several times as the little girl, standing close to her father for support, challenged her uncle with emphatic No's every time he threatened.

Related to such strength are qualities of toughness. Admired men were often described as difficult (*wa'r*) or tough (*jabbār*). Large in stature and physically strong, such men assert their will. Women claim, for instance, that "real men" control all their dependents and beat their wives when the wives do stupid things. One woman, whose daughter was about to marry one of the most respected men in the camp, said, "My daughter wants a man whose eyes are open—not someone nice. Girls want someone who will drive them crazy. My daughter doesn't want to be with someone she can push around, so she can come and go as she pleases. No, she wants someone who will order her around."

Although her remarks about women's desires must be taken with a grain of salt, since they were intended to show me (and presumably all the people to whom I would convey her words) what a wonderful and compliant bride her daughter would make, they nevertheless indicate what she believed men wanted to hear about themselves. In general, women share the men's idealization of the assertive person and the view that such people are the source of order in the community and household. However, there are limits on how much a man should assert his will. Men and women always condemn the excesses of a harsh or volatile husband, and women privately appreciate a certain amount of kindness in a man.

The correspondence between these qualities of assertiveness and the quality of potency, as described by Bourdieu (1979) of a Kabyle man of honor, are striking.[4] Bourdieu sees the "rules of honour" as those of the logic of challenge and riposte, in which a challenge both validates an individual's honor by recognizing him as worth challenging and serves as a "provocation to reply" (Bourdieu 1979, 106). Inability to reply and counter the challenge results in a loss of honor. As he notes, "Evil lies in pusillanimity, in suffering the offence without demanding amends" (Bourdieu 1979, 113). In both the Awlad 'Ali and the Kabyle codes, men of honor share a general orientation toward assertiveness and efficacy.

The final element in the Bedouin network of honor-linked values is self-mastery, one aspect of which is physical stoicism. Bedouins think physical pain and discomfort should be borne without complaint.[5] When a youth from our community underwent a serious operation in Cairo, I visited him in the hospital. His non-Bedouin roommates, all of whom had undergone the same operation, remarked on the fact that he had not complained once, whereas they had suffered terribly, moaning and complaining to all who would listen. The young man's father turned to me with pride, glad that his son had confirmed the Bedouin ideal in practice. It may well be that people disapproved of my continual complaints about my flea bites for the same reason. They always told me to try to be tougher.

The stoic acceptance of emotional pain is another aspect of self-mastery. To weep is a sign of weakness, so men of *aṣl* do not cry, regardless of the intensity of their grief. In describing his reaction to the death of a favorite aunt, one young man said, "Men don't cry. I got a terrible headache because the death was so hard on me [*ṣa'bat 'alayy*]." Mastery of needs for and passions toward others—the true sources of that dependency so antithetical to honor—seems to be related to the development of *'agl,* a complex concept, fundamental in most Muslim cultures, from Morocco to Afghanistan,[6] that can be glossed as reason or social sense. It is said that angels have only *'agl,* whereas Adam was a combination of *'agl* and passion, or carnal appetite (*shahwa*). Animals are at the other extreme from angels, having no *'agl.*

Children are born with almost no *'agl* but develop it in the process of maturing,[7] as is clear in the Awlad 'Ali description of the four stages in the male life cycle. First is childhood, a time of no responsibility when a boy merely gratifies his needs and plays. On reaching majority (*sinn ir-rushd*), when fasting and praying begin in earnest and a man becomes responsible for blood-payments of his tribe, he begins the years of youth (*shabāb*). The Bedouins have mixed feelings about this period, which lasts until about age forty. These are the great years of love and life; yet because he is governed by his passions, a man is considered flawed in religious and social terms. At forty, however, he begins to be "wise" or "reasonable" (*'āgil*). He is said to know right from wrong and to be complete. The last stage, old age (*shēkhūkha*), can be merely a continuation of the period of being *'āgil,* unless senility sets in. *'Agl,* then, is an aspect of maturity.

The value of self-control, or the possession of *'agl,* is especially apparent in the political realm. The most respected men in the Western Desert are those called on to mediate disputes. The person who does not anger easily, who is even-tempered and patient, dispassionate and fair, is "asked for in tribal hearings" (*maṭlūb fil-mi'ād*). Mediators are usually drawn from the ranks of the leaders of the smallest sociopolitical units, the *byūt* or residential sections, and referred to by the term *'awāgil,* the plural of the adjectival form of *'agl.*[8] Reason and age are embedded in this title, since most section leaders are the most senior men in a group of agnates.

Only the insane and the dim-witted do not develop *'agl* over time; like children, they have no social sense, showing no self-control in eating, drinking, defecating, or sometimes in the satisfaction of sexual needs. Although they are tolerated in Bedouin society and are not outcasts, both are disqualified from participating as equal members of society. They remain dependents all their lives, usually under the care of kin. Because their lack of *'agl* or social sense prevents them from conforming to the society's rules and cultural ideals, they are without honor.

The relationship between certain ascribed characteristics or principles on which hierarchy might appear to be based (such as age, wealth, and gender) and the actual statuses of individuals can now be fleshed out. It is not age per se that entitles one to authority over others or to higher social standing, as the positions of idiots and the insane demonstrates. Age tends to go with increasing self-mastery as well as responsibility for others. Age also brings increasing freedom from those on whom one depends or who have authority over one, because as time passes they die. Wealth provides the means for *gadr* (power) in that it allows a person to be generous, to host lavishly, to reciprocate all gifts (hence, to meet all challenges), and finally, to support many dependents. A wealthy man can support more wives, more children, and more clients, thus increasing the number of people over whom he has authority or who owe him deference. Gender affects the extent to which an individual can control property and people and, consequently, the degree to which he or she can embody the ideals of independence.

If individuals fail to embody the honor-linked values just outlined, they lose the standing appropriate to their age, level of wealth, gender, or even genealogical precedence (in the case of Saʿādis, for instance, or people from illustrious lineages). Specifically, they lose the respect on which their authority is based. Acts of cowardice, inability to stand up to opponents, failure to reciprocate gifts, succumbing to pain, miserliness—all are dishonorable and lead to a loss of respect. Inability to control desire for women is particularly threatening to a man's honor. Conversely, exemplary behavior on the part of any individual, of whatever age, level of wealth, or gender, is recognized and rewarded with respect.

The following actual cases illustrate effectively how failure to demonstrate the virtues of honor can result in a loss of social standing. The first concerns Zarība, a distinguished-looking old man in his sixties who had been one of the most respected and wealthy men in the area. He had inherited a large herd from his father, but over the course of ten years he had begun to squander his wealth. People said he was attracted to and bought for his family any useless new thing that appeared in the markets. He acted inappropriately in other contexts as well. For instance, one day he appeared at the house of an old woman he had known since his youth, complaining that his clothes were dirty and begging her to wash them for him. She agreed, but wondered what he was to wear in the meantime. He suggested that he would wear one of her dresses. The one she happened to pick out was fairly translucent. He kept laughing and commenting on how his genitals were showing. People interpreted his bizarre and unseemly behavior as a sign that he had lost his mind. Most important, however, he began to chase women, selling his property, including sheep, to buy gifts to attract these women and convince them to marry him. Especially because of his desire for these women, he became the laughingstock of the area.

Zarība's case illustrates the priority of honorable behavior over ascribed positions based either on age or wealth. He violated the code of honor by failing to control his passions; he chased women and was shameless in that he made obscene comments. By being irresponsible toward his family, and thus not fulfilling his role as provider, he violated the pact assuring that the dominant provide for the weak. Although older than most of the men with whom he associated, he no longer received their respect.

The man who needs women is called either a fool (*habal*) or a donkey (*ḥmār*), both epithets alluding to an absence of *'agl*. The bestial insult is applied to the man who seems not in control of his sexual appetites. Men who took many wives, whether wealthy (as was one man reputed to have married thirty-two women during his lifetime) or poor (as was another who took whatever money came his way to pay the bride-price for another wife, even though he could not feed or clothe the ones he had) were often called donkeys. The term was also applied to adulterers and men who frequented prostitutes. These men were described as *bitā' ṣabāya*, literally, belonging to women. Depending on the consequences of their acts they were either denounced or merely ridiculed. Disapproval was severe when the men neglected their familial responsibilities, failing to provide adequately for their dependents. When it did not jeopardize the welfare of dependents, the same behavior merely exposed the men to ridicule. Behind their backs, women described such men's interests in obscene gestures and bawdy jokes; they considered them fools for being driven by sexual desire.

Greater contempt is reserved for the man who, not simply a slave to his passions, compromises his independence by admitting dependence on a particular woman. This sign of weakness permits the proper power relations between the sexes to be reversed. One old woman told me, "When a man is really something [manly], he pays no heed to women." "A man who listens to his wife when she tells him what to do is a fool," said a young woman. Another old woman explained, "Anyone who follows a woman is not a man. He is good for nothing." Many agreed, adding, "If a man is a fool, a woman rides him like a donkey." If the women feel this way, the men feel all the more strongly about it.

A man forfeits control and loses honor either through a general lack of assertiveness vis-à-vis women—almost a personality defect—or through an excessive attachment to one woman, culminating in a fear of losing or alienating her. The unassertive man is described as flabby, flaccid, or nice—a most pathetic character. One such man was criticized for not daring to scold his wife and for being afraid to demand his meals when he came home. He always called his daughters if he wanted anything because his wife wouldn't budge. She visited around the camp all day, and he never questioned her.

Even if not flabby as a personality—in fact upholding most of the values of the honor code—a man can seem foolish, and hence be dishonored, if he becomes overly attached to a woman. The flavor of kin reactions to the violations of the ideals of independence can best be imparted through describing the events surrounding one such violation.

Rashīd, a man in his early forties from an important family, took a second wife fifteen or twenty years his junior. For the first two weeks after his wedding, Rashīd spent every night with his new bride, who had been placed in a household separate from that of his first wife, the mother of his six children. Although it is customary to spend the first week exclusively with the new bride, he did seem to be delaying the start of the proper rotation schedule. Even when he finally returned to spending nights with his first wife, he did not carry through with the expected alternation of nights but spent most nights with the new bride. People in the community began to criticize him mildly, commenting that his children were beginning to miss him.

One day, after a growing unhappiness (unknown to all but the women who shared her household), his bride suddenly ran away, seeking refuge in the house of some neighbors belonging to a saintly tribe. The other woman in her household, Rashīd's paternal first cousin and his elder brother's wife, spotted her just as she reached the neighbor's house. She ran to inform Rashīd, who began to pursue his bride but then stopped, presumably realizing the utter impropriety of such a move. Instead he asked his cousin to go talk to her, to try to persuade her to return. With tremendous embarrassment she went, entering a house she had never visited (violating social convention), and was refused by the bride.

Rashīd then set off in his truck to his bride's brother's house, some twenty kilometers away, to inform her family. (She was under the guardianship of her brother, since her father had divorced her mother, remarried, and moved to a separate household two hundred kilometers away.) Her mother and brother immediately came to get her and took her home with them. Rashīd spent the night alone. People in the household reported that he did not sleep; he moped around.

Rashīd's elder brother, the family spokesman and its most respected member, was informed of these events the next day when he returned from a trip. He consulted at length with Rashīd's other brothers and cousins in the camp. These men all thought it best that Rashīd divorce her for insulting them: she had compromised Rashīd's pride, which reflected on them as kinsmen; they wanted to turn the tables and make her family look bad. They preferred to leave the bride at her home and, as an insult, not even demand the return of the bridewealth, to which they would have been entitled because she wished the divorce. But Rashīd wanted her back, so a few days later his elder brother went to negotiate the bride's return, furious for having to endure the humiliation of begging.

He was not the only angry one. One of Rashīd's cousins later commented, "Rashīd is an idiot. You don't go chasing a woman when she leaves!" Had he beaten her or given her some cause, that would have been better. Rashīd's mother, an outspoken old woman, ranted, "He's an idiot [*habal*]. I never heard of such a fool. The woman goes and throws herself at the Mrābṭīn.[9] If you are a man you don't go after her, for God's sake. Idiot! I've never seen such a thing. What you do is leave the girl there—don't even tell her family she has run away. Let them hear in the marketplace that their daughter is at the house of strangers. [This would constitute a scandal, not only because people would be talking about their kinswoman in public but also because suspicions would arise about her chastity.] He's no man!" The other men in the family were unanimous in their criticism of Rashīd's wish to take her back—one was so disturbed that he avoided the household for several months after the bride did return. Even Rashīd's cousin, in whom he had confided and who was more sympathetic, commented as she watched him soon after the bride's return, "He's an idiot. He can hardly believe she's back. He's so happy." She had earlier scolded Rashīd's nephew for looking forlorn and sympathizing with his uncle, saying, "You get upset over a woman? Don't ever get upset over a woman. Thank God we have men and money. There are lots of women. You can always get another." She followed this with a song to the same effect:

> Money we have aplenty
> if she leaves, we'll get someone else . . .
>
> il-māl 'indinā mayjūd
> in rāḥat njībū ghērhā . . .

For a few weeks after the bride's return, Rashīd did not visit his first wife. Men and women in the community began to comment again. However, most of them did not know that the bride had discovered an amulet under her bed, which Rashīd had finally confessed to placing there, to prevent her from leaving again. A few members of the household were privy to this extraordinarily well-kept secret, but they were so embarrassed (for Rashīd's sake) about his dependence that they did not want anyone to know.

The public disapprobation that followed from this man's failure to realize the ideals of tough, assertive independence resulted in the community's loss of respect. By relinquishing control over his feelings, he allowed himself to be controlled by another person. His attachment to his bride was interpreted as a weakness of character: his mother, brothers, and cousins criticized him as lacking in *'agl,* and even the children, his nephews and nieces, all told me that they no longer feared him. Through this episode Rashīd lost the status appropriate to his age, that of the man of honor who is master of himself and others—a status that he had until then held.

These cases illustrate how important acting in terms of the moral virtues of the honor code is for achieving or legitimizing a higher place in the social hierarchy. Persons in such positions have a greater responsibility to uphold the cultural ideals, and it is their embodiment of the ideals that justifies their responsibility for, and control over, others. It is perhaps ironic that greater control entails more stringent requirements of conformity, rather than license to break the social rules, but this seems to be characteristic of what Bourdieu calls "elementary forms of domination." He notes of the Kabyle that "the 'great' are those who can least afford to take liberties with the official norms, and that the price to be paid for their outstanding value is outstanding conformity to the values of the group" (1977, 193). Bourdieu links moral virtue to power, writing that "the system is such that the dominant agents have a vested interest in virtue; . . . they must have the 'virtues' of their power because the only basis of their power is 'virtue' " (1977, 194).

A holyman (fgīh) from a Mrābiṭ tribe writing amulets

Limits on Power

Where individuals value their independence and believe in equality, those who exercise authority over others enjoy a precarious status. In Bedouin society, social precedence or power depends not on force but on demonstration of the moral virtues that win respect from others. Persons in positions of power are said to have social standing (*gīma*), which is recognized by the respect paid them. To win the respect of others, in particular dependents, such persons must adhere to the ideals of honor, provide for and protect their dependents, and be fair, taking no undue advantage of their positions. They must assert their authority gingerly lest it so compromise their dependents' autonomy that it provoke rebellion and be exposed as a sham.

Because those in authority are expected to treat their dependents, even children, with some respect, they must draw as little attention as possible to the inequality of their relationships. Euphemisms that obscure the nature of such relationships abound. For example, Sa'ādi individuals do not like to call Mrābiṭ associates Mrābṭīn in their presence. My host corrected me once when I referred to his shepherds by the technical word for shepherd, saying, "We prefer to call them 'people of the sheep' [*hal il-ghanam*]. It sounds nicer." The use of fictive kin terms serves the same function of masking relations of inequality, as for example in the case of patrons and clients.

Those in authority are also expected to respect their dependents' dignity by minimizing open assertion of their power over them. Because the provider's position requires dependents, he risks losing his power base if he alienates them. When a superior publicly orders, insults, or beats a dependent, he invites the rebellion that would undermine his position. Such moments are fraught with tension, as the dependent might feel the need to respond to a public humiliation to preserve his dignity or honor. Indeed, refusal to comply with an unreasonable order, or an order given in a compromising way, reflects well on the dependent and undercuts the authority of the person who gave it.

Tyranny is never tolerated for long. Most dependents wield sanctions that check the power of their providers. Anyone can appeal to a mediator to intervene on his or her behalf, and more radical solutions are open to all but young children. Clients can simply leave an unreasonable patron and attach themselves to a new one. Young men can always escape the tyranny of a father or paternal uncle by leaving to join maternal relatives or, if they have them, affines, or even to become clients to some other family. For the last twenty years or so, young men could go to Libya to find work.

Younger brothers commonly get out from under difficult elder brothers by splitting off from them, demanding their share of the patrimony and setting up separate households. The dynamic is clear in the case of the four brothers who constituted the core of the camp in which I lived. Two had split off and lived in separate households. Another two still shared property, herds, and expenses. While I was there, tensions began to develop. Although the elder brother was more important in the community at large, and the younger brother was slightly irresponsible and less intelligent, for the most part they worked various enterprises jointly and without friction. The younger brother deferred to his older brother and usually executed his decisions.

But one day the tensions surfaced. The elder brother came home at midday in a bad mood only to find that no one had prepared him lunch. He went to one of his wives and scolded her for not having prepared any lunch, asserting that his children had complained that they were hungry. He accused her of trying to starve his children and threatened to beat her. His younger brother tried to intervene, but the elder brother then turned on him, calling him names. Accusing him of being lazy (because he had failed to follow through on a promise involving care of the sheep that day), he then asked why the younger brother let his wife get away with sitting in her room when there was plenty of work to be done around the household. Then he went off toward his other wife carrying a big stick and yelling.

The younger brother was furious and set off to get their mother. The matriarch, accompanied by another of her sons, arrived and conferred at length with the quarreling men. The younger son wished to split off from his elder brother's household; the other brother scolded him for being so sensitive about a few words, reminding him that this was his elder brother, from whom even a beating should not matter. His mother disapproved of splitting up the households. Eventually everyone calmed down. But it is likely that a few more incidents such as that will eventually lead the younger brother to demand a separate household.

Even a woman can resist a tyrannical husband by leaving for her natal home "angry" (*mughtāẓa*). This is the approved response to abuse, and it forces the husband or his representatives to face the scolding of the woman's kin and, sometimes, to appease her with gifts. Women have less recourse against tyrannical fathers or guardians, but various informal means to resist the imposition of unwanted decisions do exist. As a last resort there is always suicide, and I heard of a number of both young men and women who committed suicide in desperate resistance to their fathers' decisions, especially regarding marriage. One old woman's tale illustrates the extent to which force can be resisted, even by women. Nāfla reminisced:

My first marriage was to my paternal cousin [*ibn 'amm*]. He was from the same camp. One day the men came over to our tent. I saw the tent full of men and wondered why. I heard they were coming to ask for my hand [*yukhulṭū fiyya*]. I went and stood at the edge of the tent and called out, "If you're planning to do anything, stop. I don't want it." Well, they went ahead anyway, and every day I would cry and say that I did not want to marry him. I was young, perhaps fourteen. When they began drumming and singing, everyone assured me that it was in celebration of another cousin's wedding, so I sang and danced along with them. This went on for days. Then on the day of the wedding my aunt and

another relative caught me in the tent and suddenly closed it
and took out the washbasin. They wanted to bathe me. I
screamed. I screamed and screamed; every time they held a
pitcher of water to wash me with, I knocked it out of their
hands.

His relatives came with camels and dragged me into the
litter and took me to his tent. I screamed and screamed when
he came into the tent in the afternoon [for the defloration].
Then at night, I hid among the blankets. Look as they
might, they couldn't find me. My father was furious. After a
few days he insisted I had to stay in my tent with my husband. As soon as he left, I ran off and hid behind the tent in
which the groom's sister stayed. I made her promise not to
tell anyone I was there and slept there.

But they made me go back. That night, my father stood
guard nearby with his gun. Every time I started to leave the
tent, he would take a puff on his cigarette so I could see that
he was still there. Finally I rolled myself up in the straw mat.
When the groom came, he looked and looked but could not
find me.

Finally I went back to my family's household. I pretended
to be possessed. I tensed my body, rolled my eyes, and
everyone rushed around, brought me incense and prayed for
me. They brought the healer [or holyman, *fgīh*], who
blamed the unwanted marriage. Then they decided that perhaps I was too young and that I should not be forced to
return to my husband. I came out of my seizure, and they
were so grateful that they forced my husband's family to
grant a divorce. My family returned the bride-price, and I
stayed at home.

Nāfla could not oppose her father's decision directly, but she
was nevertheless able to resist his will through indirect means.
Like other options for resistance by dependents unfairly treated,
abused, or humiliated publicly, her rebellion served as a check on
her father's and, perhaps more important, her paternal uncle's
power.

Supernatural sanctions, which seem to be associated with the weak and with dependents, provide the final check on abuse of authority. Supernatural retribution is believed to follow when the saintly lineages of Mrābṭīn are mistreated, their curses causing death or the downfall of the offender's lineage. In one Bedouin tale, when a woman denied food to two young girls, she fell ill, and blood appeared on food she cooked—a punishment for mistreating the helpless. Possession, as Nāfla's tale illustrates, may also be a form of resistance. It seemed that many of the possession cases I heard about were linked to abusive treatment such as wife beating, but unlike Nāfla's they were not faked.

All these sanctions serve to check the abuse of power by eminent persons who have the resources to be autonomous and to control those who are dependent on them. At the same time, moreover, figures of authority are vulnerable to their dependents because their positions rest on the respect these people are willing to give them.

Ḥasham: *Honor of the Weak*

Most analyses of honor take the perspective of those at the top of the hierarchy who are able to realize the social ideals. Yet it is important to ask how those at the bottom resolve the contradiction between their acceptance of these ideals and their own limited position, which rarely allows them to realize the ideals themselves. The tensions between Bedouin cultural ideals for the individual and the realities of hierarchy are most acute for these people. As Bedouins, they share with their superiors a high regard for autonomy and equality, the values of honor. Individuals of lower status, especially young persons and women, may have *aṣl*, or noble origins, through their tribal affiliations or merely as Bedouins, in contrast to Egyptians. But as dependents, the extent to which they can realize the ideals of behavior that validate *aṣl* is limited. Their lack of control over resources handicaps them with regard to the generosity and ability to provide that lie at the heart of power (*gadr*). By definition, their independence and capacity to stand alone are minimal, and they can assert their wills only in highly circumscribed social situations. Moreover, opposition to those who provide for them and have authority over them is only successful when their superiors' decisions are clearly unreasonable or their treatment of dependents disrespectful.

One way those at the bottom resolve the contradiction between their positions and the system's ideals is by appearing to defer to those in authority voluntarily. This situation is merely the obverse of the point made earlier, that a person in authority must earn respect through moral worthiness: the free consent of dependents is essential to the superior's legitimacy. What is voluntary is by nature free and is thus also a sign of independence. Voluntary deference is therefore the honorable mode of dependency.

The value placed on voluntary submission can be judged from various situations. One young man, in recounting the events that led to his dropping out of school, highlighted the importance of the concept of voluntary submission to the discipline of school. He described how one day his schoolteacher called him and his cousin to the office and threatened to beat them for disrupting a class. The young man responded, "Don't you dare hit us. You can't. We are here studying of our own free will. We are not peasants. We have men behind us. You'll see what will happen if you lay a hand on us."

He did not return to school for the rest of the year. During the summer, when his older brothers saw the teacher in the local market they threw rocks at him and escaped. This is an extreme example, complicated by the fact that the teacher was an Egyptian and thus, in this young Bedouin's mind, an inferior sort lacking all the moral virtues, hence with no right to impose his authority. The young man's outburst implied that whereas perhaps peasants might put up with such treatment, Bedouins would not.

Women are always dependents to some degree. Bedouin ideology holds that they are to be "ruled" by men and should be obedient. Yet, again, as Bedouins with tribal affiliations, they can have *aṣl*. As with other dependents—for instance, young men—women's submission is personally demeaning and worthless to their superiors unless perceived as freely given. On several occasions women and girls contrasted Bedouin women with Egyptian or peasant women in terms of the latter's docility in the face of coercion. For example, in describing a new bride from a peasant area, people said, "She's from the east. Look, she works so hard, serves her mother-in-law without a word, deals with all that filth and those children [her husband's father's]—an Arab [Bedouin] girl would never put up with that. She would refuse." At the same time, they criticized the husband's family for wanting a girl of such lowly origins, insinuating that the groom's mother had only wanted a servant who would not give any trouble.

People pity a woman who seems to obey her husband because she has no choice, either because she comes from an extremely poor family or because she has no male kin who would or could support her if she wished to leave her husband. But they also regard such a woman with some contempt, describing her not only as calm or docile (*hādya*) but also as pathetic (*ghalbāna*) and poor (*rāgdat rīḥ,* literally, "sleeping in the breeze").

Those who are coerced into obeying are scorned, but those who voluntarily defer are honorable. To understand the nature, meaning, and implications of voluntary deference we must explore the concept of *hasham*. Perhaps one of the most complex concepts in Bedouin culture, it lies at the heart of ideas of the individual in society. Rarely did a day pass without one form or another of this word arising spontaneously in conversation, yet the meaning seemed to shift depending on the context. In the leading dictionary of modern standard Arabic, various words formed from the triliteral root *hashama* are translated by a cluster of words including modesty, shame, and shyness. In its broadest sense, it means propriety. It is dangerous to accept any one of these terms, however, lest we prematurely assume that we understand what the Awlad 'Ali mean.[10] As Paul Riesman (1977, 136)

A young woman, wearing her gold necklace (frajallāt) *and silver bracelets* (dimlij), *with her swaddled infant*

points out, regarding a similar concept among the Fulani of Upper Volta, "the existence of a convenient term for a complex entity risks creating the false impression that in knowing the term we know the entity which it designates."

In any case, dictionary searches to determine cultural meanings are of questionable validity. The controversy provoked by Antoun's (1968) reliance on dictionary definitions in his classic article on Arab women's modesty is instructive. *Hasham* is in fact one of the key words on which he bases his analysis. He writes, "*Hishma* refers to bashfulness or self-restraint and *ihtishām* to modesty or respect, both related to the triliteral root form that means to cause to blush." Thus far the definition suffers only from vagueness. He then adds, "But another form of the same root *mahāshim* means pudenda. Many Quranic references to modesty and chastity are literally references to the protection of female genitalia" (Antoun 1968, 679). These definitions constitute part of his evidence for interpreting women's modesty as tied exclusively to sexuality.

Abu-Zahra's (1970) reply to Antoun's article is multi-faceted. One part of her criticism focuses on his reliance on lexigraphic explorations of "museum words" either unknown to the "illiterate villagers" he discusses or whose referent varies across Arabic dialects (Abu-Zahra 1970, 1081). Consulting the most definitive Arabic dictionary herself, she turns up no mention of pudenda as a meaning of the word *mahāshim*. Furthermore, she cites very different meanings for the words in both Tunisian and Egyptian spoken Arabic. In attempting to understand how the concept of *hasham* informs Awlad 'Ali society, then, the word's meaning should be sought not in obscure dictionaries of classical Arabic but in everyday usage.

In daily parlance, words from the root *hashama* are used in various grammatical forms, each having a slightly different sense. The two poles of meaning around which usage clusters are those referring to an internal state and those referring to a way of acting; thus, *hasham* involves both feelings of shame in the company of the more powerful and the acts of deference that arise from these feelings. In the first instance, *hasham* is conceptualized as an involuntary experience (we might even call it an emotion); in the second, as a voluntary set of behaviors conforming to the "code of modesty." The experience is one of discomfort, linked to feelings of shyness, embarrassment, or shame, and the acts are those of the modesty code, a language of formal self-restraint and effacement. The cultural repertoire of such behaviors includes the most extreme and visible acts of veiling and dressing modestly (covering hair, arms, legs, and the outlines of the body) as well as more personal gestures such as downcast eyes, humble but formal posture, and restraint in eating, smoking, talking, laughing, and joking.

Hasham is closely tied to the concept of *'agl,* the social sense and self-control of honorable persons. Just as the possession of *'agl* enables persons to control their needs and passions in recognition of the ideals of honor, so it also allows them to perceive the social order and their place within it. Children, who are said not to have much *'agl,* must be taught to *tahashsham* (v.); the primary goal of socialization is to teach them to understand social contexts and to act appropriately within them—which means knowing when to *tahashsham.* Mothers often scold their children with the imperative, which can be translated as "behave yourself" or "act right" and which implies, "have some shame."[11] The dual connotations of appropriate ways of feeling and voluntary behavior control are apparent here.

The concepts of *hasham* and *'agl* are closely wedded in notions of the ideal woman. The woman who is *'agla* (reasonable, characterized by *'agl*) is well-behaved; she acts properly in social life, highly attuned to her relative position in all interactions. There is also a spillover into general comportment, which should conform to the behavior appropriate to modesty. People say of a woman who is *'agla* that she knows when to speak and when to listen. This description draws attention to the fact that she is deferential, since in Bedouin society the superior speaks and the inferior listens. A leader or important person is one said to have the "word" (*kilma*). The ideal woman is described as having a soft voice (*ḥissha wāṭī*), not a "long tongue."

The negative case of the woman who lacks *'agl* or does not *taḥashsham* can take one of two forms: she can be described either as willful (*gāwya*) or as slutty (*qḥaba*). The second aspect refers specifically to sexuality, which will be considered in the next chapter, where I argue that conformity to sexual norms is merely an aspect of deference to those who more closely represent the social ideals. The first, *gāwya*—from the root *qwy*, to be strong or powerful—clearly pertains to hierarchical relations. The Bedouins use this particular adjectival form in reference only to females. It means something like "overly strong" and suggests excessive assertiveness. The negative connotations of this sort of assertiveness derive from its inappropriateness for those in positions of dependency or social inferiority. For example, the word is applied to a woman or girl who is contrary or argumentative with her elders, who refuses to do what she is told, talks back, or does things without permission. Grown women who refuse requests or disobey husbands or in-laws are also labeled willful and are perceived as lacking in *ḥasham*. Those who "talk too much" invite disciplinary action.

Bedouins attribute such disrespectful behavior to improper upbringing, specifically overindulgent treatment. Although mothers threaten and discipline boys as much as girls, they say that girls should be treated with less indulgence lest they become willful, and boys should not be disciplined as much lest they become fearful. Boys should also be indulged, presumably so they will gain a sense of power, rather than weakness, in interactions with others. Women rationalize their belief that boys should be breast-fed longer than girls through these ideas. One old woman said, "The more willful the boy, the better."

The different beliefs about the value of assertiveness for boys and girls correspond to their future positions in the hierarchy. Even though *ḥasham* really applies only to specific social situations involving persons of unequal status, women are so often in such positions that they must be trained to be modest in general demeanor—to be deferential, soft-spoken, obedient, and cooperative—or at least to be more sensitive to the social contexts in which modesty would be appropriate. Girls will grow up to be dependents, perhaps exchanging their positions as daughters for those as wives. At best, women, as matriarchs, can come to control some property and have influence over those men, usually sons, on whom they must depend to negotiate business and deal with the world of non-kin. Boys will nearly always grow up to become providers, if not for large groups of dependents, then at least for their own wives and children, and thus will not need to defer to many.

And yet there seems to be some ambivalence in Bedouin attitudes toward women's willfulness. Whereas to say that a woman *taḥashsham*s is always a compliment, to say that a woman is willful is not necessarily an insult. Women tend to view willful girls with some awe, and not a small amount of respect, even if as socializers they must scold them continually to keep them in line. Knowing the tremendous value placed on modesty, I was surprised when some older women, discussing the camp's adolescent girls, agreed that the only ones worth anything were the three most assertive—they were the liveliest and brightest, although they certainly gave their mothers trouble. But one of these girls' mothers said with some pride that she had been willful, just like her daughter, when she was young.

In fact, women are admired for many of the same qualities as men in Bedouin society. As Bedouins and people with *aṣl,* they are expected to express most of the same honor-linked virtues that legitimate the authority of their providers. The difference is that they can only express these virtues in contexts of social equality— that is, when they do not *taḥashsham*—when the ideals guiding their behavior are those of boldness and strength, not passivity. For example, a woman is expected to be energetic (*ḥurra*), industrious, enterprising, and tough (in both the physical and the emotional sense). Women do heavy work, putting up tents, gathering firewood, and getting water, and laziness is severely criticized.

Intelligence, demonstrated in verbal skill in storytelling and singing, is also valued. Cleverness or enterprise, another sign of intelligence, is shown through success in business ventures, such as small-scale chicken and rabbit raising or sewing and weaving. The active capabilities of women are even celebrated in the ideals of feminine beauty. For Awlad 'Ali, who abhor slenderness, weakness, or sickliness in women as much as in men, the beautiful woman shines with the rosy glow of good health (*hamra*) and has a robust figure (*m'anigra*).

Women who want to be respected must display, in addition to assertiveness, the moral virtues of generosity and honesty. The good woman (*wliyya zēn*) does right by her guests; she does her "duty" (*ṣāḥbit wājib*). The greatest offense is stinginess. Unwillingness to share personal belongings or the attempt to amass material goods at the expense of co-wives or other women in the household is frowned upon. In this context, women's possessions do not include valuable property but rather small items such as bars of soap, perfume, cloves, and henna. No one is expected to share the personal wealth received at marriage or later, such as gold jewelry and clothing. Women in charge of household resources—primarily food—are expected to be generous with them and are criticized for failures to offer special foods to other members of the community. I heard bitter stories about how particular women had hidden pots of food from women passing by; the most vividly recalled incidents involved inhospitality to pregnant women. Some of these stories were fifteen years old and had not faded with the passing of time.

It should be clear from this digression into the expectations regarding women's conformity to the cultural ideals that dependents, including women, strive for honor in the traditional sense. They share with their providers the same ideals for self-image and social reputation, which they try to follow in their everyday lives. Yet the situations in which they can realize these ideals, in particular those of independence and assertiveness, are circumscribed. Just as through defiance dependents can expose the authority of their providers as a sham, so can the more powerful expose their dependents for what they are—lacking in the key values of independence and ability to stand up in a confrontation.

It is perhaps this realization of vulnerability to humiliation that provokes feelings of *ḥasham* (shame, shyness, or embarrassment) in the presence of those higher in the hierarchy. It is rare to hear of someone who is shy or ashamed in general. Most often, the preposition *from* is used with the verb, to suggest that persons are "ashamed from" (or, in more idiomatic English, in front of) particular others. This interpretation is supported by the fact that two other words are used almost interchangeably with the phrase "he is ashamed/shy in front of": "he is afraid of" (*ykhāf min*) and "he respects" (*yiḥtaram*).

Although we cannot know the subjective experience of shame, which seems to range from a basic lack of ease to extreme discomfort, we can deduce some of its qualities from several incidents. Once when I visited a strange household I felt dizzy and sick to my stomach, probably from the strain. When I described my symptoms to the people with whom I lived, they all nodded knowingly, saying I had been *mitḥashma* (adj.). Although I heard about other cases as severe, more common was a muted experience of shyness that individuals were anxious to escape as soon as possible.

Awlad 'Ali conceive of relative weakness or vulnerability in the idiom of exposure, the corollary being that protection involves nonexposure. The ideal form of nonexposure is avoidance, but when encounters must take place, the next best thing is cloaking or masking. *Ḥasham,* then, in its manifestation as emotional discomfort or shame, is that which motivates avoidance of the more powerful, and in its manifestation as the acts of modesty prompted by these feelings, it is the protective self-masking that occurs when exposure to the more powerful is unavoidable.

The categories of persons from whom a young man might *taḥashsham* are his father and male agnates of his father's generation, together with men of the same generations from lineages of equal status to his own, and his older brothers, especially if they have succeeded the father in controlling the patrimony. Clients *taḥashsham* from their patrons and from anyone of the same status as their patrons. Women *taḥashsham* from some older women, especially their older affines, and from most older men, both kin and affines. They do not, however, *taḥashsham* from men who are clients, no matter how old, especially if they have known them for a long time. The general rule is that persons *taḥashsham* from those who deserve respect—those responsible for them and/or those who display the virtues of honor.

The idiom of exposure may have its roots in the way the life cycle is viewed. Because children are born helpless, the ultimate dependents, they are not only utterly vulnerable but also totally exposed to their powerful caretakers, who see them naked, defecating, eating, drinking. They have no self-control. As they grow and develop self-control and social sense, however, they become less dependent and have some choice in whether to obey their caretakers. They are also less exposed; they wear clothing, defecate in private, and are able to have secrets.

People feel embarrassed in front of their elders not just because the latter control resources and currently have authority, but also because the elders may have known them in an earlier state of extreme weakness and exposure. By the same token, individuals do not feel fear or shame in front of anyone they have seen exposed or vulnerable. Women never *taḥashsham* from younger men even if they depend on them and know that they control more resources, or from their husband's or kinsmen's clients—possibly because they have seen these men exposed or at least dominated by fathers, patrons, or whomever. Their common weakness vis-à-vis the more powerful unites these categories of dependents in relative equality, despite gender and social differences.

The cultural salience of the link between exposure and vulnerability or weakness is confirmed by the explanatory paradigms that Bedouins use to interpret illness and misfortune. The "evil eye," magic, and possession—the three most common sources of illness and misfortune—all work through the victim's exposure to more

Young men and clients feel at ease with each other

powerful forces. Holymen (*fgīh*) tend to diagnose illnesses as caused by being "looked at" (*manzūr*). Magic works through the victim's exposure to a charm or amulet, or merely to water in which a charm was soaked. Bedouins even believe that a new mother's milk can dry up if she is exposed to the gold coins (*frajallāt*) on another woman's necklace. Serious illnesses are usually caused by solitary encounters in deserted places with *jinn* (spirits), which, if they get too close, can "ride" the person and possess him or her. The experience of such encounters is always described in terms of fear. Fright also causes other illnesses, such as hepatitis, whose symptoms of yellowness are believed to be caused by the rise of bile accompanying a frightened gasp.

Safety in encounters with powerful forces, supernatural or social, is enhanced by avoiding encounters in the first place or by placing barriers between oneself and the force. The most popular protection against the evil eye, the *jinn,* and magic is an amulet, one or more pieces of paper on which a holyman has written Koranic verses or, more frequently, scribbles that people mistake for the verses. The word Awlad 'Ali use for amulet is *hjāb,* meaning a protection, cover, or veil; elsewhere in the Arab world the word refers specifically to women's veils.

Likewise, to protect oneself from more powerful people one must *tahashsham,* in the sense of acting modestly. That this involves cloaking or masking is apparent from the range of behaviors that Bedouins consider signs of modesty. First, there is dressing modestly, which for women includes veiling the face, a literal cloaking. Also masked are the "natural" needs and passions; so to *tahashsham* from someone involves neither eating nor drinking in front of him or her, nor smoking (or, in Arabic, "drinking") cigarettes. One also assumes a rigid posture and does not speak or look the superior in the eyes. These acts imply formality on the one hand and self-effacement on the other, both means of masking one's nature, of not exposing oneself to the other.

Complete avoidance is the best protection; there is no danger of exposure if there is no interaction. Not just individuals but whole categories of unequals avoid each other. Sexual segregation and, to a lesser extent, generational segregation characterize the everyday social world of the Awlad 'Ali, and they are justified in terms of the *ḥasham* felt by those lower in the hierarchy. Thus, the Bedouins do not attribute the separation of the women and the young from the adult male world to the men's wish to exclude the others; rather, they understand it as the response of the weak to their discomfort in the presence of the more powerful. The response of women when adult men intrude into their world certainly attests to the validity of this interpretation. Upon a respected adult man's entrance, the only sounds are the rustlings of posture and clothing being adjusted and of wide-eyed children moving closer together, and then a hush falls on a roomful of garrulous women and boisterous children. The mood changes. Even well-born young men fall silent and seem uncomfortable in the presence of their older agnates; they do not laugh or joke but sit quietly, listening and ready to serve. Not surprisingly, they too prefer the world of their peers, of adult clients, or even of the women, their mothers, aunts, and grandmothers. By minimizing contact between those of unequal status, segregation limits the time the weak must spend feeling uncomfortable and acting with such restraint.[12]

Inequality is thus expressed as social distance, which is marked by *ḥasham*'s formality, effacement, and, ultimately, avoidance. Social intimacy, as between equals and among kin, is expressed in terms both of the absence of *ḥasham* and of the willingness to share everything, to expose oneself. These assumptions underlie the ritualized exchanges between hostess and formal guest. Whenever guests indicate they have finished eating, they are reprimanded by their hostesses: "What? Is that all you're eating? What's the matter with you? Are you *mitḥashma?*" The guest always responds, "Of course I'm not *mitḥashma.*" The rhetorical purpose of this exchange is to suggest that theirs should be a relationship of intimacy and equality, not inequality and social distance.

Ḥasham indexes hierarchical relationships. It is so accurate that when a young woman married into our community, some of the first questions she asked her husband's young kinswomen concerned who *taḥashshams* from whom. This was her way of finding out about the status hierarchy in the community, information necessary for her own appropriate social responses. In their answers, the young women used smoking as a sign of *ḥasham* in relations between men, and veiling in relations between men and women.

What is all this protection for? What do the weak fear? These questions are difficult to answer, but I would suggest that at the bottom of *ḥasham* lies the fear that an encounter with someone more powerful will show one to be controlled—a state contrary to the ideals of autonomy and equality. Perhaps the fear or discomfort is due to the precariousness of self-image and of image in others' eyes. Since women and, even more so, young men and clients share the cultural ideals of honor and measure themselves in its terms, masking and avoidance may be protection against being exposed as falling short of these ideals, which anyone who is not independent inevitably must.

Ḥasham is not thought of as a passive protection; it is conceived as arising spontaneously from the individual, and it cannot be coerced or imposed by the strong. People are held responsible for acting modestly. Whether *ḥasham* is a response to feelings of weakness and fears of exposure or just the modest acts that protect a person in such situations matters little: even if no feelings of vulnerability toward particular individuals are involved, by acting modestly a person shows at least some recognition of his or her relative position in the hierarchy, as well as respect, if not for the individuals with more authority, then for the system that gives those persons their authority. It is not compliance, but a form of self-control, and it preempts the need for a show of strength by the powerful—a show that would reveal the subordinate's weakness. Initiated by the dependent, *ḥasham* is a voluntary act, a sign of independence, and as such, it is part of the honor code, applying to the dignified way of being weak and dependent in a society that values strength and autonomy. This strategy for the honor of the weak thus reinforces the hierarchy by fusing virtue with deference.

4

MODESTY, GENDER,
AND SEXUALITY

Gender Ideology and Hierarchy

The moral discourse of honor and modesty is the means by which
Awlad 'Ali rationalize the social hierarchy and inequities in the
freedom of individuals to make choices about their lives and to
influence others. Nowhere is this clearer than in Bedouin gender
ideology. In Bedouin thought, the network of values associated
with autonomy that I have called honor is generally associated
with masculinity, as earlier descriptions of the "real man" suggested; modesty (*hasham*) is associated with femininity. Bedouins
would not deny that some women can achieve more honor, in the
strict sense of the term, than some men or that some men or
categories of men (dependents such as young and lowly men) are
more deferential than some women (older women and women
from important families). Nevertheless, in the abstract, maleness
is associated with autonomy and femaleness with dependency.
This association corresponds to and reinforces the realities of both
the Bedouin social system, with its basis in agnatic bonds, and the
Bedouin economic system, in which senior men control resources
and provide for others and women are the quintessential depen-

dents.¹ Because Awlad 'Ali couch hierarchy in the language of moral worth, the association implies that men's precedence is due to their moral superiority.

The Bedouin valuation of masculinity over femininity is reflected in myriad sayings, institutions, rituals, and symbols, just as it is tempered by others. Although there are important sociological reasons for devaluing females, as Bedouins articulate in explaining their preference for sons over daughters, this devaluation is generally justified by reference to their moral inferiority. In Awlad 'Ali ideology, the primary source of this moral inferiority is the association of femininity with reproduction, which, although positive in itself, is tainted by its concomitants: menstruation and sexuality.

This identification of women with both menstruation and sexuality is thought to preclude them, in different ways, from achieving the moral virtue of those who uphold the honor code. It also determines the path they must take to gain respectability, the path of modesty. In this chapter I will show why chastity or sexual modesty, as an aspect of the social deference of *hasham,* is essential to a woman's honor. I argue that the denial of sexuality that is the mark of *hasham* is a symbolic means of communicating deference to those in the hierarchy who more closely represent the cultural ideals and the social system itself. This denial is necessary because the greatest threat to the social system and to the authority of those preferred by this system is sexuality itself.

The Social Value of Male and Female

One of the ways Bedouins express the value of males over females is their avowed preference for sons. Both men and women say things like, "Men gather women together [marry wives] to have sons. Daughters are worthless." Pregnancies are thought to differ depending on whether a boy or a girl is being carried. If a woman

*Children gathering khubbēza,
a wild edible green*

is fat and swollen, feels heavy, and sleeps a lot, people predict she will give birth to a girl; a woman carrying a boy is said to be light, remaining so throughout the term of pregnancy, and she sleeps little, especially in the last month.

People greet the birth of a boy with more enthusiasm than that of a girl. In describing her activities as a midwife, one old woman proudly told of the happy time she delivered two boys in one day. She explained:

> To give birth to boys is better. Everyone present rejoices. They run to tell the father that he has a son. If it is a girl, everyone is upset: those who delivered her, those in attendance. They don't go to tell the men. No one eats dinner. Even the tent goes into mourning. When it is a boy, the tent is happy, the father is happy, the uncles are happy, and the mother—I can't tell you how happy she is!

When women visit a new mother, they enter ululating and eagerly offer their congratulations if she has delivered a son. If she has given birth to a girl, they offer the phrase "Thank God for your safety [*al-ḥamdullāh 'ale slāmtik*]." People generally greet the birth of a girl with the philosophical statement, "Whatever God brings is good." One father, hearing that his wife had delivered a daughter (her fifth daughter, out of seven children), commented, "It's all the same." But his fifteen-year-old daughter was less neutral; she responded to the news with the disparaging rhyme "A little girl, may she have cramps [*bnayya, a'ṭīhā layya*]," for which the older women immediately rebuked her, saying, "Shame on you, girls are nice!" People acknowledge that the death of a male infant is more disturbing than the death of a female, although both elicit reactions of sadness mingled with resignation to the will of God.

Yet the stated preference for boys is not reflected in the way boys and girls are treated in their early years or in the affection their mothers, fathers, and others show them as infants and toddlers. Although people believe that boys should be breast-fed longer than girls, as we saw in the last chapter this is a function not of preference for boys but of ideas about the relationship between indulgence in childhood and the development of fearlessness. In fact, weaning depends largely on idiosyncratic factors and circumstance, and its timing varies considerably from family to family, and even within a family, regardless of gender.

There is good sociological reason to prefer sons. The tribal system is organized around the principles of patrilineality and agnatic solidarity and is based on relationships between men. However important affines and cognatic kin are economically, socially, and affectively, tribal segments can only grow through the addition of males. Strength is measured in numbers of men. It is therefore not surprising that men unequivocally prefer sons.

Because the tribal system is so male-oriented, the interests of men and women do not always coincide. Women's attitudes toward sons and daughters are more complex and ambivalent than men's, a fact the Bedouins recognize. They say, "A girl is in her mother's interest, and a boy in his father's [*il-binit fī maṣlaḥit umhā wil-wad fī maṣlaḥit būh*]." The preference for sons in any particular family is tempered by a desire for daughters who will help with the household work. Even if a household of girls is pitiful, people recognize the practical difficulties of managing a household of men and boys. The ideal, then, is to have many sons and a few daughters. Mothers and daughters are close and interdependent, spending a great deal of time together. Mothers rely on their daughters for help with work, for companionship, and, later in life, for care, and most relationships between mother and daughter are emotionally close.

Yet, on the whole, women share their husbands' preference for sons because of the way social and economic life is organized. Sons are a woman's social security. She is initially happy to give birth to sons because this secures her position in her marital community and with her husband. Later, once the sons inherit from their fathers, she depends on them for support (Bedouin women, like women in our own society, tend to outlive their husbands). In the case of divorce, a woman often lives in the household of an adult son (if she has one), gaining a position of some independence and power, his wife or wives performing services for her, and his children living near her.

The heart of the problem with girls, as far as their mothers are concerned, is that because residence is virilocal and descent patrilineal, unless they marry patrilateral parallel cousins, daughters leave their natal groups and their mothers, and their children belong to another tribe. One woman explained, "A daughter will leave, she'll marry and abandon you. She won't even get news of you. But if you are fortunate, a son will support you and look after you when you are old. Girls may be more tender [*ḥanūn*], but they leave. That is, unless they marry within the camp."

A daughter who marries outside the camp can only come to visit when her husband or his kin allow it, and she can rarely be spared from her own household for any length of time. The social distance between her children and her natal group varies, depending on numerous factors, but, despite fondness for maternal relatives, the jural and political distance cannot be surmounted. An old woman's statement about a daughter who had married into another group living nearby confirms the importance of this factor. She explained that she preferred her daughter to all of her sons (prosperous, respected men in whose camp she lived as a matriarch) because the daughter came to visit and cared for her when she was ill, whereas her sons didn't even ask after her (an exaggeration). Nevertheless, she preferred her sons' children to her daughter's because the latter "belong to someone else."

Although the tribal system organized around patrilineal descent and inheritance and virilocal residence by definition slights females, preventing them from attaining the social statuses open to men and peripheralizing them in the patriline, it does give them a place, however temporary, with their brothers in the tribe and lineage. No one denies that women can have the nobility (*aṣl*) of genealogy or even that they can pass a bit of it on to their children (Abou-Zeid 1966, 257). In Bedouin thought, women's secondary status is based on a kind of moral inferiority defined by the standards of the honor code by which individuals are measured.

The "Natural" Bases
of Female Moral Inferiority

Male and female are symbolically opposed in Bedouin thought. Above all, females are defined by their association with reproduction, not so much in its social aspect of motherhood, but in its natural aspects of menstruation, procreation, and sexuality. These natural qualities are symbolically highlighted in the colors of female dress, especially in the ubiquitous red belt, whereas male dress communicates men's more cultural (and religious) qualities. Women's association with nature is seen as a handicap to their ability to attain the same level of moral worth as men. Women's lack of independence from nature compromises them vis-à-vis one of the crucial virtues of honor, the self-mastery associated with 'agl (social sense or reason).

Beliefs about women's moral inferiority in terms of other honor-linked values besides self-mastery also abound. Most of the statements I heard about these beliefs were asserted by men; women rarely volunteered them, although they also rarely contested them. For example, men are said to be stronger and more fearless than women. Women are said to fear the dark and not to be able to "take much" (*mā yithammalūsh*). Men's talk is said to be full, whereas women's is empty or ignorant. Some say that whenever two women talk, the Devil is there between them. Most important, men are said to be more honest and straightforward. One man illustrated this point with this version of the Fall from Grace:

> God created Eve from Adam's bent lower rib. That is why women are always twisted. They never talk straight.
> In the Garden of Eden, Adam and Eve had everything. One day the Devil was playing a flute [*zummāra*], and Adam and Eve listened. He stopped playing and said to Eve, "Eat these tasty fruit (off the tree that God had forbidden to them), or I won't play for you anymore." Wanting to hear

the music, she agreed. They had thought the reason they were forbidden to eat the fruit was that it was poisonous, but when Adam saw that Eve did not fall ill or die when she ate it, he went ahead and ate too. As he was swallowing, he thought better of it and the fruit stuck in his throat. This is why men have Adam's apples.

When God saw that Adam and Eve had disobeyed him, He banished them to earth. Eve landed in the west, and Adam in the east. They began looking for each other, she traveling eastward, and he westward. The halfway point was Mt. 'Arafat (near Mecca). Eve arrived there first. When she saw Adam coming, she immediately sat down and acted as if she had been there all along. When he approached her, they greeted each other and embraced. Eve turned away and tried to pull out of the embrace. She did not let on that she had been as anxious to find him as he had been to find her. To this day women are like that. They always try to pull away and pretend they don't care.[2]

These signs of moral inferiority are not exclusively female, however. Everyone recognizes that men can also be dishonest, ignorant, cowardly, and so forth. If that were not the case, these values would hardly provide the standards by which moral worth could be assessed and hierarchy justified.

It is the association with nature that is special to females, the source of both their positive and negative value. Bedouins do not devalue all that is natural and related to reproduction. For instance, as reproducers, women are responsible for giving birth to the children that are so desired and adored. Everyone wants children, and men want as many as they can have and support. Women, overworked, fatigued, and not in the best health, want fewer merely because they cannot cope with the work involved in bringing them into the world and caring for them. Yet if they have trouble conceiving or carrying pregnancies to term, they turn to ritual specialists, folk healers, or doctors for help. Fertile women are valued, admired, and envied. Barren women face a sad life, certain that their husbands will, at the least, take second wives.

The association of females with fertility extends from their role as reproducers to ideas about general plenty. A saying that often came up in response to news of the birth of a girl was "A year of girls is a year of bounty" (*sanat banāt sanat khēr*)—that is, baby girls bring good pasture, so milk and butter are plentiful; in a year of boys there is no rain, no pasture, and no milk.

Girls are linked symbolically to rain (necessary for both the pasture and the barley crop on which livelihood depends) in a more explicit way through rituals that were performed formerly in times of drought. Awlad 'Ali have a calendar of seasons based on the movement of constellations through the winter sky, which they rely on to time barley planting and to predict the lushness of spring pastures in the desert, both of which depend on the amount and timing of rainfall. Rain is essential in the period known as *jōza,* which occurs around mid-December. In the past, when there was no rain during this month the children performed a ritual to bring rain. Central to the ritual was a doll called the *zirrāfa,* fashioned by lashing together a bread shovel (used in bread baking) and a weaving shuttle, both items associated with female activities. The doll was clothed in a red dress, a red belt, and a silk kerchief, "like a virgin."[3]

Women's relationship to certain life-cycle rituals also reflects their symbolic association with fertility. Women are more closely linked to life, and men to death. Not only do men slaughter animals, but they also exchange sacrificial sheep at ceremonies, including funerals. Women do not slaughter, and although they attend all ceremonies, they do not bring gifts or make exchanges at funerals. Following childbirth, however, women pay visits to new mothers and bring them gifts, whereas men do not visit or, as a rule, give gifts to new mothers. At all other ceremonies, both men and women attend and have parallel, if separate, gift exchanges.

The possession of a womb for fertility carries with it other positive moral qualities. In the following folktale, told to me by

A woman's veil can be manipulated to indicate degree of social comfort

an old woman during a discussion of the relative value of boys and girls, the difference in moral nature between a compassionate and loving daughter and an abusive and heartless son is rooted in their physiological differences.

There once was a woman with nine daughters. When she became pregnant again she prayed for a boy and made an oath to give up one of her daughters as an offering if she were granted a son. She did give birth to a boy. When they moved camp, riding off on their camels, she left behind one daughter.

Soon a man came by on a horse and found the girl tied up. He asked her story, untied her, took her with him, and cared for her.

Meanwhile, the boy grew up and took a wife. His wife demanded that he make his mother a servant. He did this, and the old mother was forced to do all the household work for her daughter-in-law [a reversal of proper relations between mother-in-law and daughter-in-law].

One day they decided to move camp. They loaded up the camels and traveled and traveled. The old mother had to walk, driving the sheep. She got tired and was eventually left behind. Lost, she wandered and wandered until she came upon a camp. The people in the camp called to her and invited her in. They asked her story. She told them she had not always been a servant and recounted her tale. When the people in the camp heard this story they went running to tell one of the women. It turned out that she was the old woman's daughter who had been abandoned as a child. She came, questioned the old woman, and, once convinced that it was really her mother, embraced and kissed her, took her to her tent, washed her clothes for her, fed her, and cared well for her.

By and by, the son came looking for his mother. He rode up to the camp and asked people, "Haven't you seen an old servant wandering around?" The woman who (unknown to him) was his sister invited him into her tent. She demanded that a ram be brought and slaughtered in his honor. She then asked him, "Where is the *riḥm* [womb] of the ram?" The brother looked at her in surprise answering, "A ram has no *riḥm*, didn't you know?"

She then revealed her identity and told him her story. She refused to let him take his mother back and scolded him for having so mistreated her.

The moral of the story turns on the double meaning of the triliteral root *raḥama*, from which the word *riḥm* (womb), as well as a word meaning pity, compassion, or mercy, is derived. Thus the story links wombs (femaleness) with compassion and caring. The old woman who told me the story added this commentary:

> You see, the male has no womb. He has nothing but a little penis, just like this finger of mine [laughingly wiggling her finger in a contemptuous gesture]. The male has no compassion. But the female is tender and compassionate [*idh-dhakar mā yirḥamsh, l-anthā thinn wtirḥam*]. It is the daughter who will care for her mother, not the son.

From this story and the old woman's comment, it is clear that despite the avowed preference for boys in Bedouin culture and society, certain positive values are associated with females, particularly in their relationships to other women, especially their mothers. The contrast between the son's abuse of his mother and the daughter's care and forgiveness is striking, and it is tied to a difference in their nature, for females possess wombs.

The positive value accorded females through their association with fertility is countered by the negative value of fertility's partners, menstruation and sexuality. Each of these two factors impedes women's abilities to realize the ideals of honor in a different way. Menstruation compromises women's virtue by undermining their piety. As a natural force over which they have no control, it also represents inescapable weakness, and lack of self-control or independence. Sexuality, as I will show, threatens the whole male-oriented social order. Insofar as women are more closely associated with sexuality through their reproductive capacities, they represent not the embodiment of that social order, as do the mature men at the top of the hierarchy, but its antithesis. And because honor is attained through embodying the cultural ideals, in this sphere, too, women are morally inferior.

Piety is an aspect of morality that women cannot easily attain because of their "natural" pollution through menstruation. One version of the Fall from Grace relates how Eve had not menstruated in the Garden of Eden but only began to bleed when she hit the ground in her fall. Women's monthly menstruation commemorates the fall into earthly sin, or at least to that which is not godly. Although there are five pillars of Islamic faith and practice (declaration of faith in the unity of God and Muhammad's prophecy, prayer, alms, the pilgrimage to Mecca, and the Ramadan fast), prayer is the duty that defines piety most vividly on a daily basis. Women are handicapped because menstruation is considered polluting. A menstruating woman cannot pray.[4] In fact, the polite Bedouin term for menstruation is "that which forbids prayer" (*ḥirmān iṣ-ṣalā*). Islamic convention stipulates that a menstruating woman may not enter a mosque or touch holy objects, the Koran in particular. Furthermore, her fasts do not count, which means that she must make up at some other time during the year the days of the Ramadan fast that she misses. Bedouin women exaggerate the uncleanliness of menstruation by abstaining from bathing or even hair combing while menstruating. The bath that marks the end of the flow is also a ritual ablution; after this bath, a woman may resume prayers, not to mention sexual intercourse. In contrast, men face no "natural" restrictions on the performance of their religious duties. Most Bedouin men (at least in the community in which I lived) try to pray five times a day, both showing their piety and assuring their continual purity in the ritual ablutions that precede each prayer.

The uncleanliness associated with menstruation is not restricted to the days when a woman is actually menstruating; rather, it taints all females from the onset of menarche until menopause, and even after. Men are symbolically associated with purity, the right (the sacred), and the color white.[5] Men tend to sit on the right side of the tent, and women on the left. When asked why, people simply explain that men are "preferred" (*afdhal*), a term with religious connotations. White is, along with green, one of the colors of Islam, and pilgrims to Mecca wear unseamed white cloth. The quintessential item of Awlad 'Ali men's clothing is the *jard,* a white woolen blanket worn over the robes and knotted at one shoulder like a toga. Women are associated with uncleanliness, the left, and the colors red and black (whose symbolic significance will be discussed in the next section). They never wear white. Even when women go on the pilgrimage to Mecca, they prefer not to don white pilgrim's garb, but would rather retain their traditional black headcloth, if not also a black full-length dress, and their red belts, the essential pair in women's dress.

The religious basis of the purity/impurity distinction and the intensity of feelings on this subject were vividly exposed when I unthinkingly threw an item of women's clothing into a washtub of men's clothes. The women gasped and rushed to remove the item, scolding me for mixing men's and women's clothing. They told me that women were unclean and that their clothes and children's clothes were washed separately from those of men and of postmenopausal women, whose clothing (other than underwear) could be washed with men's. By way of explanation, they merely said, "Men pray." The implication was that men were pure and religious, as are postmenopausal women, who, for the most part, also pray regularly. Young women in their reproductive years tend not to pray so regularly, often excusing themselves on grounds that, thanks to their many children, they are too messy and too harried to take the time to perform the proper ablutions in preparation for prayer. Yet even if they wished, they could not pray regularly because of menstruation.

The religious and ritual distinction between males and females is also evident in the ban on women slaughtering animals. All animals must be ritually killed according to Islamic rules: the person must face Mecca and slit the throat quickly in one stroke while pronouncing *allāhu akbar* (God is great). According to Bedouin custom, only men may slaughter, a restriction that often creates inconveniences for people. A common sight in the camp was that of girls running frantically from household to household carrying rabbits by the ears or chickens by the feet in search of a man to slaughter the animals their mothers wished to cook. The ritual impurity of females is apparent in solving the problem of who may slaughter in the complete absence of men. I was told that when no man can be found, a postmenopausal woman is permitted to sacrifice the animal, but only if she places the knife in the hand of a circumcised boy. She grasps his hand in hers as she actually slits the neck, but it is the boy who must utter the religious formula. The unequivocal purity of maleness per se is clear: even a nonpraying boy is considered more pure than a praying, nonmenstruating woman.

A more serious source of female moral inferiority is sexuality, with which women are intimately associated through their reproductive functions. Pregnancy is itself incontrovertible evidence of sexual activity with no equivalent among men, and fertility activated by sexuality is what defines younger women as females. Indeed, since fertility calls attention to their sexuality, women downplay it;[6] they even try to keep pregnancies secret for as long as possible, disguising the size of their bellies with their wide belts. Childbirth, although positive in that it produces the children so prized in Bedouin society, is considered polluting. Some men will not even eat food cooked by a new mother. The ambivalence about reproduction is reflected in the mixed attitudes toward women who have just given birth. A new mother, described as closer to God because her prayers are more readily answered, is also identified with the unclean menstruating woman: she is sexually taboo (for forty days after giving birth), is discouraged from bathing, and may not perform her prayers until she ceases bleeding.

Why would the association with reproduction, and especially

the sexuality necessary to it, contribute to the moral inferiority of women? The answer has two parts, corresponding to two values in the Bedouin honor complex that sets the standards for moral worth. The first value concerns the individual's relationship to his or her natural passions and functions; specifically, it is the value of independence and self-mastery. Sexuality and reproduction, like menstruation, are negatively valued as "natural" events over which females have little control, thereby providing the avenue through which others come to control them. As such they diminish women's capacities to attain the cultural ideal of self-mastery. Men want children to perpetuate lineages, and women are the vehicles; their value as reproducers leads men to want to control them. Through sexuality and pregnancy, women lose control over their own bodies. Paradoxically, the children, who later secure a woman's position, initially make her more dependent on her husband, thus increasing his control: she is tied to him by her children, whom she would lose if she left through divorce or her own choice. Even in her daily life she has less freedom to travel and visit or merely to control her own schedule.

The association of lack of independence with women's sexuality and reproduction is obvious from the instances in which Bedouins characterize particular women as either masculine (*mtdhakkara*) or like men (*kēf ir-rājil*). The former are older, postmenopausal women who, having ceased menstruating, are no longer reproductive and are less sexually active (usually being divorced, "left," or widowed), more pious, and less controlled by others. The women described as being like men are women without men. One divorcée who refused to consider remarriage was teased about being like a man. Another woman whose husband had "left" her (had ceased sleeping with her but had not officially divorced her) told me she was "living like a man." A slightly older woman who had divorced quite young and never remarried was often referred to as masculine. These women had two basic things in common: they were not under marital control, and they were not reproducing. Because the Bedouins for the most part do not have any systematic or reliable form of birth control, only for men and postmenopausal women can sexuality be divorced from reproduction, hence concealed.

The second value of the honor complex that women's association with sexuality prevents them from embodying is conformity to the ideals of the social order inherent in the concept of *'agl* (social sense). We have seen that mature men are expected to conform to and uphold—in fact embody—the social order and its ideals to justify their positions at the top of the hierarchy. But sexuality, as I will show, is a threat to the social order. It follows, then, that greater *'agl* implies distance from sexuality and that females, being closely tied to sexuality, have less of the honor that accrues from greater *'agl*.

Red Belts and Black Veils: The Symbolism of Gender and Sexuality

Gender symbolism, in particular the symbolism of the two distinctive items of women's clothing, the red belt and the black veil, illuminates Awlad 'Ali ideas about the female association with sexuality. For women, sexual knowledge and activity go with marriage, and the transition from virgin to woman is radical. The positive value of fertility, discussed above in the context of rain rituals and the symbolic associations with plenty, is tied explicitly to virgins and not to adult, married women, for whom its unambiguous character is lost. The transition is dramatically marked by a change in a girl's clothing.[7] In traditional weddings, the bride is completely covered by a man's white toga (*jard*) from the minute she is brought from her father's house until the defloration, which usually takes place in the early afternoon of the wedding day. From then on she begins to wear married women's clothing, which consists of two critical pieces: the black headcloth that doubles as a veil and the red woolen belt. These represent Bedouin womanhood. People often said to me, "Wear a veil and a

An unmarried girl covers her hair with a kerchief, and a married woman wears a black headcloth that can be used as a veil

belt and you'll be a real Bedouin woman [*tganna'ī wthazzamī wtigbī bduwiyya*]."

The red belt that every married woman wears symbolizes her fertility and association with the creation of life. Red, as we saw in the symbolism of the rain ritual, is associated with femaleness and fertility. It is the color of weddings and circumcisions, both ceremonies that celebrate sexuality and fertility. On both occasions a large red blanket is draped on the tent or even on the automobile carrying the bride to her groom's home. Belts are also linked to fertility; the onset of menarche is followed by the gradual transition to wearing some kind of belt, usually only a colorful kerchief until marriage, when the red belt is required. To go without a belt is considered highly indecent or shameful. When I first arrived in the field, I wore blouses and full-length skirts. The adolescent girls criticized me for not wearing a belt, although the skirts had waistbands. I began to wear a kerchief around my waist and everyone was pleased.

When questioned about the meaning of women's belts, one man explained that young girls did not need to wear them because "they don't know anything," the implication being about sexuality. Then, somewhat embarrassed, he explained that for an adult woman to go without a belt signaled that she was "ready for anything," again implying sexuality. In fact, the only time women remove their belts is when they sleep with their husbands, so the association is not spurious. Most women defended the belts as customary and condemned women who did not wear them (the Egyptians, for example) as shameless, but they also explained that they needed to wear them because they had to work hard and might strain their backs if they did not wear belts. Even this argument provides indirect support for the association of belts with fertility and reproductive capacity, since menstruation is also sometimes called "the back" and is thought to originate in that part of the body, just as children are said to come from "the back."

Consideration of colors other than red for belts confirms this interpretation. One day I tied a black kerchief around my waist and was immediately reprimanded. When I asked why, one woman responded that it was forbidden (*ḥarām*) to wear dark colors around one's waist because it showed a refusal to be grateful for "the life God brings." A woman in mourning for a close relative substitutes a white cloth for the red belt. Although I was unable to get an explanation for the white belt's meaning, it may represent the loss of interest in life, since the end of mourning and a woman's return to ordinary life and concern with the living are marked by resuming the red belt; those in mourning also stop using henna (which dyes hair red) and refrain from dyeing wool for weaving (red being the dominant dye color). Whether white in this context has associations with purity, religion, and masculinity I do not know.

The red belt cannot be worn if the black veil is not also worn. In the towns, where Bedouins have been influenced by Egyptian fashions, many women dispense with the red belt, but they usually retain the black headcover. Everywhere in the Muslim world the head is covered as a sign of modesty. Bedouin men also cover their heads, and they consider those who do not brazen and lacking in religion. Bedouin women's headcovers double as veils. They do not wear stiff masks, as in the Persian Gulf area, or permanent veils covering nose and mouth, as in Morocco. Rather, their not-quite-opaque black headcloth is draped and knotted in such a way that it can be lifted to cover the whole face, dropped to reveal it, or draped in intermediate ways depending on the status of the person with whom the woman is interacting. The complex rules and social meaning of veiling will be explored in the final section of this chapter.

Black is a color with numerous connotations, most of which are negative. Black is often opposed to white, the color of religion and purity. In Bedouin expressions describing human character, for instance, well-meaning, sincere, and nonmalicious people are "white-hearted," and those who act in bad faith or with malicious intent are "black-hearted." Social respectability translates into a white face, as when people assert that they have nothing to be ashamed of or to **hide. However,** someone who has been shamed or whose reputation **has been** besmirched is said to have had his or her face blackened. **Veils** literally blacken the face; thus, they symbolize shame, particularly sexual shame.

The veil is not the only article of women's clothing that is black. In the past, women wore black overdresses when they traveled long distances or paid formal social calls. Older women still wear these dresses, but many younger women have abandoned the practice. Nevertheless, all women still wear a black shawl, called a *milāya* (an item of Egyptian peasant and *baladi* dress), whenever they make formal visits. One clue to the meaning of the black overdress and shawl, and ultimately the black veil, can be found in the comment of a woman as she watched her young, lower-status neighbor set off to a wedding in the village nearby. The young neighbor was wearing a black overdress made of translucent rather than opaque cloth. The older woman noted that many considered these new overdresses unrespectable and provocative, and their wearers shameless.

This association of black with shame is confirmed in a rich folktale of mother-son incest a woman related one evening to an audience of women and children. The moral of the story places the origins of women's black veils in their antistructural sexuality. But the tale also carries messages about the complex relationship between women, sexuality, and morality. In the version below, the asides and comments of the woman telling the story are in parentheses.

> Once there was a barren woman who asked a traveling holyman [*fgīh*] for some medicine to make her fertile. He gave her something that looked like eggs and instructed her to cook them but not to eat them until the next morning. She cooked them, then left to fetch water. While she was gone, her husband returned, peeked in the pot, found the "eggs," and ate them.
>
> When she came home and saw the empty pot, she was

alarmed. "Oh no!" she said, "now you'll get pregnant." Her
husband didn't believe her but later realized that he was
pregnant. Time passed. Then one day he felt labor pains. He
came to his wife and asked her what to do. She replied, "Go
out and squat behind that bush and deliver the baby. If it's a
boy, bring it home. If it's a girl, just leave her there." He
went and pushed and pushed, hanging onto the bush until he
gave birth. He took off as fast as he could.

A bird came along and carried away the baby girl. He put
her in a nest high up in a tree and brought her food every
day. She grew up to be the most beautiful girl imaginable.
No one surpassed her in beauty.

Now, under this tree was a spring. Muḥammad būh
Sulṭān, living in a castle not far from there, had a beautiful
horse which he sent out with a slave to be watered there.
But when they approached the spring, the horse reared and
refused to drink. Muḥammad būh Sulṭān was furious when
they returned, shouting, "What do you mean she wouldn't
drink?" So he beheaded the slave. The next day, he sent out
another slave to water the horse. The same thing happened.
So the third day, he decided to go himself. When they approached the spring, again the horse reared, but as it did, he
caught a glimpse of the girl's reflection in the pool and immediately fell in love with her.

He went to an old woman and told her he wanted the
girl. She said she could help him, but he must bring her a
small tent, a ram, a cooking pot, and a grindstone. He did.
She went with this stuff and started pitching the tent under
the tree in which the girl lived. She set about doing everything wrong, trying to pitch the tent upside down and putting the poles on the outside. The girl called down, "Grandmother, not like that. You've got it upside down!" The old
lady responded, "Oh please, come down and help me. Show
me how." But the girl refused. Finally the old woman managed to pitch the tent.

Then she started sacrificing the ram, taking the knife to its
leg. The girl called down, "No, Grandmother, that's not

how you sacrifice a ram. You slit its neck." The old woman said, "Oh please, child, come down and show me how to do it." The girl refused.

Next the old woman built a fire and put the pot on it, bottom side up. The girl called down, "Oh, Grandmother, that's not how you cook. Put the pot right side up." The old lady said, "Please come down and show me how." The girl again refused. Then the old lady took the ram without killing it and tried to cram it whole into the pot. Again the girl called down, "Grandmother, that's not how you cook meat." The old lady again begged her to come down, but she refused.

After getting the ram into the pot, she set about grinding some wheat. Instead of putting the wheat on a cloth, she put it directly on the ground and started grinding. The girl called down, "No, no, Grandmother, it is forbidden [*ḥarām*] to put God's blessing [*niʿmat rabnā*] on the ground. Lay down a burlap sack or something first." The old lady ignored her. The girl climbed down, took the wheat, and placed it on a sack.

Now Muḥammad būh Sulṭān had hidden himself nearby, and when the girl stooped over he jumped out and grabbed her, put her on his horse, and took off. She cried and screamed all the way, "Damn you, Grandmother! Damn you, Grandmother!" She did not stop screaming until they got to the castle. Then he talked to the girl. He said, "Please live with me. If you want me as a father, I'll be that. If you want me as a brother, I'll be that. If you want me as a husband, I'll be that." She married him. (She knew what was in her best interest!)

The only other person in the castle was his mother, an old woman. Now, Muḥammad būh Sulṭān decided to make the holy pilgrimage to Mecca. Before he left, he gave his mother and wife a ram, saying, "If one of you dies, the other will slaughter this ram over her. If my mother dies, bury her in the courtyard." Then he went to his wife and told her, "For my sake, do anything my mother asks of you, even if she asks you to take out your own eyes." (She had gorgeous eyes.) Then he set off.

Immediately, the mother-in-law started picking on the girl. She asked her to take out her eyes and the girl agreed. The old lady, with these beautiful new eyes, threw the girl out of the castle. Now blind, the girl left. She walked and walked until she encountered a *"magass"*[8] being chased by a large snake. He begged her to hide him from the snake, promising that she could have anything she wished if she would help him. So she hid him in an empty grain bin. When the snake was gone, he came out and thanked her. Then he asked what she wished for. She asked for a castle twice as big as her old one, a new pair of eyes, and an orchard full of every conceivable fruit tree. He granted her these wishes, and they lived together in the castle.

When Muḥammad būh Sulṭān returned from the pilgrimage, the woman he found started weeping. "We slaughtered the ram over your poor old mother," she said. Indeed, he found a grave in the courtyard. But he found his wife quite changed. "Why is your skin so tough? Why has your body aged so?" he asked. She replied, "You've been gone a long time." So they lived for a while as man and wife. (Muḥammad and his mother.)

Then one day, the woman announced that she was pregnant. (A lie, she was too old to conceive.) She said she had a pregnancy craving [*tawaḥḥamat*] for some grapes. So Muḥammad sent a slave to the castle that had sprung up in his absence to ask for some grapes. The slave went off to the castle and said to the mistress who greeted him, "The wife of Muḥammad būh Sulṭān has a craving for some grapes, won't you give us some?" The woman answered, "What a lie! That's not his wife; that's his mother!" She told the *magass* to cut out the slave's tongue so he wouldn't talk. The slave came back empty-handed with his tongue cut out. Muḥammad was furious. The next day he sent another slave, who also returned with his tongue cut.

Finally, he decided to go himself. When he got there he

said, "Don't you have any grapes for the wife of Muḥammad būh Sulṭān? She has a pregnancy craving." He heard
the woman respond, "What a lie, that's not his wife; that's
his mother." He was shocked and asked, "What do you
mean?" Just as the *magaṣṣ* was about to cut out his tongue
the woman recognized her husband and stopped him. She
related what had happened in his absence: how his mother
had taken her eyes, thrown her out, and buried the ram
whole in the courtyard.

Muḥammad returned to his castle and demanded that his
"wife" dig up his mother's grave. She tried to dissuade him,
pleading, "No, no. Why do you want to see her?" He insisted, and when they dug it up he found the ram. Furious,
he threw his mother into the fire. [The listeners, mostly
young girls, were shocked. The woman telling the story
commented, "That's what she deserved!"] Then he brought
his true wife back to live with him.

They say that it is because of what his mother did that
women's veils are black.

Although this tale is so rich and complex that it could be ana-
lyzed on many levels, I will note only a few points. By linking
women's black veils to the shameful act of incest, it supports the
association of females with a negatively valued sexuality. It is
telling that women are associated not just with the ordinary sexuality of marriage, but also with an illegitimate sexuality that violates social and religious norms. Mother-son incest threatens the
primacy of bonds between men and the control of fathers over the
marriages of sons—the foundations of the Bedouin social order. In
this tale, there is no father, only a mother. Furthermore, the old
woman's sexual desire is not redeemed by a potential contribution
to procreation, as she is postmenopausal and infertile. Thus, the
black veil of shame is closely tied to a sexuality stripped of its
positive association with fertility and out of the control of senior
men. I will return to this point in the next section.

By presenting two types of women, the tale carries even more important messages about female moral worth. From the discussion of gender thus far, it might seem that Bedouins perceive women's moral inferiority to men as absolute, associating women, on the one hand, with "nature," symbolized in the balanced pairing of the red belt of fertility with the black veil of sexuality, and men, on the other hand, with white, the color of religion, that which is most "cultural."[9] But the tale clearly distinguishes between good and bad females, opposing the evil old mother driven by sexuality and the beautiful, virtuous woman.

Through its depiction of a good woman, this tale indicates that female moral worth is variable and hints at the ways women can counteract their moral inferiority. First of all, the good woman is the most male woman, symbolized by the father giving birth to her. In social life, the equivalent might be a woman who maintains close ties to male kin. Second, she is pious, which identifies her with a critical source of moral virtue. The young woman's good character is demonstrated by her inability to let the old woman commit the sacrilege of letting wheat touch the ground. Third, she is respectful, obeying both her husband and his mother to the point of giving up her eyes. Finally, she is chaste, claiming not to want a man and protesting violently when forcefully abducted. In short, through proper action, in particular through *hasham,* a woman can at least partially overcome the inferiority that is hers through her "natural" functions. To understand why this is so, the place of sexuality in the Bedouin system must be explored.

Sexuality and the Social Order

The roots of sexuality's negative value in Bedouin thought lie primarily in the social order. Where common descent and consan-

guinity provide the primary, and only legitimate, basis for binding people together, the sexual bond is a threat in that it unites
individuals outside of this conceptual framework of social relations. This interpretation conflicts with Mernissi's (1975); she lo-
cates Moroccan society's negative valuation of sexuality in the
religious order, arguing that Islamic doctrine and belief associate
women with chaos (*fitna*) and enjoin men to avoid women lest
they succumb to female seductions instead of directing their energy toward God and the social order. I argue, rather, that this
negative attitude toward sexuality is identified with religion only
because piety constitutes one of the standards of moral worth in a
Muslim society. Insofar as Islamic belief and practice represent the
highest ideals of Bedouin society, identification of the prevailing
social system and status quo with Islam is inevitable—it accords
the society legitimacy. But religious ideals are then confused with
social ideals, and personal honor comes to depend on conformity
to both.

There *is* a religious basis for the belief that sexual intercourse is
polluting. For example, it is forbidden to pray or to enter a
mosque in the unclean state following intercourse. Yet to counter
this pollution men and women need do no more than observe
certain restrictions and perform simple purificatory acts. Awlad
'Ali explain that intercourse must be followed immediately by
bathing to minimize the chance of encountering anyone while still
"unclean"; they add that care must be taken to avoid spilling the
bath water anywhere people are likely to walk. The soap used in
these baths should be kept away from children or those who pray.
To appear before children in the clothes worn during intercourse
is believed to cause them eye problems.[10] Furthermore, Bedouins
said it was forbidden (*ḥarām*) to go with one's pollution (*wasākha*)
to places such as gardens where there was food or any sort of
"God's bounty" (*ni'ma*).

But, as Mernissi (1975, 1–2) points out, Islam recognizes sexuality as a relatively positive fact of life, a strong motivating force that

must find a legitimate outlet. She notes that no antipathy between spirituality or religiosity and carnality, no split between mind and body, exists in Islam as in Christianity. Men and women are enjoined to marry; not even members of the clergy are expected to be celibate. The Bedouins share these beliefs, and most Bedouin men and women marry. Within marriage, both men and women have rights to sexual satisfaction, and long-term refusal or inability to provide sexual services by either husband or wife is considered sufficient grounds for divorce.

Thus, Islam, in symbolizing the highest good in all Muslim societies, including the Awlad 'Ali, and in codifying aspects of sexuality and sexual behavior as threatening, contributes to the negative view of sexuality. However, the source of the force and tenacity of this attitude lies not in Islamic ideology, but in the tribal social-structural model, based on the priority of relationships of consanguinity and organized in terms of patrilineal descent. Sexuality, even in its socially legitimate and religiously sanctioned guise of marriage, although necessary for the reproduction of society and the perpetuation of lineages, does not rest easily within this framework. Only patrilateral parallel-cousin marriage fits this model, which is why it is the preferred and culturally ideal marriage form in much of the Middle East. Frequently practiced by Awlad 'Ali, patrilineal parallel-cousin marriage is legally sanctioned in the institution of "the claim to the daughter of the paternal uncle" (*mask bint il-'amm*), and it carries a positive affective tone.[11] This form is ideal because it follows the patrilineal principle, subsuming the marital bond under the prior and more legitimate bond of kinship.[12]

Sexuality, together with the bonds it establishes between individuals, is not just a conceptual threat to the conceptual system that orders social relations, but a threat to the solidarity of the agnatic kin group itself. This threat, particularly to the extended patrilocal residential group, is often noted in the literature on similarly organized societies, from traditional China (Wolf 1972) to Zinacantan (Collier 1974). Collier (1974, 92) notes that in systems where resources are held jointly, the interests of in-marrying women are bound to be different from those of the men they marry and at cross-purposes with those of senior agnates, whose concern is the preservation of lineage unity. In-marrying women's loyalties are to their children, not to their husband's kin group. They may pressure to split the joint households of adult brothers in order to increase access both to resources and to the power accruing to the person at the top of the domestic hierarchy in an independent household. However, it should be noted that wives do not necessarily initiate moves to fission; often they serve merely as excuses or scapegoats for younger brothers wishing to escape their elder brothers' authority and to seek independence, in contradiction to the explicit ideology of the solidarity of patrikin (Denich 1974, 256).

At marriage, men, too, develop competing interests, but to a lesser degree than women. Their children are part of their lineage, so any interest in them is consonant with lineage interests. But, as Riesman notes for the patrilineal Fulani, the sexual bond leads to the dispersal of the agnatic group.

> The sexual bond, the bond that must not be evoked by uttering the partner's name, detaches a man from his agnatic group by uniting him with his wife. And the more fertile this bond is, the more the man approaches true independence with respect to this group. . . . As a result, to the extent that women in their huts symbolize legitimate sexuality, hence the right to progeny, they are in fact a necessary cause of the dispersal of men. (Riesman 1977, 58)

Sexuality and marriage also threaten the authority and control of elder agnates, who represent the interests of the agnatic group. The Bedouins recognize the competing nature of sexual bonds and kinship bonds, as the following popular wedding ditties, referring to the groom on his wedding night, indicate.[13]

When he shuts the door behind him
he forgets the father who raised him

kēf yrud il-bāb warāh
yansā būh illī rabbāh

He reached your arms stretched on the pillow
forgot his father, and then his grandfather

ṭāl dhrā'ak 'al l-imkhadda
yansā būh wyansā jaddu

This challenge to the hierarchical relationship between providers and dependents, or elders and juniors, is at the heart of Bedouin attitudes about sexuality. When a woman leaves her kin's residential sphere at marriage, their control over her must thenceforth be shared with her husband and his kin. When she bears children, her attachment to her husband's group grows, competing with her loyalty to her own natal group, despite her continued membership in her own patrilineage and tribe. For a young man, as Peters (1965, 129–31) points out in reference to the Cyrenaican Bedouins, marriage undermines the exclusive authority of senior agnates by giving him a domain of authority of his own, however minuscule. Senior agnates, for their part, studiously ignore junior agnates' weddings, subconsciously recognizing the threat such weddings pose to their authority. Similarly, among the Awlad 'Ali the groom's father and elder paternal uncles are never among the men firing rifles to celebrate the engagement or marriage of a son or nephew, and the father never joins the group that fetches the bride. Needless to say, sexuality outside of marriage (rare indeed) intensifies the challenge to the control of senior agnates over their dependents.

The more closely individuals identify with the interests of the patricentered system, the more they perceive the threat to the system as a threat to their own authority. This even holds true in the relations between men and women. Sexual desire is an internal force that is difficult to master, thus representing a potent challenge to one of the keystones of honor, self-control. Succumbing to sexual desire, or merely to romantic love, can lead individuals to disregard social convention and social obligations intimately implicated in the honor-linked values, marking the failure of *'agl*—as we saw in the cases of men called idiots or donkeys. Sexuality can lead to dependency, which is inimical to the highest honor-linked value, independence. Men can forfeit their positions of responsibility as independent providers by coming to depend on women to gratify their sexual desire. Women, not to mention others, lose respect for such men, and may use this dependence to their own advantage, thus reversing accepted hierarchical relations between men and women.

At every point, the threat to the solidarity of the agnatic group and to the authority and control of its elders is counteracted by social and ideological strategies. Patrilateral parallel-cousin marriage is the logical strategy for defusing the threat of the sexual bond in this social system. In this case, the sexual bond does not violate the basic principles of the social order simply because the couple is already bound by relations of identity and closeness through their bond as kin. And since the term for patrilateral cousin extends beyond actual first cousins to include any patrikin of the same generation—hence, any members of the same tribe, as defined at various levels of segmentation—the range of marriages that need not be construed as challenges to the social system is quite broad. Also, the preference for endogamous marriages assures that many Bedouin women will be of the same lineage or tribal segment as their husband and his kin; these wives are not the "worms within the apple of a patrilocal domestic group," as Collier (1974, 92) so graphically puts it, but individuals who share interests with their community of marriage.

The priority of the bonds of kinship over those of marriage are asserted and enforced in other ways. Bedouin women retain their tribal affiliation, their contact with their own patrikin, particularly brothers and fathers, and their reliance on their own kin for moral, economic, and social support. Rarely cut off from their own kin, they are never utterly dependent on their husbands, and, having alternative paths to support and respect, they rely less on a strategy of binding sons to themselves for security than do women in other patricentered systems, such as the Chinese (Wolf 1972). Their loyalties remain with their patrikin as well; thus, a woman's kinsmen may demand that she leave her husband if they fight with him or with any member of his lineage.

The control of senior agnates over the choice of marriage partners is another means of limiting the threat marriage poses to the system. Families arrange marriages for young people. Love matches are actively discouraged, and thwarted when discovered. In much of the Middle East, the explicit ideology—that men arrange marriages—is contradicted by the influence women exert over marriage choices. Among Awlad 'Ali, although there was a great deal of variation in who arranged marriages, men seemed to take the lead in higher-status tribes and lineages, whereas women had more say in families of less importance or wealth. In any case, men certainly conducted the official ceremonial marriage and bride-price negotiations. Taking the decision out of the hands of the two people to be married bolsters the authority of the kin group over individuals and over the couple as a unit.

The predominance of kinship bonds is further reinforced by downplaying the married couple's separateness and independence. The marital bond itself is not sanctified; it is dissoluble and not exclusive (at least for men). Divorce is common and fairly easy to obtain:[14] of the fifty-three adults in the fourteen households that constituted the camp I lived in, eighteen, or approximately one-third, had been divorced at least once, five more than once. Divorce carries no stigma; divorced women easily remarry and command almost the same bride-prices as virgin brides. Polygyny is condoned, if relished less by women than men.

Even in terms of residence and economic power, the conjugal unit is barely allowed to exist in its early years. Most new couples live in extended households in which the patriarch controls resources. The new husband rarely has financial independence but works jointly with his brothers. The young bride receives gifts such as clothing not from her husband but from her father-in-law, who brings gifts to all the women in the household—his wives, daughters-in-law, daughters, sisters, or whoever happens to be living with him. In the past, except in very difficult circumstances, a new couple had a tent of their own, to which the bride was brought on her wedding day. It was pitched in front of the camp (traditionally a row of tents), and after the honeymoon week the rest of the camp moved forward to join the new tent. Nowadays, brides are brought to rooms that have been added on to the groom's father's house. In neither case was the conjugal household considered separate, for resources were not split and the new couple had no resources of its own.

On the level of ideology, every attempt is made to minimize the significance of the marital relationship and to mask its nature as a sexual bond between man and woman. Marriage is spoken of as a bond between groups, families, lineages, or tribes; stress is on the creation of affines (*ansāb*). The Bedouins never refer to marriage by the usual Arabic terms *jawāz* or *zawāj,* whose direct reference to pairing or coupling, hence private sexuality, they find crude and overly explicit. They prefer the euphemism *bani il-bēt* ("setting up a tent or household" or "building a house"), which simultaneously suggests the establishment of a household and the building of a lineage. This expression deflects attention from the significance of marriage as that which joins a man and woman and stresses its significance as that which establishes and contributes to the growth of kin groups.

The modesty code is the final strategy for undermining the bond of sexuality. If the threat to the social system can be experienced as a threat to individual respectability, then the social order will be reproduced by the actions of individuals in their everyday lives. This is precisely what happens with Awlad 'Ali. To achieve virtue, those most disadvantaged by the social system must suppress in themselves that which threatens the social system, espe-

An independent old woman with her niece

cially in front of those who represent and who have most to gain in the system.

Ḥasham *Reconsidered:*
Deference and the Denial of Sexuality

The modesty code minimizes the threat sexuality poses to the social system by tying virtue or moral standing to its denial. To overcome the moral devaluation entailed by less self-mastery and control over one's own body and by closer association with that which threatens the social system, people must distance themselves from sexuality and their reproductive functions. For Awlad 'Ali, closeness to the "natural" force of sexuality provides an axis along which moral worth may be readily gauged. The more women are able to deny their sexuality, the more honorable they are.

This association is clear in *hasham,* the sine qua non of virtuous womanhood. To describe a woman as someone who *tahashshams,*[15] referring both to the emotion that motivates sexual propriety and to the acts that mark it, is the highest compliment. Women so described are those who act chastely, denying any sexual interests and avoiding men who are not kin. The modest woman admits no interest in men, makes no attempt to attract them through behavior or dress, and covers up any indication of a sexual or romantic attachment (even in her marriage). The woman who does not is called a "slut" (*qhaba*) or a "whore" (*sharmūṭa*).

The surest way not to attract men's attention is to avoid them. Although the exigencies of the division of labor and the nature of women's work make seclusion impractical for Awlad 'Ali, women avoid men in other ways. The woman who *tahashshams* does not let herself be seen by men unless it is absolutely unavoidable or unless, as with certain categories of men (described below), it is unnecessary to avoid them. She does not go to market and does not appear when guests or strangers visit her household. If contact is unavoidable, she veils. In addition, she acts and dresses so as not to draw attention to her beauty. Makeup is frowned on (except *kuḥl*), and her cherished long braids and gold earrings must be covered with the headcover (*ṭarḥa*). The modesty of Bedouin women's dress has already been remarked. But everyone recognizes that modest dress and even veiling are no guarantee of modesty. Older women complained that younger women were not as modest as they had been: younger women's veils were of thinner material, and worse, they raised their heads and talked to men through the veils—in short, they did not act correctly. As noted in the last chapter, the behavioral correlates of modesty are a variety of self-effacing and formal acts, including refraining from talking, eating, and laughing. To act immodestly in any of these ways in the company of men is interpreted as shameless flirtation. I was once taken to task by the adolescent girls in my household for having flirted with some men I was interviewing. Their evidence was that I had been animated, letting my face and eyes become too expressive.

Good women deny interest in sexual matters and deny their own sexuality. An important goal of the socialization process is to teach girls to do this. One little girl who laughed at the enormous size of a donkey's genitals was reprimanded by her older sister, "Let's have no *quḥub* [whorishness]!" Another girl confided in her uncle's new wife, "To tell you the truth, I don't even know what this love is. I hear about it in songs and hear about this one giving her necklace and that one her ring, but I don't know what they are feeling." The older woman responded approvingly, "That's my girl." Adolescents are criticized for any indication that they wish to marry. If they get carried away singing and clapping at a wedding or hover as the defloration is taking place, their mothers taunt them, "What are you so interested in? Are you looking forward to your own wedding day?"

Much socialization takes the form of humorous teasing, as in the following incident I witnessed. Western-style negligees, quite common in urban areas, had just begun to be peddled in the desert areas. Two adolescent girls, generally intrigued with urban accoutrements, were enthralled and purchased frilly nightgowns for their trousseaus. Their grandmothers were outraged, and one demanded that her granddaughter bring her the negligee as she sat with a group of women. She showed it to the visitors, asking if it was not the most shameless thing they had ever seen, and then she pulled the sheer, lime-green nightgown over her bulky dress and danced provocatively around the room. When she threatened to go outside to show it to the men, the women wailed with laughter and dragged her away from the doorway. The other grandmother then proposed taking a match to the negligees. Finally the chastised girls were told to try to return them to the peddler.

The girl who *taḥashshams* cries when she hears that someone has come to ask for her hand. The good bride screams when the groom comes near her and tries to fight him off. She is admired for her unwillingness to talk to the groom or answer any of his questions, as reported by the young men who listen outside the window on the wedding night.

Even married women must deny any interest in their husbands, much less other men. One young woman reported that her older cousin had pinched her between the legs when she caught her peeking at an attractive man through the side of the tent. People accuse a woman of lacking *ḥasham* if she indicates that she desires her husband sexually, especially when she reaches middle age or has grown sons. Stories of older women who get pregnant meet with mild signs of disapproval despite the admiration for fecundity. One woman in our camp caused quite a stir when she made her older children sleep with their grandmother to indicate her availability to her estranged husband; after he returned she was radiant and even joked that she should be given bridal gifts (see Ṣafiyya's story in chapter 7). An angry woman will insult another by referring to the size of her genitals (the presumption being that the larger the genitals the more voracious the desire).

Modest women mask sexual or romantic attachments. Women rarely use their husbands' names but refer to them simply as "that one" (*hadhāk*) or, if they are affectionate, "the old man" (*shāyib*) or "the master of my house" (*ṣāḥib bētī*). At least in front of others, they are formal and distant with their husbands, showing no public affection and acting terribly embarrassed if it is shown toward them. Although quick to admit the ubiquity of jealousy, the Bedouins do not respect a woman who lets on that she resents a co-wife whom the husband prefers or spends more time with. They consider such resentment an indication of excessive desire or interest in the husband. To maintain reputation, most women couch objections to co-wives or dissatisfaction with polygynous husbands in material terms, complaining about inequalities in the distribution of material rather than emotional favors.

The importance of the denial of sexuality to women's modesty is clear from this discussion of the good woman. But why is the denial of sexuality more crucial to women's virtue than to men's? In its ordinary aspect, as deference for providers and social superiors, *hasham* is an avenue to honor that is equally crucial for the essentially dependent female as for those males who are dependent for whatever reason and duration. Yet in its other aspect, as sexual shame and modesty, it is more essential to women than to men. As we saw earlier, men's honor also rests on their mastery of "natural" passions and functions, including sexuality; but because men are less organically linked to sexuality, they are correspondingly less pressed to deny it. The primary forces men must master in themselves are fear, pain, hunger, and dependency. Thus, only insofar as sexuality leads to dependency must men deny it, and they can do so by condemning and avoiding its representatives, women. Women are more closely associated with the sexuality that threatens the whole male-oriented social order through their reproductive activities and their inability to conceal sexuality because of pregnancy. This close association means that they represent not the embodiment of that order, as do the mature men at the top of the hierarchy, but its antithesis. It is therefore more incumbent on women to deny their sexuality in order to assert their morality.

It is important to note, however, that the devaluation and denial of sexuality implied by *hasham* are not equally necessary to women's honor in all social contexts. *Ḥasham* is critical in public and in situations where women interact with hierarchical superiors or strangers. The situational character of *hasham* is marked by the preposition it takes—*min,* "from." People do not expect women to act modestly or to experience shame about their sexuality in interactions with peers and close associates. In same-sex groups of women who are close kin, age-mates, or familiar for other reasons, conversations are often bawdy, and Bedouin girls and women do not seem priggish or delicate. Many interactions between women and certain categories of men—nephews in particular— are also extremely relaxed and intimate; as long as a woman is chaste and acts modestly with other men, her allusions to sexual interests meet only with bemused tolerance. For example, a lively and funny woman who had left her husband temporarily to stay with her mother (suffering because her only son was in prison) joked, "I've been five months away from 'the old man,' not a taste! I left him to another woman. The least they [her mother's household] could do is give me a little tip." Her cousin, relating this incident to her friends back home, laughed and commented affectionately, "She has no shame [*mā taḥashshamsh*]!" This was not a condemnation.

In public women avoid their husbands, but in private they may be affectionate and familiar. The woman with whom I lived claimed that she had no objection to eating with her husband but refused to do so when other women were around. She looked very embarrassed when her husband tried to put his head in her lap while I was sitting with them, even though I had lived with them for over a year and knew them both quite well. The formality and distance between husbands and wives is exacerbated when men, particularly elder men, are present, but even in front of younger men or children men mask affection for and interest in their wives. People say that a man's children won't *taḥashsham* from him if they witness his affection for their mother; attachment to women is interpreted as dependency, which compromises a man's right to control and receive the respect of his dependents.

The situational character of sexual modesty is the clue to its meaning. In the last chapter I showed that Awlad 'Ali conceptualize *hasham* as both the shame of lesser moral worthiness (the emotion of embarrassment/shame/shyness) and voluntary deference for those of greater moral worth who have control over one (expressed in acts of modesty). Thus, it is relevant only to specific social contexts—interactions with superiors. I now argue further that sexual modesty in Bedouin society is tied to the same specific contexts and can best be understood as an aspect of deference. (This interpretation allows sense to be made of the otherwise inexplicable patterns of Awlad 'Ali women's veiling, as I will show in the next section.) Because men of honor, those responsible for dependents, embody the values of the system and also represent it and bear responsibility for upholding it, sexuality is a challenge not only to the system but to these men's positions as well. To express sexuality is therefore an act of defiance, and to deny it an act of deference.

By showing sexual modesty before these representatives of the male system, those lower in the honor-based hierarchy express their respect for the social system. When I asked one man why women *tahashsham,* he replied, "From respect [*ihtiram*] for their tribe [lineage], their husband, and themselves." Unable themselves to identify with the system through the embodiment of its highest values, women, as well as young and poor men, defer to those who do, thereby gaining for themselves the honor garnered by those with *'agl,* the social sense to conform to the social system. Not surprisingly, the woman who *tahashsham*s is also described as *'agla.*

This association of sexual modesty with respect for the more responsible is reflected in the way the Bedouins conceive of virtuous women. The ideal woman who *tahashsham*s is called "the daughter of a man" (*bint ir-rajil*). When I asked girls why a young bride cries when someone comes to ask for her hand, they answered, "So everyone will know her father is a man and that he raised her." On the question of premarital sex or elopement, the most egregious violations of the modesty code, the same connections are asserted. Whenever I questioned women about the motivations of girls who engaged in premarital sex or eloped, they explained, "They are sluts who don't care about their fathers and aren't afraid of their kinsmen." As we saw in the last chapter, deference and fear are extremely close conceptually and are often used interchangeably in Bedouin utterances.

This analysis of the relationship between sexual modesty and deference for those more responsible allows us to reinterpret a phenomenon that has long puzzled observers of Arab social relations: the dishonor brought on kin by a woman's sexual misconduct. In part, this sharing of dishonor can be attributed to the identification with kin described in chapter 2. But shared social identity does not explain why kinsmen are more dishonored than the woman herself or why killing her wipes out the shame. If we understand women's chastity as an aspect of deference, however, we can see how Bedouins interpret infractions as acts of insubordination and insolence. Because men's positions in the hierarchy are validated by the voluntary deference shown them by their dependents, withdrawal of this respect challenges men's authority and undermines their positions. In the eyes of others, a dependent's rebellion dishonors the superior by throwing into question his moral worth, the very basis of his authority. Thus, a woman's refusal to *taḥashsham* (deny her sexuality) destabilizes the position of the man responsible for her. To reclaim it, he must reassert his moral superiority by declaring her actions immoral and must show his capacity to control her, best expressed in the ultimate form of violence.[16]

The greater dishonor of adultery for the woman's kin than for her husband can also be understood in these terms. If sexual immodesty is an affront to those who depend on a woman for validation of their authority, then those most responsible for her would be most dishonored. Her husband's authority over her is always limited by the primary authority of her kin in a system so thoroughly patrilineal that women, even after marriage, retain their ties to, identification with, and dependence on patrikin. As Meeker (1976) points out in a brilliant discussion of honor in the Middle East, Arabs contrast in this respect with the Black Sea Turks, among whom the husband gains full authority for his wife at marriage; he is thus correspondingly more dishonored by her infidelities and bears the responsibility for her punishment.

The Meaning of Veiling

The best test of the validity of this interpretation of *ḥasham*—that denial of sexuality is equated with deference—is its power to explain the pattern of women's veiling. Bedouins consider veiling synonymous with *ḥasham*, or at least a fairly accurate index of it. Symbolizing sexual shame as it hides it, veiling constitutes the most visible act of modest deference. When the new bride quoted in the last chapter asked her young friends, "Who *taḥashsham*s from whom in the community?" she got a list of the men for whom particular women veiled.

Veiling is both voluntary and situational. Awlad 'Ali view it as an act undertaken by women to express their virtue in encounters with particular categories of men. They certainly do not perceive it as forced on women by men. If anyone besides the woman herself has responsibility for enforcing the veil's proper use, it is other women; they guide novices (brides) along, teasing young women for veiling for men who don't deserve their deference and criticizing them for failing to veil for men who do.

Although Anderson (1982, 403) correctly notes that "veiling refers actions to a paradigm of comportment in general rather than to chastity in particular," he overstates the case in his effort to combat prevailing misconceptions about its exclusively sexual

Veiled women cleaning rice

motivation (see Antoun 1968; Mernissi 1975; Dwyer 1978).[17] Veiling communicates deference, but its vocabulary is that of sexuality or chastity. The folktale of mother-son incest recounted earlier makes that point, as does the fact that Bedouin women do not veil for other women no matter how identified with the lineage and social system they are. The most compelling piece of evidence is the timing of veiling in the life cycle. Girls start veiling only at marriage, when they become sexually active, and women gradually abandon the practice as they pass menopause. When I asked one close woman friend why virgins did not veil, she laughed, made the obscene gesture of coitus, and asked, "Hasn't a man entered the married woman? She *taḥashshams*." Exceptions to proper veiling prove the rule. When I asked a widow in early middle age why she did not veil, she answered, "I'm not buying or selling [the reference being to marriage and sexuality]." Those women described earlier as "like men" or "living like men" also veil less often than women living with husbands, confirming this interpretation of the meaning of veiling as that which covers sexual shame.

The final indication of veiling's association with sexuality is that women resort to it when embarrassed by references to sexuality even in the company of men for whom they ordinarily do not veil. During my first visit to the Bedouin household in which I was later to live, I naively pulled out my notebook and asked the head of household who was married to whom. All the women present blushed and pulled their veils over their faces. I realized I had done something wrong, but it was a long time before I understood what. When a woman told her husband about a marriage engagement that had been concluded in his absence, she held her veil over her mouth. At a gathering of kinswomen brought together by a wedding, an older woman began teasing her nephew, a patriarch in his own right, about his marital life. At this point in the conversation, the younger women, who had been sitting a bit apart with their backs to the man, suddenly veiled and moved to another room. In another instance, the divorcée who was "living like a man" and did not usually veil, suddenly paled and pulled her veil over her face when the one-and-a-half-year-old daughter of the senior lineage head with whom she was sitting revealed a bare bottom as she played nearby.

To veil because one is ashamed of sexuality, one's own or in general, is not the same thing as veiling, either voluntarily or by force, to prevent seduction or arousal. If veiling was intended to prevent sexual interest, there would be no sense to the Bedouin system, which allows women to interact unveiled and quite familiarly with numerous men whom they could easily attract sexually and whom they are not prohibited by Islamic law from marrying. Conversely, they would not veil for categories of men with whom sexual relations would be incestuous and out of the question, such as close kinsmen.

If, however, we interpret veiling as the covering of sexual shame, we can better understand why Bedouin women veil for some men and not others. Veiling, and *hasham* generally, indicate a woman's recognition of sexuality's place in the social system and her wish to distance herself from it, thus asserting her possession of *'agl,* or the social sense to conform to the system's ideals. As I showed earlier, this distancing is her way of showing respect for the system, in the person of those who represent its interests and more thoroughly embody its ideals. Through deference to those higher in the hierarchy she gains the kind of honor open to the weak or morally inferior.

Women generally veil for their fathers, elder uncles and lineage elders, their elder male cousins, and elder affines. They are more likely to veil for married than for unmarried men. They always veil for older nonkinsmen or strangers, unless these men are clearly of low social status or non-Bedouins. If a woman's father is dead and responsibility for the family has been assumed by her elder brother, she is likely to veil for him. Women do not veil for husbands, younger brothers, cousins, or affines or for their husbands' dependents, such as clients, or men of lower status than their husbands. If there is a large age differential between a woman and her husband, she often does not veil for his juniors, even though they may be older than she is. In ambiguous cases, generation, as embedded in kinship relation, takes precedence over actual age.[18] Only insofar as the principles of kinship and affinity are coterminous with hierarchy do they determine the unarticulated rules of veiling, and when men lose honor through cowardice, excessive dependence, dishonesty, or whatever, women cease to veil for them.

The operating principle here is that women veil for those who have authority over them or greater responsibility for the system. They do not veil for those lower in the hierarchy—dependents and those without honor. Husbands are excepted because as sexual partners they probably share their wives' shame. Non-Bedouins, of course, have no responsibility for upholding or embodying the ideals of the system and get no respect from Bedouin women. Since Bedouins characterize the Egyptians as deficient in all the key dimensions of morality (see chapter 2), when Bedouin women visit Alexandria or Cairo, they walk unveiled in the streets;[19] but they veil closely, even if riding in a car, when they pass through Bedouin towns in the Governorate of Matruh.

Women veil less as they grow older, in part because they encounter fewer men senior to them or responsible for them. As the older men in a community die off, women are surrounded by their sons and nephews, from whom they do not *tahashsham* because they not only have seen these men exposed and vulnerable as children but also have shared with them a dependency on elders. As elders themselves, these women, who have been responsible for rearing these young men, become more identified with the social system. Furthermore, as they are less sexually active, they are automatically distanced from the "natural" sexuality usually associated with females and so feel less shame. They are more like men and aspire to the moral virtues of assertiveness, responsibility, self-control, and piety that justify men's positions in the hierarchy.

The system is flexible, leaving room for women to make judgments about relative status and even to negotiate status.[20] For example, a woman who had spent her early years with her maternal kin never veiled for them when she returned to their camp for visits; when her mother criticized her, she countered with the argument, "They were all young when I left." A bride married to an older man failed to veil for a few of her affines; when her husband's kinswomen asked her why, she responded that she had decided to veil only for men older than her husband and quipped that she had discovered no one who was. Women also manipulate their veils to communicate degrees of deference, from the extremely formal total covering of the face to the token gesture of draping the veil sideways to cover only part of the face.

Under certain circumstances, ceasing to veil is a bid for status. Women who consider themselves highly virtuous often declare this by not veiling. One woman who rarely veiled defended herself by claiming that her "face was white," meaning she had nothing to be ashamed of. Women reaching middle age declare their changing identities by veiling for fewer men. Older women and high-status women (from honorable lineages or married to wealthy men with many dependents) veil for fewer people than do young and low-status women (poor women or wives of clients), thus asserting their moral parity with mature men.

The only category of people for whom women generally veil that does not, at first glance, appear to follow this principle is that of strangers or nonkin. Indeed, women are more likely to veil for nonkin than for kin of equivalent age and status. To understand this phenomenon, we must invoke the identification with kin discussed in chapter 2. If status in the larger society is also tied to the honor complex, it follows that it depends on the respect shown men by their dependents. Because women identify with their male kin, they share their kinsmen's interest in intergroup status. Their gestures of sexual modesty, then, including conspicuous veiling in public, enhance their kin's honor and social standing by showing others that their women respect them. Conversely, failure to veil or to deny sexuality, like sexual misconduct, affronts kin and saps their honor. Veiling for strangers thus demonstrates respect for kin in absentia.

Veiling, for Awlad 'Ali, is best understood as a vocabulary item in a symbolic language for communicating about morality. Avoidance and self-effacing gestures of various sorts, including downcast eyes and restraint in eating, talking, and relaxing, are other "expressions" in this specialized language of modesty. All of these vocabulary elements are gestures of deference to hierarchical superiors who more closely adhere to Awlad 'Ali honor-linked values, but veiling is unique in that it is peculiar to women and has a specifically sexual meaning. As we saw, sexuality is the most potent threat to the patrilineal, patricentered system and to the authority of those who uphold it, namely, senior agnates, and women are those most closely identified with sexuality through their reproductive activities. Therefore, to show respect for that social order and the people who represent it, women must deny their sexuality. They do so by denying sexual interests—avoiding and acting uninterested in men, dressing modestly so as not to draw attention to their sexual charms, and veiling. By distancing themselves from sexuality and its antisocial associations, they escape moral stigma and gain the only kind of honor open to them: modesty, the honor of voluntary deference, which is the moral virtue of dependents in Bedouin society.

Morality is by definition voluntary. As with forced obedience, the modesty of women coerced into seclusion or into veiling would be worthless, both to the women and to those whose status is validated by the deference they receive from their dependents. *Hasham* cannot be forced; others can only suggest that a particular situation is a context in which one should feel shame and act modestly. A person with *'agl,* or social sense, a person who wants to be good, will *tahashsham* when it is appropriate.

I have described an ideological system that supports social, political, and economic inequality, despite the fact that egalitarian principles are clearly valued. The central theme of the moral system through which individuals live this ideology is that separate paths to honor exist, appropriate to the socially and economically independent on the one hand, and to the dependent on the other.

Moral worthiness can be expressed through the honor code or the modesty code, depending on one's rank, whether actual or potential. Moreover, these codes provide yardsticks by which individuals' legitimate rights to hierarchical positions are measured. People achieve honor by displaying the honor-linked virtues associated with Awlad 'Ali ideals, ideals related mostly to autonomy. Women and other dependents are morally inferior because of their dependency (hence, lack of autonomy), but they can achieve honor by showing deference to those on whom they depend. Because females are associated with sexuality and sexuality threatens the authority of those who represent the system and its ideals—mainly males—women show deference by suppressing their own sexuality in front of men. This form of deference is sexual modesty.

Finally, honor and modesty are dialectically related in the establishment of family or lineage honor. A family has honor when its men are "real men," embodying the ideals of Bedouin society, including supporting and protecting their dependents, and the women and dependents are modest, deferring to their providers and thus validating these men's claims to their high positions in the hierarchy. If the men fail, their women lose honor, and if the women or other dependents fail, the men lose honor. Thus, all members are responsible for the honor of all those with whom they identify as kin.

My concern with this ideology of honor is not so much with its causes or roots—a question much debated in the literature on circum-Mediterranean societies (see, for example, Antoun 1968; Bourdieu 1977; Denich 1974; Goody 1976; Ortner 1976; Paige 1983; Schneider 1971; Sharma 1978; Tillion 1966; Yalman 1963) and arguably unanswerable, given the complexity of human social life—but rather with its effects on individuals. I assume that social and economic systems cannot reproduce themselves in a particular form without the actions of individuals, and individuals are guided by ideas, especially cultural notions of morality and virtue. For the Awlad 'Ali Bedouins, these ideas are tied up with honor and modesty. The system is thus reproduced by the actions of individuals motivated by a desire to embody the good—that which wins respect, confers respectability, and allows for self-respect. How the ideology of honor and modesty engenders a discourse of morality, shapes individual actions, and, most important, affects sentiments and experiences in relations with others is the subject of Part Two.

Part Two

DISCOURSES ON
SENTIMENT

5

THE POETRY
OF PERSONAL LIFE

Turning from the logic of the Awlad 'Ali ideological system to
the ways in which, in its incarnation as a moral system, it can be
understood to shape what individuals do and say, and perhaps
even feel, we are led into the intimate realm of Bedouin personal
life. It is here that the ideals of the moral system should engender
ways of acting and speaking, particularly with regard to sentiments. But, as I suggested in the introduction, one cannot talk
about Awlad 'Ali personal life without talking about poetry, that
vital and highly valued expressive form that carries such moving
messages about the life of sentiment. So, before exploring the
discourse of Awlad 'Ali personal life, I will give a sense of how
poetry is used and how people respond to it, along with some
background on the genre most associated with the sentiments of
personal life, the *ghinnāwa*.

On Poetry in Context

While in the field, I was rarely able to tape-record anything but
wedding festivities. Laughingly accusing my machine of being a

tattler, people were reluctant to let me record their ordinary conversations or the songs that often punctuated these conversations. I
was usually out of batteries anyway, since there was nothing people
loved more than listening to tapes. They enjoyed the wedding tapes
I had made, despite the fact that the singing was barely audible over
the din of multiple conversations, crying babies, and excited children. But one special tape was the most frequently requested. I had
recorded it one afternoon when I happened to catch the spontaneous conversation and songs of two women sewing a tent together.
They were comfortable with me and with each other, and, save for
the children, we were alone in the household. As they shredded and
sewed fabric for a patchwork to decorate the tent walls, they began
to sing, responding to each other's songs in turn. 'Azīza initiated
the singing with the following verse, which can be interpreted to
mean that the poet had tried patience, but since it got her nowhere,
she finally gave up.

> Patience brought no fulfilled wishes
> I wearied and hope's door closed . . .

> iṣ-ṣabr mā gadḥā ḥājāt
> mallēt wir-rajā bābu gafal . . .

Her friend answered with a poem implying that it was better to
replace love with patience. 'Azīza rejoined with a poem about the
persistence of memories; her friend countered with an exhortation
to forget those who cause pain. 'Azīza then resumed her original
theme of patience with the following poem:

> If patience availed her in despair
> the self would commit no offense, even small . . .

> in fādhā ṣ-ṣabr 'al-yās
> l-'ēn mā jināya dāyra . . .

Here she evoked a despair so overwhelming that patience could
exert no control over it or over the things it might drive its victim

to do. In response came a song I had heard in another context warning of the ill effects of bringing up tales of old loves.

Whenever I played this tape for women in the community, they sat quietly and listened intently. They always looked solemn and pained. Some shook their heads sadly and commented, "Her luck is bad!" or "This is news that makes you cry." Some even wept. Although much more will have to be revealed about the use of poetry in Bedouin social life to allow a full appreciation of why this tape was so cherished and why it provoked such strong reactions, a few elements can be outlined here.

One reason these women appreciated this particular tape so much was that the poems answered each other—the interchange became a form of conversation.[1] Improvisational talent and ability to play with linguistic forms are highly valued in Bedouin culture. Even if the women were repeating poems everyone had heard, their ability to summon them up at the appropriate time was still admirable.

Bedouins are sensitive to the graces and evocative power of oral textual elements such as sound, alliteration, intonation, and rhythm, elements that are highlighted in recitation. When sung, much of the effect of the *ghinnāwa* depends on the delivery (usually plaintive), the singer's skill, and the quality of his or her voice. 'Azīza's singing was extremely mournful, and her friend had a beautiful voice.

Some of the Bedouins' appreciation may be more elusive for the outsider to uncover, as it is based in part on shared cultural background, including familiarity with a large corpus of poems. Although Awlad 'Ali appreciate original metaphors and new images, they do not insist on them. Even familiar and ordinary images, such as the ones in these poems—all of which center around traditional, and one might presume tired, themes—derive great connotative richness from subliminal intertextual comparisons. Individuals know so many poems that each new one undoubtedly evokes image-traces and feeling-tones from others with shared words, phrases, or themes. People are reminded of "sister" songs, variations on a theme, or poems used on similar occasions.

Alternatively, some poems may call up specific situations in which they were last heard or in which they properly belong, as, for example, love stories. By drawing images and experiences from the shared world of a small, culturally homogeneous community, poems gain meaning.

But I would argue that the Bedouin women were moved by the tape mostly because they knew the difficult conditions under which 'Azīza lived, and they cared about her, having known her all their lives. They interpreted the intrinsically vague songs, traditional and formulaic, as revealing personal statements. They understood the formal poetic elements just described to be tools for articulating, conveying, and evoking sentiments, whose meaning and poignancy derived from and referred to the context of 'Azīza's life.

The women knew that 'Azīza, who had been born in the community and had spent all but a few of her thirty-three years there, had recurring problems with the moody and poverty-stricken brother she lived with. Barely able to support himself and unable to keep a wife (he had married four, all of whom had left him after not being able to conceive), he resented having to support his divorced sister. His attitude was a great shame to her, since, as noted earlier, a woman is always supposed to be able to depend on her father, and later on her brother.

Her marital history was sad. Her husband had taken a dislike to her shortly after their marriage and had become abusive. She escaped home, only to be met with her father's death. After the funeral she was persuaded to return to her husband's household, where his other wife (her half-sister) mistreated her and then got her into trouble with her husband, who had been spending most of his time away from home, working in Libya. He divorced her, and she refused to remarry, in part because she was raising her son alone—a woman cannot take a child from another husband into her new marital community, and she would have lost him had she remarried. She had been allowed to bring him with her in the first place because he was only an infant when she left her husband; in an unusual move, she had then gotten hold of his government registration papers, which she hoped would enable her to keep legal custody of him. Yet she lived in fear that he would be taken away from her.

To make matters worse, 'Azīza had a hideous and painful skin disease that had first appeared during the difficult period prior to her divorce. It erupted at intervals and then receded. She had visited holymen and doctors, none of whom could help her; all seemed to attribute it to unhappiness or stress. She conceded that her condition worsened whenever she dwelt on her misfortune. Others noted that her sores reappeared whenever she had a fight with her brother.

Her revelation of painful personal sentiments in poetry moved people. Knowing the circumstances of her life, they realized that the despair of which she sang came from her unhappy marriage, her illness, her poverty and loneliness. When she sang about memories and her inability to forget, they understood that despite the passage of time, she was still preoccupied with her failed marriage and wounded by her husband's unfair treatment. By singing about patience, 'Azīza betrayed her hope that some reward would come from her suffering. Her discouragement troubled the listeners as well as her friend, who had tried her best to give comfort and advice through poetry—but they all knew how few signs of hope really existed.

The intrinsically ambiguous *ghinnāwas*, so seemingly impersonal, bound as they are to formula and tradition, were in this context revealing personal statements that allowed those who knew 'Azīza to glimpse how she experienced her difficult situation. The insight the poems afforded these women, then, contributed as much to their appreciation as did formal aesthetics or internal poetics. Indeed, unless marked by particularly striking metaphors or haunting images, most poems have little impact in the abstract; context is crucial, not just for the appreciation but even for the understanding of a poem's meaning.[2] Awlad 'Ali are

Two women talking as they warm themselves by the glowing ashes from the bread oven

in fact hard-pressed to interpret poems without contextual information—whenever I asked anyone the meaning of a particular poem, their first question was "Who said it?"

Because Awlad 'Ali interpret poems as personal statements in specific social contexts, I slight poetics, formal analysis, and comparisons with other forms of Arabic poetry in favor of analyzing the way individuals use *ghinnāwa*s and the role poetry plays in Bedouin social life and thought. In the chapters that follow, I ask what people are saying about their experiences through their poems, what their goals are in reciting them, and to whom they are addressing the poems. In this regard, I share some interests with more contextual- or performance-oriented students of oral literature, who focus on the individual and the social situation of recitations, the uses to which recitations are put in social interactions, and the creativity involved in manipulating traditional forms such as songs, proverbs, and folktales (T. B. Joseph 1980; Mills 1978; Sapir and Crocker 1977; Seitel 1977). Yet, in focusing on the social use of these discourses, these studies sometimes lose sight of the expressive aspect of the arts as reflections on and statements about profound human experiences. I try to keep both in sight.

The Poetry of Self and Sentiment

The genre of poetry 'Azīza and her friend recited is the *ghinnāwa*. Their use of poems in conversation and the reaction of others illustrate much about poetry's role in Bedouin life. Awlad 'Ali delight in reciting and listening to *ghinnāwa*s. They attach special weight to the messages conveyed in poetry and are moved, often to tears, by the sentiments expressed. In fact, their definition of a good poem is that it moves the people who hear it. They say, "Beautiful poetry makes you cry," and note that poems can move others to change their minds and actions. Such visceral responses are contingent on the hearer's knowledge of the person reciting the poem, the life circumstances to which the poem is a response, and the general contours of social relations in Bedouin society. Awlad 'Ali perceive poems as personal statements, even when they know the poems to be conventional and formulaic.

The *ghinnāwa* is the only genre of poetry and song mentioned in earlier studies of Awlad 'Ali that remains a vital part of every-day life and is still performed at wedding and circumcision festivi-ties (Falls 1908, 1913; Hartmann 1899; and Smart 1966, 1967), at least in the eastern part of Egypt's Western Desert, that part that has been most transformed over the past few decades.[3] The word *ghinnāwa* means "little song," yet, because it is either recited or sung in what is almost a chant and is distinguished from songs with rhyme and melody that more closely fit our own concep-tions of songs, I call it poetry.[4] The Bedouins themselves classify it, along with other types of poetry and song, as *gōl*, a general term that means simply anything said.[5]

The *ghinnāwa* is clearly distinguishable in form, context, and content from other genres of Awlad 'Ali poetry and song. These other genres are usually composed of numerous rhythmic verses, are sometimes rhymed, and are recited or sung by specialists, mostly men, whereas the *ghinnāwa* is composed of only one line of approximately fifteen syllables, divisible into two hemistiches, and can be sung or recited by anyone. Men and women do so with varying frequency depending on their talents, their social circumstances, and the vicissitudes of their personal lives and in-terpersonal relationships.[6] When recited, usually in the midst of conversations but also in sweethearts' dialogues in traditional ro-mances, *ghinnāwa*s are spoken in a breathless, drawn-out monotone stressing the long vowels, with a pause in the middle to mark the beginning of what must be considered the second hemistich. When sung, either when people are alone working or at formal occasions such as weddings or circumcision ceremonies, *ghinnāwa*s are "char-acterized by a high-pitched chanting, the repetition of words within the verse and the stretching out of single syllables into whole melodic passages" (Smart 1966, 206).[7] The most intriguing

aspect of the sung form is word order. Not only are words repeated, but the order is reversed. To clarify this description, it is
best to work with an example:

> Tears increased, oh Lord
> the beloved came to mind in the time of sadness . . .

<pre>
 1   2   3   4
dami' zād yā mawlāy
   5   6 7 8   9
khaṭar 'azīz fī wān iz-za'al . . .
</pre>

The words were sung in the following order:

fī wān (78)	in the time
fī wān (78)	in the time
fī wān iz-za'al (789)	in the time of sadness
fī wān (78)	in the time
'azīz fī wān iz-za'al (6789)	beloved in the time of sadness
fī wān (78)	in the time
fī wān (78)	in the time
'azīz fī wān iz-za'al (6789)	beloved in the time of sadness
fī wān (78)	in the time
fī wān (78)	in the time
fī wān dami' (781)	in the time tears
dami' zād yā mawlāy (1234)	tears increased oh Lord
fī wān (78)	in the time
fī wān (78)	in the time
khaṭar 'azīz (56)	beloved came to mind
khaṭar 'azīz fī wān iz-za'al (56789)	the beloved came to mind in the time of sadness . . .

The number of repetitions is variable, based on the whim and
mood of the singer, and there is much room for individual play in

highlighting the language, creating suspense, and manipulating emotional tone and intensity. The only general rule about word order is that all but the first word of the second hemistich are always sung first, followed by the words of the first hemistich, and, near the end, the whole song from beginning to end including the missing first word of the second hemistich is sung more or less in the correct order.[8]

Like most oral poetry, the *ghinnāwa* is formulaic and traditional.[9] Individuals either appropriate poems whole from the cultural repertoire or compose them extemporaneously, drawing on a traditional stock of themes, metaphors, phrases, and structures. They appear to care little about matters of authorship (see Appendix). How traditional the form is can be seen by comparing the examples collected by the German explorer J. C. Ewald Falls in 1906 (Falls 1908) with my own. The hundred or so poems he published bear a striking resemblance to ones I recorded nearly seventy-five years later in the same vicinity; several are even identical.

The genre is also widely found. Not just Awlad 'Ali but also the tribal groups of Cyrenaica compose and recite *ghinnāwas*, although the Libyans call this genre *'alam* or *ṣōb khalīl* (names known to but not used by Awlad 'Ali). Libyan folklorists (including Jibrīl 1973; Qādirbūh 1977; and Al-Ghannāy 1968) consider it one of the more important genres of Libyan folk poetry and song.[10] Again, there is considerable overlap in the poems they collected and ones that I recorded, hundreds of miles away and across a border that has been closed for a number of years. Quite a few poems are virtually identical; many more share images, phrases, metaphors, and themes.

To say that the poems are formulaic and traditional is not, however, to deny the tremendous creative possibilities of the genre. Elements and structures are combined in seemingly infinite ways to express new meanings (see Appendix). One index of the variety possible is that among the four hundred and fifty poems I recorded in the course of my stay, only a few were duplicates. Most important, as 'Azīza's case showed, this poetry finds its true expressiveness in and ultimately takes its meaning from the social contexts in which it is embedded. It is in the contexts of peoples' lives that I analyze Bedouin poetry.

More than anything else, the subject matter of this much-loved genre distinguishes it from other genres of poetry and song and accounts for its special place in Bedouin society. The *ghinnāwa* is the poetry of personal sentiment. It is about feelings people have, feelings about situations and human relationships. Even a cursory look at the poetic vocabulary of the *ghinnāwa* betrays this content. The simple formulas, so prevalent that they practically define the genre, are the terms for the self and the beloved. One of the following six terms appears in the majority of poems I heard.

The three conventional terms that are used to refer to the self in *ghinnāwa*s are each actually parts of persons. These synecdoches share one quality: they are nouns that allow poets to speak about themselves in the third person, an element of depersonalization whose significance I will take up in the final chapter. The most common and likewise least specific term of self-reference is *'ēn* (eye). This term opens up metaphorical possibilities associated with real eyes and their functions, including weeping, that are only sometimes explored. Often the eye just stands for the self;[11] on occasion it takes the reverse meaning of the beloved, as in the English expression "apple of my eye." The prominence of eyes and imagery of eyes is by no means peculiar to Awlad 'Ali culture but is reflected in songs and idiomatic expressions in other Arab societies and in cultural beliefs about illness and misfortune with regard to the "evil eye."

The second most common term for self is *'agl,* which suggests the link between self and sentiment or feelings. Its meaning in *ghinnāwa*s differs from its meaning in other contexts, such as those discussed in chapters 3 and 4. In poetry *'agl* does not mean propriety or social knowledge, as in ordinary talk; the closest translation might be "mind," or even "psyche," given a meaning with less of a cerebral or intellectual connotation than our concept implies. Bedouins explain that the *'agl* is in the heart—one woman pointed to her heart as she said something about her *'agl*. The Libyan folklorist Qādirbūh actually glosses *'agl* as *qalb*, the Arabic word for heart, in his exegeses of *ghinnāwa*s. A comment one Bedouin made to me about singing confirms that poetry is linked to feelings of the self. She explained, "Those who sing feel something strongly in their hearts [*'agl*]."

A third common poetic term of self-reference is *khāṭr*, a term difficult to translate. That it refers to the heart or feelings, what we might consider the inner person, is suggested by the most common context in which the term is used in ordinary talk. After funeral ceremonies are over, anyone who visits the bereaved asks how they are by asking after their *khāṭr*. For example, someone would ask a bereaved niece, "How is your heart/soul over your aunt [*izzāy khāṭrik 'ala 'amtik*]?" As with *'agl*, Qādirbūh, along with Jibrīl, glosses *khāṭr* as "heart." My inclination is to translate it as "soul," since it seems to refer to the inner person. Unlike the English "soul," however, it carries no metaphysical or religious connotations[12]—the word that comes closer to that meaning is *rūḥ*, or "spirit," which the Bedouins also use in poetry to refer to the self.

That many of the sentiments of the heart or self explored in *ghinnāwa*s are those associated with love and attachments to others is even clearer from the other three vocabulary items characteristic of the genre. These are the interchangeable terms for the loved one: *'azīz*, *'alam*, and *awlāf*. These terms may describe either the persons the poems are about or those to whom the poems are addressed.[13] All can, but need not, refer specifically to a lover or sweetheart, and none is gender-marked. The first word's close association with the genre was brought home to me by an amusing incident. One evening after dinner I was chatting with a group of women and children. Suddenly a young boy, no more than five, began to sing loudly, showing off. Following the pattern and melody of the *ghinnāwa* but being too young to know any of the words, he merely repeated the phrase "Oh beloved, oh beloved" (*yā 'azīz, yā 'azīz*). The second word for the beloved, *'alam*, is even used as the name of the genre in Libya. The third term, *awlāf*, comes from the root meaning "to be used to" or "familiar with," which I discussed in the context of the closeness that binds those who live together (chapter 2). This term leaves ambiguous the gender and number of the people being referred to, and it appears most often in poems sung about families or children, underscoring the fact that *ghinnāwa*s are not just about romantic love but also about all sorts of attachments to others.

Although the range of sentiments expressed in *ghinnāwa*s is wide and the objects of these sentiments varied, two generalizations can fairly be made, both of which are borne out by the case of 'Azīza described above. First, with the exception of *ghinnāwa*s sung at weddings and circumcision celebrations, the sentiments of poetry tend to be negative or dysphoric. Even the poems of love and passion, described in metaphors of fires and flames, usually dwell on the painful aspects of the experience. I once asked an old woman why so many of the poems seemed to be about sadness. She laughed and said, "She who gets what she wants is happy and shuts up." A number of individuals corroborated my observations that people turned to poetry when faced with personal difficulties: one woman remarked, "I sing when I feel depressed/frustrated [*mtd̲h̲āyga*, literally, pressed in upon]." And an old man said, "I sing to soothe myself. Especially in times of trouble—that is when you sing."

Second, although nearly all of the poems I heard had to do with powerful sentiments arising in interpersonal relationships, the most common references were probably to romantic love relationships between men and women. The *ghinnāwa* is the quintessential language of courtship and love. Not only are the dialogues of lovers in traditional Bedouin romantic tales always in this form, but in the past real youths and girls are also reported to have exchanged poetry, usually of the improvised competitive song and response type (see Appendix), when they met at the wells or in more formal contexts such as weddings, sheep shearings, grain threshings, tattooing ceremonies, or an institution known as the *mijlās*.[14] However, the increasing segregation of the sexes concomitant with the changing division of labor, the demise of the latter four institutions, and the transformation of wedding rituals have limited the occasions for such interchanges.[15] As one older man noted with regret, "There are no longer occasions for singing." When a group of women I was visiting discovered that their young nephew had composed a song for a young woman he had met, they laughed and exclaimed that it was "like the old days." The modern equivalent, rare even so, is for young unmarried literate Bedouins to exchange poems in written form.

The remaining links between *ghinnāwa*s and romantic love have become more indirect: subject matter, of course, and the fact that *ghinnāwa*s are still sung publicly at the two occasions most tied to sexuality, weddings and circumcision celebrations (the latter being identified with weddings in many ways, including the very term by which they are known, *faraḥ*).[16] *Ghinnāwa*s are not, however, exchanged between men and women; indeed, the songs sung at these feasts are more often songs of praise or congratulations than the more personal type described above. Men rarely sing *ghinnāwa*s at weddings anymore; that is the province of the women, who sing at various stages of the wedding festivities, including the "night of henna" (*lēlt il-ḥinna*) before the wedding day and the procession to fetch the bride (*zaffa*). The bride's family and friends sing songs bidding her farewell, wishing her well in her new home, warning her not to put up with poor treatment, and bemoaning their loss. The groom's kinswomen congratulate their kinsman on his victory, bless the marriage, welcome the bride, and glorify the groom's family, and sometimes the bride's, depending on relations. Rivalry between the families is often reflected in these poems. The songs are usually exuberant rather than plaintive, both in singing style and in message.[17]

Likewise, the songs women sing at circumcision celebrations tend to congratulate the circumcised boy and his parents and kin, often referring to the boy as a groom. But, just as at weddings, the festivities also provide an occasion for singing about other things. At one unusually elaborate circumcision feast the boy's father installed a loudspeaker system and hired a dancer and a troupe of Bedouin musicians. Many of the local young men who attended as guests also sang; among the genres heard was the *ghinnāwa*. This was the only time I ever heard men sing in public, so I assume it has become rare. The women with whom I sat listening all seemed nostalgic and quite appreciative.

Formal public occasions like weddings and circumcision feasts, although the highlights of social life, are sporadic. My interest in the poems was sparked by the frequency with which individuals punctuated their conversations with them, and I concentrate on this use of poetry.[18] People sing *ghinnāwa*s when alone or with friends of the same sex. Smart (1966, 206) notes that shepherds sing *ghinnāwa*s when alone at night. I heard women singing them while working alone or while sitting around with other women, with no men nearby. Most of the time people recite, rather than sing, *ghinnāwa*s. They do so in the middle of conversations, usually with intimates.

Two features characterize the *ghinnāwa*s sung or recited in these informal contexts. People tend to sing about themselves and their situations in life, and, in the context of conversations, the poems they recite are usually either comments on the situation being discussed or concise, and often poignant, expressions of their sentiments about the situation.[19] Also, as I noted above in the case of 'Azīza, men and women most often recite poetry about their relationships to loved ones. In short, the *ghinnāwa* is the poetry of personal life, the poetry of intimacy. As we shall see, this discourse on sentiment is also a discourse of defiance.

6

HONOR AND POETIC
VULNERABILITY

Discourses on Loss

Poetry is not, of course, the only medium in which Awlad 'Ali express sentiment and make statements about their experiences in personal life; they also do so in ordinary language and plain behavior. Yet, as suggested in the introduction, individuals use poetry in their everyday lives in a striking way: to express special sentiments, sentiments radically different from those they express about the same situations using nonpoetic language. Thus, each mode of expression can be considered a distinct discourse on personal life. *Discourse* here refers not simply to linguistic form, as in the distinction between formalized and everyday speech acts.[1] Rather, I use the term more in the sense that Foucault (1972, 1980) uses it, to mean a set of statements, verbal and nonverbal, bound by rules and characterized by regularities, that both constructs and is patterned by social and personal reality.[2]

This use of the term *discourse* as a shorthand for a complex of statements made by numerous people in different social contexts is justified by the existence of a pattern in the sentiments expressed in the two media. People often turn to poetry when faced with personal difficulties, but the constellations of sentiments they communicate in response to these difficulties in their poems and in their ordinary verbal and nonverbal statements overlap very little. The discourse of ordinary life for those confronted with loss, poor treatment, or neglect (among the most frequent elicitors of poetry) is one of hostility, bitterness, and anger; in matters of lost love, which will be explored in the next chapter, the discourse is one of militant indifference and denial of concern. Poetry, on the contrary, is a discourse of vulnerability, expressing sentiments of devastating sadness, self-pity, and a sense of betrayal, or, in cases of love, a discourse of attachment and deep feeling.

Before analyzing the intriguing incongruities between the two discourses, I want to lay out the contours of the poetic and mundane discourses by presenting a few cases that illustrate the pattern of individual responses to loss and show how widely the two discourses ramify in social life. It will become clear that the mundane discourse is explicable by reference to the ideology of honor and modesty, whose logic has already been uncovered; the sentiments people express in ordinary life are informed by and consonant with the ideals of this moral code. (Explication of the poetic discourse will be the subject of the final chapter.)

Matters of Pride

A case of rejected love illustrates the pattern of dual responses and introduces the tension between the honor code's ideals and emotional entailments and those of poetry. In chapter 3 (see p. 94) I presented the case of Rashīd, the man whose bride ran away. His inability to mask his dejection from his close kin had seriously jeopardized his right to respect. But outsiders and even many in the camp who knew him less well were unaware of these signs of his attachment to her, and hence of his dependency and weakness.

What they saw was another response, supported and encouraged by his kinsmen and friends.

Almost immediately after the woman fled, Rashīd looked for someone to blame. In the community, the question on everyone's lips was "Who ruined her [*man kharrabhā*]?" meaning something like, Who made her unhappy or poisoned her thoughts? Rashīd, along with his brother, undertook an intensive investigation of the events preceding her departure. When they had eliminated the possibility of some woman or child in the household having upset her, they began to consider sorcery as an explanation. Rashīd was convinced that his senior wife must have been responsible. A visit to the local holyman (*fgīh*) to divine the reason behind the bride's act confirmed this suspicion, and the hushed accusation sped through the community. In the face of opposition from many of the camp's women, Rashīd persisted in blaming his first wife, angrily refusing to talk to her or visit her and sleeping alone in the men's guest room.

Rashīd's kinsmen, who viewed this as a family, not a personal, crisis, also reacted with anger. Although some suspected the senior wife and shunned her, others directed their anger at the bride. They took her flight as an insult to the lineage, and many echoed the sentiments of Rashīd's paternal first cousin, who defiantly sang a traditional wedding song to the effect that there were many more women where that one had come from. The men blustered, "If she doesn't want us, she can just have her divorce, and we won't even ask for the bride-price back."

After some negotiation and pressure from her family, the bride agreed to return. A day or so later, I was talking privately with Rashīd. I asked him how he felt and he answered with a statement about how everything was all right because "the woman" knew that she had done something wrong. I then asked disingenuously if he ever recited poetry. He looked embarrassed, because I had mentioned something that was not appropriate in conversations between men and women, but offered the following poems on the assumption that I would not realize their significance.

Cooking with a liquid of tears
at a funeral done for the beloved . . .

blūlhum ghēr dmū'
il-khāṭr 'azā dār fil-'alam . . .

Her bad deeds were wrongs that hurt
yet I won't repay them, still dear the beloved . . . [3]

'azīz lil-kfā mā hān
sayyāthā khaṭā wāj'ātnī . . .

Any doubts I harbored about whether these poems expressed his personal sentiments regarding the situation were put to rest a few days later. It was evening, and Rashīd sat with his returned wife. He asked me to join them, requesting that I bring my notebook, and he instructed me to read them "the talk of the other day." I realized he was referring to the poems he had recited for me. As I read them aloud, he seemed embarrassed and acted almost as if he had never heard them before. He looked blank when I asked him to explain them. The next day his wife confided that these poems were about her. He had used this indirect means to communicate his sentiments to her.

The poems revealed sentiments of grief and pain caused by the loss, a far cry from the anger and the wish to attribute blame that his public accusations of sorcery had communicated. When I shared these poems with some of my women confidantes, they were touched. Yet these were the same women who had condemned Rashīd as foolish or unmanly when he had earlier betrayed sadness over his bride's departure and expressed his desire to have her back. Their differing attitudes toward statements made in poetry and those in ordinary interaction suggest that poetic revelations are judged by different criteria than are nonpoetic expressions.

The same dual pattern characterized the responses of Mabrūka, Rashīd's senior wife, to the events of this marriage. When she first got wind of the sorcery allegations, she responded angrily and threatened to return to her kinsmen and demand a divorce. She also made bitter jokes about her "magic," where she obtained it, and how powerful it was. For instance, when she sent a special pot of food to one of the other women in her co-wife's household, she sent it with a message warning them to beware—the food might have "something" in it, a reference to magical potions. But two poems she later recited referred to this incident in a different way. The first indicated how wronged she felt by the accusation. The second conveyed her sense of isolation and loneliness in the community, as visiting is both essential to maintenance of social relationships and viewed as one of life's great pleasures.

> They slandered me then found me innocent
> now the guilt must fall on them . . .
>
> ithimū khāṭrī bagwāl
> ṭalaʿ barā wdhnūb ādkadhū . . .
>
> I could not make my visiting rounds
> the married man's house was full of suspicion . . . [4]
>
> ʿalēh mā gdirt njūl
> tammat birībtu bēt il-ghanī . . .

A clearer illustration of the dual patterning of the expression of sentiment was her early reaction to the news of the marriage. Mabrūka's immediate response was to blame her brother-in-law for the decision, suspecting him of having encouraged his brother to take a second wife so the lineage could have more children. Although she had been close to his wife for fifteen years, she stopped visiting her household and refused to help her with the major project of sewing a tent, even though all the other women in the community contributed their labor. When presented with the customary wedding gifts due the first wife, she threw them on the ground and refused to accept them until her sister-in-law begged her to.

She justified her anger by the blame she placed on her brother-in-law, some material injustices, and violations of conventions in the handling of the marriage. For example, she refused to accept her wedding gifts because they were not identical to those given to the bride—a bone of contention was a pair of Western-style sandals the bride had received, whereas Mabrūka had not been offered any shoes. She refused to attend the wedding because the new bride was not going to be brought into her household but would be set up in a house with her husband's brother and his wives—not customary procedure, as she pointed out to everyone. When I asked how she felt about the wedding, she remarked on these injustices and claimed that she was only angry because things were not being done correctly.

Shortly before the marriage took place, I was sitting with her and a group of her daughters and nieces, when, with an initial prompt from me, she began to recite poems, one after another. These indicated a rather different set of responses to the event and another emotional tone. The following sample, only a few of a long string, represents a range of sentiments she expressed that day. In the first poem, she described the sensation of being overwhelmed not just by anger but by "despair" (*yās*), the sentiment of extreme despondency that figures heavily in *ghinnāwa*s:

> Held fast by despair and rage
> the vastness of my soul is cramped . . . [5]
>
> msāk yās wghēẓ
> barāḥ khāṭrī dhayyigibhun . . .

Another poem expressed her sense of abandonment through metaphors of nature:

> Long shriveled from despair
> are the roots that fed my soul . . .
>
> shjirat khāṭrī min il-yās
> zamān mōta 'urūghā . . .

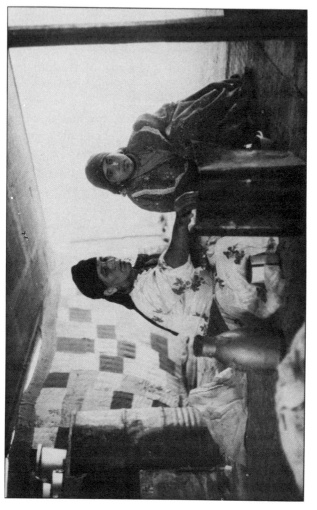

Woman and her niece making tea on a kerosene burner with a windbreak made of an old olive oil tin

In another she appealed to her absent husband for some consideration in response to all she had given him. This poem used imagery
of ships and harbors, which I could not carry into the translation:

> I took upon myself your love
> kindly make me a place to rest . . .
>
> shaḥanit khāṭrī bghalāk
> bifdhūlak marāsī dīrlī . . .

Related to this theme was another poem suggesting she was being
neglected in her suffering by someone who had the power to cure
her. Her husband could have relieved her by paying attention to
her and trying to please her.

> They left me to suffer
> wise ones, they had but withheld the cure . . .
>
> tarākū 'alē mashkāy
> 'aggāl lū bghaw dāy māsakun . . .

These early poetic responses to the prospect of her husband's second marriage expressed not so much the anger and blame evidenced
in the rejection of her wedding gifts and in her constant threats to
leave as misery and vulnerability. Toward the end her poems took a
different turn, providing commentary on her angry behavior:

> She raised her prices
> closed her door and refused to provision them . . .
>
> 'allat s'ārhā 'an-nās
> gfilat bābhā mā mayyarat . . .

and finally:

> Better had they calmed me
> but since they opposed me I opposed them . . .
>
> lū kān hāwadūnī khēr
> min ḥāsh 'ānadū 'ānadithum . . .

Anger and blame are such common responses that people act carefully to avoid any possibility of being blamed. The fear of being blamed for "ruining" the bride again, or for making anything else go wrong in the marriage, led to a great unwillingness on the part of many community members to visit the household she lived in. The same type of fear underlay the absence of another woman's maternal kin from her husband's marriage to a second wife. They thought it likely their kinswoman would opt for a divorce, since she had only been married a year and was young, beautiful, and childless, hence highly marriageable. If she left, however, they would most likely be blamed for putting the idea into her head. Attributing blame when hurt is a response learned early in life: when young children come crying to their mothers, they are more likely to be asked, "Who did it?" than "What's the matter?"

There is one alternative to anger in cases of loss other than death, namely, a show of indifference or defensive denial of concern. This behavior is particularly characteristic in matters of love (see chapter 7), but it also applies in the most trivial of loss situations. For example, Awlad 'Ali consider long thick hair one of women's most treasured assets and a mark of beauty. Its loss would thus be significant. Someone observing a woman combing her hair might remark that she was losing a great deal of it, a common enough occurrence given women's generally poor health. She would probably respond with the phrase "*in shāllah mā yrawwiḥ*," literally "God willing it won't return," but in idiomatic translation, "Good riddance" or "May it never come back." The same phrase greets a child who disobeys or who defiantly refuses to come when called. People also speak of misplaced objects and memories of past pleasures in the same way.

A show of indifference can be a sign of stoic acceptance of a situation over which an individual has little control. Separations represent the type of loss to which stoic acceptance is the rule. The poems of separation, however, were among the most numerous and poignant people sang, expressing the sentiments of sadness and longing and, through metaphors of illness, the effects of the loss. A few examples suggest the range. The following one implies that the natural world mirrors the dark inner state of the person left behind:

> The night of the beloved's parting
> cloud cover, no stars and no moon . . .
>
> laylat frāg ʿazīz
> ghṭāṭ lā njūm wlā gmar . . .

Another describes through metaphors drawn from physiological experience the painful effects of separation. Blindness comes from excessive weeping.

> Separation from intimates is hard
> the heart dries up and the eye goes blind . . .
>
> frāg ish-shgīg ṣaʿīb
> il-galb ṣāf wil-ʿēn ghāwnanat . . .

A third alludes directly to the effort to be stoic in partings:

> Strong-willed in the send-off
> the self did not cry until they parted . . .
>
> shdīd ʿazm fit-taṣmīl
> il-ʿagl mā bkā nīn fārgū . . .

A more defensive denial of concern can be the response to rejections or slights, as one woman's visit to her natal community illustrates. Migdim was a woman in her sixties, the favorite paternal aunt of the core agnates of my community. The old woman often came to visit; she would stay a week or two or as long as she could be persuaded, spending a few days in each of the core households to divide her time among her many nieces and nephews. One night she came to stay in the household I was living in, where her niece Gaṭīfa, married to her nephew, the Haj, and another nephew and his wife lived. Gaṭīfa, always solicitous and happy to see Migdim, invited her to sleep in her room, since her husband was away. But just as they were bedding down for the night, the Haj returned unexpectedly from his trip. Feeling uncomfortable ejecting him from his room and wife, the old woman insisted she would move. I offered her my room, which was next to the room of her other nephew and his wife of several months. I stayed behind to speak with the Haj, and Migdim and her grand-nieces went to my room, where the other man's wife offered them the use of her blankets and pillows. But then *her* husband returned and complained about the missing blankets; he was also irritated because the children would be in his section of the house. So Migdim moved again, this time to an empty room where she spent an uncomfortable night with practically no bedding.

The next day, Migdim was unusually silent. She said nothing about her trials of the night before. But then she recited some poems that showed how she felt about the disgraceful mistreatment she had received at her young nephew's hands. These poems convey surprise and pain at his inconsiderate behavior.

> I never figured you'd do
> wrongs like these, oh they hurt . . .
>
> mā niḥisbūk tdīr
> sayyāt kēf hādhēn yaṣ'abū . . .
>
> Forced by drought in the land
> to seek refuge among peoples of twisted tongues . . .
>
> rmāna jdab l-awṭān
> 'alē nās 'āwja lghāthum . . . [6]

She explained the last poem to me. In search of pasture, people had to go to a new area where they found alien tribes whose language they could not comprehend, "people who weren't people." She was referring to her expulsion of that evening and the incomprehensibility of her nephew's disrespectful and inhospitable behavior. By drawing attention to it in ordinary social interaction, she would have admitted her humiliation. Instead, she had appeared to ignore it or not to care, a strategy that, given the code of honor, had the same effect of saving face as fighting back in anger would have had. She confessed how wounded she felt only in her poems.

Responding to Death

Death is the ultimate loss. As with other losses, Awlad 'Ali individuals respond to bereavement differently in ordinary public behavior and in the formulaic medium of poetry. But in bereavement, individuals also express their sentiments through a ritualized funeral lament called "crying" (*bkā*) that is structurally equivalent and technically similar to poetry. Significantly, this form is a vehicle for the same sorts of sentiments poetry carries, for reasons that will become clear in the final chapter.

The following three cases convey the typical cultural patterning of reactions to death and suggest the cultural terms in which death is interpreted by Awlad 'Ali. In everyday language and behavior, people react to death with anger and blame, sentiments closely associated with the impulse to avenge deaths, mirrored in and buttressed by the institutionalized complex of feuding described in detail by Peters (1951, 1967). However, in poetry and in "crying," the same angry individuals communicate sorrow and the devastating effects of the loss on their personal well-being.

The first case concerns a family's response to the fairly sudden illness and death of a girl of about seventeen. Although a physician pronounced the cause of death as cancer, the family accused the man who had frightened her by firing his rifle into the air while she was grazing some goats nearby of having caused her death. It was after that incident, her family claimed, that she had sickened. Their angry dispute with this man wore on for months until it was finally brought to a tribal court, where the girl's family demanded blood indemnity, the traditional recompense for a killing within a tribal segment (see Peters 1967).

Yet at her funeral, and for over a month after, her death was met with much "crying," the quintessential act of ritual mourning. At the news of a death, Awlad 'Ali women begin a stylized high-pitched, wordless wailing (*'ayāṭ*). Then they "cry." "Crying" involves much more than weeping; it is a chanted lament in which the bereaved women and those who have come to console them express their grief. Beginning with a phrase whose English equivalent is "woe is me," the bereaved bewail their loss in "crying." Those consoling the bereaved bewail the loss of a deceased person dear to them, usually a father or mother. Like the singing of poems, the chant takes the form of a short verse of two parts, the words repeated in a set order following a single melodic pattern. The special pitch and quavering of the voice, more exaggerated than in singing, along with the weeping and sobbing that often accompany it, make this heart-rending. The Bedouins do not equate "crying" and singing, but they recognize the resemblance when questioned. The two are structurally equivalent, both being expressions of sadness that draw attention to the mourner's sorrow and bereavement.

Generally, men do not "cry," although they sometimes weep silently; in this case, however, even the girl's brother was said to have "cried," attesting to her family's uncontrollable grief. As a rule, men offering condolences greet the bereaved with a somber embrace out of which others must pull them. Men counsel the bereaved relatives to "pull yourself together" (*shidd ḥēlak*) and console them with pious references to God's will and goodness. The only exception to men's general avoidance of "crying" is the ritual lamenting undertaken by descendants of local saints at the annual festivals at the tombs of the saints or holymen. Men of the saintly lineage sing "poems" of their forefather in a quavering voice as they move from tent to tent, blessing those who have come to pay their respects and cursing those who cross them. People describe this singing as "crying" over the saint.

Another case, this time the death of an old woman, also provoked a heated response among her kin. Shortly after returning to her husband's camp following an extended visit with her kin, the old woman died suddenly in the middle of the night. Her paternal relatives rushed to the camp, where they wailed and "cried" for two days, consoled her daughters, and were consoled for their loss.

The mourners returned to their own community angry, furious that her husband had behaved rudely to them and blaming him for her death. Some were convinced that the shock of hearing the news that he planned to marry another wife had brought on her death; others insinuated that the man had actually strangled her. The most vivid description of the old woman's death was recounted by one of her nieces, a dramatic storyteller. In animated tones, she described how she had arrived in the aunt's camp to find that her aunt's body lay where she had fallen, the legs exposed and the face barely covered by her veil. No one had prepared her in proper Muslim fashion, placing drops of water in her mouth and tying her jaw shut. Throwing herself on the floor of the tent and letting her tongue hang out and saliva drool from the side of her mouth, the niece mimicked the awful state in which she had found her aunt. She recounted how she had scolded the people there, "What is the matter with you? Haven't you ever seen a corpse before? At least you could treat her as decent human beings would. You could have covered her, shown her a little respect!" She then told how she had assisted the women in preparing the corpse for burial and how she had ordered her kin to provide a decent shroud to replace the inferior one the husband's kin had provided. She personally was absolutely convinced that her favorite aunt had been strangled and that the husband was the culprit.

The senior agnate (and informal leader) of her paternal kin's community had been traveling when the news of the old woman's death arrived. By the time he returned, everyone else had already come back from the funeral. Informed of the death, he interviewed the men and women who had attended about what they had witnessed. At their descriptions, he kept exclaiming, "Damn him!" and muttering, "We'll make him swear the oath!" He was referring to the ultimate recourse in determining guilt, the swearing of an oath at a saint's tomb by the accused and his kin. But when he went to question the old woman's daughters and other witnesses in the husband's camp, he determined that there had been no trouble between her and her husband and was satisfied that she had died of natural causes. The furor subsided, and people began to concede that she might have died of a broken heart caused by the recent death of her only son. Nonetheless, the initial reaction had been one of angry accusation, balanced by the mournful "crying" of the funeral.

The third case is the most telling. This reaction to a homicide shows explicitly how the manifest anger and desire for revenge on the part of the murdered man's kin are counterbalanced by the terrible sense of suffering revealed not just in "crying" but also in singing or reciting poetry.[7] This case differs from the other two in that there was genuine cause for anger and someone who deserved blame. The killing of the youngest adult man in the group of agnatic kinsmen who constituted the core of the community had occurred seven years before my arrival. He had died from wounds inflicted by a couple of men from another tribe, who had provoked a fight in retaliation for an earlier beating he had dealt a kinsman of theirs. The event was described to me in vivid detail numerous times by various members of the group. The initial reaction to the news of the fight was always described in the same way: everyone, women and children included, rushed toward the hostile group's camp, throwing rocks and wailing. The young man was still breathing when they found him. The men took him to the hospital in Alexandria, where he died a few days later. By

Young men herding sheep to the market

all descriptions, the grief and ritualized mourning that followed were extraordinary and prolonged.

There was not only grief, but also a great deal of anger, directed at the family of those responsible and at others as well. For example, two subsections of the murdered man's tribe officially split over this incident, because one group urged a peaceful reconciliation and the acceptance of blood indemnity three years after the killing, whereas the other recognized that the offended party was entitled to revenge. Hostility still flared up between these groups on various pretexts during my stay. Meanwhile, the murderers' group had escaped to Libya, where the victim's group tried to track them and had even made one unsuccessful attempt to avenge the murder. After the attempt, the avenging group let themselves be persuaded to undergo the reconciliation procedures, and they declared their forgiveness publicly. But this was only a tactic to flush out the offending subsection; they were biding their time, hoping the other group would let down its guard and give them the opportunity to take their revenge. People cursed whenever the name of the offending group was mentioned.

The poems the close relatives of the murdered man sang revealed another set of sentiments besides anger and the desire for revenge. All suggested the suffering the death had caused. Three themes characterized the poems: sleeplessness, associated in traditional Bedouin poetry with weeping and sorrow; illness, in folk psychology a consequence of any negative emotions; and "despair," the word connoting apathy, hopeless misery, or extreme sadness.

The first poems I heard about the death were two by the elder paternal cousin of the victim. The first suggested restless search, perhaps for the object of revenge (and thus some anger); the second evoked only sad memories that intruded.

> Until he reaches his target's border
> no happy sleep is his . . .
>
> yṭūla ḥdūd mnāh
> wlā bāt fī nawm hanī . . .

Caught by a memory unawares
brought tears in the hour of pleasure . . .

khṭūra ʿalēh ghaflāt
bakkā l-ʿēn fī wān iṭ-ṭarab . . .

The victim's mother recited a poem that alluded to her inability
to forget and the sleeplessness her memories and grief brought:

Dear ones deprive me of sleep
just as I drift off, they come to mind . . .

in-nawm ḥarramō ʿizāz
in jānā yjūnā fawwalu . . .

Metaphors of illness abound in the poems of various other
kinsmen and kinswomen. Yet the poems of men and women
seem to differ. Another paternal first cousin echoed his brother's
sentiments, likening his suffering to a wasting disease from which
he cannot recover until the death is avenged (the bones being
those of the object of revenge).

Wasting away you'd say consumptive,
wanted bones, repayment would release him . . .

yḏhāmar tgūl silīl
ṭalīb ʿaẓm fī dēn salak . . .

The victim's sister sang a poem referring to the ill health resulting
from the loss:

You left me, oh loved one,
unsteady, stunted, and unhealthy . . .

khallēt yā ʿazīz il-ʿēn
tmūj lā nimā lā ʿāfya . . .

The victim's widow recited several poems late one night. Her
closest friends were surprised, saying they had never heard her
recite poetry before. These were two of her poems:

Ill and full of despair
show me what medicine could cure this malady . . .

illī marīd̲h̲ fīh yāsāt
warrūnī duwā dāhā asmu . . .

Drowning in despair
the eye says, oh my destiny in love . . .

il-ʿēn g̲h̲ārga fil-yās
tgūl yā naṣībī fil-g̲h̲alā . . .

The despair to which she referred also appeared in the poems of a
close kinswoman:

Terrible torment fills the heart
brought by despair and no other . . .

il-ʿagl fīhā ʿadhāb shdīd
min l-yās wlā g̲h̲ēr yā ʿalam . . .

Forgotten not a single day
just a patient mastering of despair . . .

il-ʿagl mā nsīhum yōm
ṣabrā mg̲h̲ēr dālī yāshum . . .

These poems give voice to the anguish and pain the death
caused, in the form of such symptoms as physical suffering, crying, disrupted sleep, brooding, and a sense of the presence of the
dead, as well as apathy and despair.[8] In contrast to the ordinary
discourse, they barely speak of anger and vengeance.

The Discourse of Honor

The sentiments expressed in ordinary public interaction are, I
would argue, those appropriate to what could be called a discourse

of honor, their consistency attributable to the fact that they are generated within the context of the dominant ideology described in the first half of this book. In chapter 3 the virtues of a person of honor were outlined as those related to autonomy. The ideal person among Awlad 'Ali is the "real man," the apogee of control who manifests his independence in his freedom from control by others and his strength or potency in his unwillingness to submit to others. He commands respect because of his high degree of self-control, physical and emotional. These ideal characteristics are valued by all, although differentially realized, and realizable, by individuals and social categories in Bedouin society. Except in direct interchanges with superiors, where deference is more highly valued, even women are expected to act in terms of these honor-linked ideals.

Only certain sentiments would be appropriate to self-presentation in terms of these ideals. Because weakness and pusillanimity are anathema, individuals strive to assert their independence and strength through resistance to coercion or through aggressive responses to loss. The prime sentiment of resistance is anger, which is focused into blame of others. An alternate strategy for asserting honor is defensive denial of concern, hence of the very existence of an attack. As Bourdieu (1979, 108) notes, "non-response can also express the refusal to riposte; the recipient of the offence refuses to see it as an offence and by his disdain . . . he causes it to rebound on its author, who is thereby dishonoured." In the examples, this response arose only in cases of offenses by social inferiors, as with Migdim, or, as we shall see, in love. Like outward-directed defenses against the imposition of the will of others on the self, the third alternative of stoicism is consonant with the ideals of honor. To admit that one is wounded or deeply affected by the loss of others is to admit a lack of autonomy and self-control, a dependency through vulnerability. These are the attributes of the weak, of the young, the poor, and the female. Thus, by responding to loss with anger and blame or with a denial of concern, individuals both live in terms of the honor code and dramatize their claims to the respect accruing to the honorable.

In a similar way, the ideology of honor provides the guiding concepts behind responses to that most radical of loss situations—death—at least in routine social interactions and communications in the nonpoetic modes. It seems reasonable to assume that a concern with autonomy and pride would predispose individuals to interpret situations of loss as personal affronts or attacks. Resistance is the honorable response to an attack, and anger is the sentiment, whether perceived as motivation or concomitant, compatible with resistance. By responding with anger to the pain of loss, people assert their strength and potency—their refusal to succumb passively to the impositions of others. Blaming others is an aggressive act that focuses anger.

Psychological and cross-cultural studies of bereavement report affective and behavioral responses to death ranging from sadness to hostility (Marris 1974; Rosenblatt, Walsh, and Jackson 1976). Although the Bedouin poetic or ritualized discourse rarely carries bellicose threats or sentiments of anger, the expression of these themes in ordinary discourse suggests that Awlad 'Ali express the range of sentiments associated with bereavement and loss, but in a culturally specific, culturally regulated, and nonhaphazard way. LeVine (1982b) argues that individuals in particular cultures selectively interpret death in the idiom of the dominant themes of interpersonal relations. Huntington and Metcalf (1979, 43) argue that "cultural difference works on the universal human emotional material. . . . The range of acceptable emotions and the constellation of sentiments appropriate to the situations of death are tied up with the unique institutions and concepts of each society." The Bedouin response provides support for these anthropological positions on the cultural construction of the sentiments associated with death, with one modification: different cultural forms may carry different sets of sentiments.

The same people who so energetically present themselves as invulnerable and assertive in loss situations, who dramatically disavow the experiences of helplessness, vulnerability, or passivity that would compromise their images of being strong and independent, portray themselves differently through their poems. In their poems and in the ritualized "crying" of mourning, they express sentiments of sadness and confess feelings of devastation: tears and ailments signal the impact of the losses; constant references to "despair" betray a sense of helplessness. In Awlad 'Ali terms, helpless passivity in the face of assaults is the mark of impotence, and vulnerability to the pain inflicted by loss suggests attachments that, in the language of honor, translate as dependency and weakness. The discourse of poetry and ritualized mourning is one of vulnerability, weakness, and dependency.

Why the Bedouins can express through poetry the sentiments of weakness that violate the code of honor, why listeners apply a different set of standards regarding conformity to the societal ideals to presentations in this medium, and what the significance of having two contradictory discourses is, are questions that will be taken up in the final chapter. To be able to consider them, however, another dimension of the use of *ghinnāwas* in social life must be explored. In the next chapter, I look at the relationship between poetry and love.

7

MODESTY AND
THE POETRY OF LOVE

Discourses on Love

Personal relationships, especially love relationships with persons of
the opposite sex, are of great concern among the Bedouins. Indeed,
they are central to the ideology of honor and modesty: love relationships pose such a threat to the system that they are the object of
stringent control through symbolic manipulation. The threat of
sexuality is contained primarily by transmuting it into an element
of the code of morality by which individual worth is judged. Modesty, including the denial of attachment to unrelated members of
the opposite sex, is construed as a moral virtue—for women, the
ultimate one. Denial of sexuality is interpreted as an aspect of self-
mastery and deference to those who represent the social order.
Women's closer "natural" association with sexuality saddles them
with a greater need to distance themselves from it in order to gain
respectability, but men, too, must deny their sexual interests if they
are to assert their autonomy.

Love relationships are also central to poetic life. As noted in
chapter 5, Awlad 'Ali associate the *ghinnāwa* more closely with
romantic love than with any other theme.[1] But poetry is a lan-

guage of love distinct from and opposed to ordinary discourse on such matters. The same pattern of contradictory responses that characterizes individuals' responses to loss may also be seen in their communications about love relationships. In matters of love, instead of an honorable discourse of anger counterposed to a poetic discourse of vulnerability, there is a modest discourse of detachment balanced by a poetic discourse of attachment and deep feeling. This dichotomy can be seen in the way people respond to situations of thwarted love, arranged marriages, divorces, and polygynous marriages.

Star-Crossed Lovers

*Ghinnāwa*s are tied up with the popular cultural theme of thwarted love, both in its ordinary and in its mythic manifestations. The real trials of individual sweethearts and the mythic ones of the tragic heroes and heroines of Bedouin traditional romances or love stories usually display a tension between the wishes of individual lovers and the demands of a system that is based on kinship, arranged marriage, and the priority of patrilateral parallel cousins. *Ghinnāwa*s are also indexically linked to romantic love, in that sweethearts exchange poems when together (although this practice was more common in the past), and when separated they sing plaintive songs to express their longing. In Bedouin romances, lovers always speak to each other in poetry.

Although Awlad 'Ali give families the unquestioned right to arrange marriages for their children, this system, like all others, has its costs. Many arranged marriages are long-lasting and not unhappy, benefiting from luck, personal maturity, support by both kin groups, preexisting bonds of affinity or kinship, and minimal demands on or expectations of the conjugal pair. Other such marriages bring only misery.

Misery arises when one partner has an aversion to the person chosen for him or her, or had wished to marry someone else and was prevented. Nāfla's marital history, presented in chapter 3 to illustrate the limits of coercion, includes several cases of aversion. In the first arranged marriage to her cousin, she already knew the groom, had no desire to marry him, and resisted successfully. In the second one, her aversion arose as soon as she saw the groom on her wedding day. This type of aversion is so common, especially for women, who tend to have less say in their marriages, that it goes by a special term with ritualized behavioral correlates. If the girl's family refuses to support her in her bid for a divorce or the husband's family refuses to grant a divorce, the couple lives unhappily.

It often happens that one of the marriage partners is unhappy with an arranged marriage because there was someone else who would have been preferred. With the decreasing opportunity for contact between adolescent girls and boys, except in the large towns where they attend school together, this may be less of a problem now than in the past. At least according to informants' tales romances and infatuations used to be prevalent. The ideal romance was secret, involving brief meetings in isolated spots, the exchange of tokens such as jewelry or other personal possessions, and most of all, the exchange of poetry.

Romances were unlikely to result in marriage for a number of reasons. Love matches are opposed in principle; they violate the ideal of family control over marriage and represent individual initiative and hence defiance of the system. To accept love matches would be to legitimize as a force in social life passion that does not derive from relationships of kinship. One man argued that romances could lead to marriage only if the couple was careful not to let anyone, especially the girl's kin, even suspect that the two knew each other and then finagled to have the families arrange the marriage. That senior men disapprove is understandable, but even women share these views. They rationalize their disapproval by claiming that love matches never work out because if a woman marries for love she is especially vulnerable to her husband; a woman following her heart probably does so at the expense of her kin group, so, alone in her marital community and without the support of her kin, she has no recourse if mistreated nor any leverage in asserting her rights.

The person most responsible for preventing love matches is the girl's paternal first cousin. By stepping in and claiming her for himself, a right given him by custom, he dashes any hopes a potential rival might entertain. Sometimes his claim is underpinned by a genuine wish to marry the girl; often he is put up to it by his kinsmen or does it to preserve the kin group's honor, which is threatened by the "shameful" desires of an immodest kinswoman. This threat to the authority of kinsmen is the crux of the problem with romance.

Cousins regularly avail themselves of their right, as endless stories, fictional and real, of star-crossed lovers and thwarted love matches attest. Many men complained that they had been prevented at varying stages of the negotiations from marrying women by cousins' interference, and many women were married to their cousins. The Haj, for example, had fallen in love with and wanted to marry three women before his present wife, but he had been prevented in each case by the girls' cousins. He had had his first romance at the age of seventeen; his telling of the story is intriguing because he mentions the role poetry played in it. He and his father took considerable pride in this defiant romance, a significant fact but one that I will wait until the final chapter to discuss; here I will only note that people enforced the social system and thwarted those who tried to contravene it. I paraphrase his story as he told it:

It was 1950. I was in love with a girl from a Mrābiṭ tribe. Her father and mine were best friends. She was tough but beautiful. I loved her and she loved me. We would arrange meetings through friends, who took messages back and forth. We only managed meetings of a few minutes. We recited poetry to one another. I never touched her; we met just to talk. I swear it was not for anything else. We are humans, not animals. This was God-given love [*min rabnā*], true love.

One day, after much scheming, we managed to arrange a special rendezvous. We were out in the desert, far away from the camps. We sat together, she a few inches away [a respectable distance], and I had my rifle across my lap. Suddenly her three cousins [father's brother's sons] came upon us. [How did they know about the meeting?] They had been keeping an eye on her.

She nearly died of fear. She knew they would kill her, or kill me. But I had a gun and they didn't. I asked her, "Would you feel safe if you were in your father's house?" She said yes. So we got up and I slowly walked her toward her camp. The three cousins walked near us, watching every move. But I delivered her safely to her father's house and had to explain everything to her father.

Her father came to see mine, told him everything that had happened. It was a big scandal. But my father was very fond of me, and her father was fond of her. He said he would be willing to give his daughter to us [in marriage]. My father was willing to pay the bride-price. No one had ever gotten away with something like this before, but they all respected me for not having run, for having bravely walked the girl home to protect her. It showed I was a real man.

But her cousins prevented the marriage. They called a tribal hearing [*mi'ād*] to settle the problem. The conditions set were that I was never to see or talk to her again. They said I must never try to get in touch with her. Then one of these cousins married her. When he died, another of the cousins married her. She is still living with him. Her husband is now a friend of mine, so I occasionally see her. I greet her when I go to their house [a sign of familiarity].

It is all over now, even the feelings. But it lasted a long time. I was very sad at the time. My father used to ask people to recite the many poems I had composed for her and her responses because they were so beautiful.² I married very late. I was thirty. This was because the same thing kept happening. It happened again twice. I loved someone and she loved me but it was not destined to be [*naṣīb*]. Each time, the cousins of the girl prevented the marriage. Finally I gave up and was willing to take any old wife.

Proud of his poetic skills, one day the Haj offered to record some *ghinnāwa*s for me. We went over the tape together, and he gave exegeses of the twelve poems he had sung. The first was a poem he had composed about the Mrābiṭ girl, a couple of years after she had married her cousin. He explained that it referred to his despair at never being able to have her and at having nothing left of her but memories. When he thought of her, he fell ill, so he wished he could just forget her.

> Thinking of them with pain
> if only they would not come to mind . . .
>
> tafākīrhun bawjā‘
> lū kān mā ‘alēnā yukhuṭrū . . .

A second poem was about a married woman he had loved. It describes the strain of trying to catch a glimpse of her from a distance, she who wasn't free to meet him. The word he uses for married woman is common to this genre, although not used in the vernacular. It comes from the same root as *hostage*.

> They've worn you out, oh eye
> married loved ones with no time for you . . .
>
> mdhāyblīnik yā ‘ēn
> awlāfun mrāhīn mā fḍhaw . . .

Poetry, from this case, is clearly the medium through which sentiments of love and longing are expressed.

The groom's female relatives dance and sing to welcome a new bride

An Arranged Marriage

Most people lead less dramatic lives; most do not pine away for those forbidden to them, and most do not die of broken hearts. People nevertheless confront difficult personal situations, which are often the consequence of the way Bedouin society structures the relations between men and women.

The complex relationship between poetry and the discourse of everyday life is reflected in the reactions of Fāyga, a young woman of about twenty-five, to her arranged marriage to a man in our community. By juxtaposing her poetic and mundane responses we can see how she grappled with conflicting feelings and motivations. Paramount in ordinary social interactions was her concern not to compromise her image as a proper Bedouin girl from a good family who knows the meaning of *ḥasham*—in both its senses, as sexual modesty and as propriety. As a good woman she should not resist a marriage arranged by her brothers, as this would constitute defiance. At the same time, she should express no interest in men, not even her husband, in order to preserve her image as sexually modest. She upheld these standards in her interactions with others in her husband's household and in her conversations with me. But in her poems, especially those she recited in the first months of her marriage, she revealed shifting feelings about the marriage, feelings very different from the ones she conveyed in her public response.

Fāyga was brought as a bride for the Haj's brother Rashīd, the man whose first wife's angry reaction I described in the last chapter. He had decided to take a second wife—perhaps because his first wife, Mabrūka, kept giving birth to sickly children—and had heard about Fāyga from a friend. As an adult, he had arranged for the marriage himself, using his friend as a go-between. Although he claimed that he had seen her before the wedding, she insisted that she had not seen him. She and her mother had been living in a household with her older brothers, her guardians in her father's absence, who were responsible for agreeing to the marriage. Because there had been no previous marriages between her family and Rashīd's, and because both Fāyga and Rashīd were of high-status families that were unrelated, the negotiations had been long and the bride-price was high. There was a big wedding.

Things seemed all right at first. Fāyga, who did not know any of the women in her husband's community, was initially shy; she rarely talked, and she ate little during the first week or two. This was normal—strangers are expected to feel uncomfortable and to *taḥashsham*. The women who lived in her household, her sisters-in-law, and visiting women teased her continually about sexual matters, loading their conversations with innuendos about her marital pleasures. She persistently feigned ignorance and inno-cence, denying any comprehension of what the women meant. They found her insistence a bit annoying, in part because it showed how estranged she felt among them, but they also rec-ognized that they should respect her for it since she did it out of sexual modesty.

About two weeks after the wedding we had the first hints that she was unhappy with her marriage. She framed her dissatisfac-tion in terms that would reinforce her image as uninterested in men and sex and devoted to her kin group. She scolded the girls one night for singing wedding songs, saying, "It is wrong to sing and dance for the bride on the night before her wedding. What are people celebrating? Her separation from her loved ones?" I do not know what happened over the next three weeks, because I left for a short trip, but when I returned her attitude had worsened no-ticeably. One day she just started crying, allegedly because she missed her relatives. Two days later she confided in her mother-in-law that she was *zāhda* (had an aversion to her husband). That night, she stayed up late talking to the women, stubbornly ignor-ing their pleas to go to her room, where, as she well knew, her husband sat waiting for her. She dragged her heels night after night.

One afternoon she promised to help me interpret some wedding *ghinnāwa*s, so I sat with her in her room. After a bit she began reciting new poems and songs. First she sang a long song, the gist of which was that sharing a husband was not good. Then came a short poem that seemed more like a proverb. It was on the same theme of the undesirability of polygyny:

> Better death, blindness, poverty, and destitution
> than a match with a married man . . .
>
> il-mōt wil-'ama wil-fagr
> wil-'āza wlā ṣōb il-ghanī . . .

She then recited a series of *ghinnāwa*s on the theme of one's divine lot, or fate in life. When I asked at one point if a particular poem was about herself, she laughed and said it was just a song. Then she asked if it was important that it be about herself and admitted, "Yes, even this one is about me." These poems seemed to express her dissatisfaction with the marriage that had been arranged for her. In the first she suggests agitation about something that could not be helped—presumably her choice of marriage partner:

> You want, oh dear one, to be disappointed
> and to fight about something not fated to be . . .
>
> trīd yā 'azīz tkhīb
> wt'ārik 'alē shī mā gsim . . .

In the second, she implies that her lot is so bad she would not wish it on a friend:

> Without pleasures is my lot
> oh God, may it not be imposed on a friend . . .
>
> gsāmī blā ghayyāt
> liṣ-ṣāḥib allāh lā yjībhun . . .

She explained the third as being about someone who wanted something she did not get. When I questioned her, she admitted that she had wanted to marry another man.

> Don't blame those who hurt you
> just say it was not meant to be . . .
>
> mā min illī yā 'ēn
> ijraḥik ghēr gūlī mā gsimsh . . .

A few days later her brother-in-law, sister-in-law, and I set off to take her on a formal visit to her father.[3] It was a difficult trip, taking us far into the desert where we had trouble finding our way and were caught in a sandstorm. We didn't stay long because her brother-in-law was anxious to return. Fāyga was disappointed; she wanted to wait to see her younger brother, who had just been released from jail and was supposed to be on his way to her father's. When we got home she said she was ill and complained that they could have dropped her off at her mother's, where her brother was sure to come next.

After we returned from this trip she began to find fault with everything about her husband's kin group. She complained to me and to the girls in the group that the men neglected and over-worked their women and children and that their lifestyle was appalling and unlike what she, coming from a town, was accustomed to. It is unclear whether by this she hoped merely to insult them or, more seriously, to provoke their anger so they would wish to send her home. She also began to recite a great deal of poetry that struck me as more negative than her earlier poems. The first poem she recited after her return was very depressing:

> On my breast I placed
> a tombstone, though I was not dead, oh loved one . . .
>
> 'alē ṣidērī ḥaṭṭēt
> shahāyid blā mōt yā 'alam . . .

The next day she recited a couple of poems, which I later shared with several women who interpreted them as indicating unhappiness with the marriage and a desire to end it. They suspected that Fāyga wished to marry someone else. The poems were the following:

> Can it be that the eye would not want
> to be happy again and its condition to clear . . .
>
> z'ama mā trīd il-'ēn
> tazhā jdīd wyrūg ḥālhā . . .
>
> If a new love match is not granted
> the ache in my mind will continue, oh beloved . . .
>
> in mā jdā ṣōb jdīd
> ṣudā' l-'agl mā zāl yā 'alam . . .

When I questioned her privately about these poems and her feelings about her marriage, she at first protested that she was unhappy because she found her husband ugly and old. (He was neither.) In a conversation a few days later, rather than mentioning a desire for another man—which she had all but admitted earlier in her poems and in her explanations of them—she took a different approach. She presented herself as a modest and asexual woman, professing a horror of sex, and as a good Bedouin with close ties to kin and a devotion to Islam. She said she wanted to have nothing to do with marriage.

> I don't like being married. I don't like men. I want to go home to my family and just live there forever. It is much better to live without a man. What good is marriage? [Do you hate all men?] No, just a man who would want to "take me" [sexually]. I did not want to marry. Many people came to ask for me, but I refused to marry. I just wanted to stay with my relatives, those dear to me. I want to pray and go on the pilgrimage. And my brother's children, I adore them.

I practically raised them. What is this marriage stuff, away from your dear ones and you can't even go to visit them. Men, I never liked them. I'm afraid of them and I am disgusted by them [*nitgarraf minhum*]. [How did you feel on your wedding night?] I was afraid and so embarrassed. Oh, I got so embarrassed [*kisift*] and disgusted. I felt sick. I couldn't eat. The whole first week I was disgusted and embarrassed. No, I want to go back home and never marry again.

Two days later she ran away, causing quite a stir in the community and considerable concern and speculation about her motives. The reactions of some individuals have already been described in chapter 3, referring to the unmanly way her husband, Rashīd, reacted. Fāyga was eventually persuaded to return, following negotiations and the rumored use of force by her brothers and intimidation by her mother.

Fāyga never gave a straight answer to the question of why she had left. When she did not answer, "Just because . . .," she insisted that her husband had suddenly looked like an evil spirit and she had fled in fright. People privately proposed a number of theories. Some said that she was merely playing hard-to-get to raise herself in her husband's esteem and to secure a place in his affections; they assumed that she wished to displace her senior co-wife. Others thought she had left because she was jealous of his senior wife. Still others suspected sorcery or magic. There seemed to be no way to choose among the hypotheses.

Through her poems, though, what people took to be the truth came out. After her return, she complained often of illness, stubbornly defended her act to all the women who pressed and scolded her, and recited or sang many *ghinnāwa*s. Nearly all her poems revolved around themes of putting up with bad luck and of suffering from longing for something unattainable. For the only time, I broke my promise not to reveal any of the women's poems to men and shared some of them with her brother-in-law, who was extremely puzzled about the true state of her feelings. I had confided that she had recited some poems to me, and he begged to hear them. He listened intently and was astounded. A backer of the theory that she was merely playing games to maneuver for a better position, he changed his mind when he heard the poems, commenting as he listened, "It's really that bad! I had not realized. She really is upset."

When I shared yet others with my closest confidantes, they confirmed that not only was she miserable, but she probably was also in love with another man. I confronted her, and she defensively asked who had told me. I pretended I had figured it out from her poems, and then she confessed that she had wanted to marry a man from another tribe, whose marriage offer her brothers had refused because of a history of hostility between the families. She said she had not really known him but had fallen in love because she heard he was young, handsome, and wealthy.

A few basic points about the use of poetry in social life can be drawn even from this fragment of a young woman's reaction to an arranged marriage. *Ghinnāwa*s seem to have been the medium in which she could voice responses not culturally appropriate for a young Bedouin woman. Acquiescence to the decisions of her brothers and kinsmen, especially regarding her marriage, was proper. Respectability required the denial of romantic love or any interest in such matters. She tried to follow the correct path, or at least to present herself as conforming to these ideals. Even when she ran away, she tried to follow the customary procedure for declaring her unhappiness. But in her poems, which increased in frequency and intensity as she became more unhappy, she expressed a different set of sentiments and presented a side of her feelings not revealed elsewhere. More intriguing than the fact that she used poetry to express such sentiments was the fact that others judged that the poems reflected her reactions more accurately and dependably than did her ordinary behavior and conversation.

Marriage, Divorce, and Polygyny

The loves of youth, fulfilled or unfulfilled, pass. Individuals have to face different kinds of crises in love once they have married, settled down, and begun their adult lives. Most Awlad 'Ali marry fairly young—girls between about fifteen and twenty, boys anywhere between sixteen and thirty, depending on their financial situations. Many first marriages do not last but break up within a few months to a year because of youthful incompatibility or in-law difficulties; most people remain with their second partners.

The behavior and attitudes of spouses toward one another are powerfully shaped by the cultural ideals of modesty. Even if over time a married couple develop attachments, they rarely display their affection publicly. They spend little time together and do not engage in extended conversation, share meals, or work side by side. They politely avoid talking about each other in conversations with others, and they do not utter each other's names. When men and women do make statements about their spouses or their marriages, they tend to express a limited range and special type of sentiment. At best they offer protestations of indifference or assertions of emotional independence. Women make jokes to suggest detachment from and lack of interest in their husbands. In situations of marital conflict, hostile insults and bitter complaints do surface, but these are always couched in material rather than emotional terms and justified by appeals to rights and duties.

Others reinforce these standards partly through teasing. I was surprised by the reception given a young woman who came running to one household crying. Shortly before, her husband had decided to take her back after "leaving" her (no longer going to sleep in her room) for two years. Now he was giving her a hard time about her chickens, which he said were messing the house; he wanted her to get rid of them. But she had been raising them for years and had used them to support her children. The women to whom she complained all concurred with one old woman who asked, "Why did you agree to go back to him? What do you want with a man? Your chickens are worth more than a husband."

It is especially improper for an older woman to complain about losing her husband as a sexual partner. Some men argued that older couples should be like brother and sister; women thought it was "a shame in the woman's face" ('ēb fī wijh il-wliyya) to have sexual relations with her husband once her children were grown. One woman in our community was highly regarded for her calm response when her husband abandoned her for his second wife. Another woman, whose story will be told below, encountered criticism for admitting desire for her estranged husband.

The attachment and emotional dependence that often develop despite social and cultural deemphasis of, even disdain for, emotional closeness between husband and wife are uncovered, at least in poetry, when the relationship is threatened. Divorce can be a critical event in people's lives. In the first few years of a marriage or before there are children, divorce, instigated by either husband or wife, rarely induces anguish. The woman returns to her family and nearly always remarries shortly thereafter. Little stigma attaches to divorce, and divorcées often command high bride-prices. Over a third of the adults in my community had been officially divorced at least once.[4]

But when divorce occurs after many years of marriage, it can be quite difficult. By this time a woman usually has many children and is unlikely to ask for a divorce, even if she is abused or unhappy, because she would have to leave her children behind, something most women cannot bear. Most commonly, then, at this stage in a marriage, a husband will divorce his wife after marital disputes or will "leave" her in favor of a younger wife. The wife has two choices in such situations: to return to her kin or to remain with her children. She often decides to stay with her children, and the husband is then responsible for providing her with food, clothing, and shelter. In the case of an angry divorce, they spend no time together and do not even greet one another in the camp. In a more friendly divorce or when the husband "leaves" the older woman (usually a first cousin) for a junior wife, the senior woman retains her position as head of the domestic household and continues to discuss business with her ex-husband, keep charge of his money, and share in confidential matters.

Ṣafiyya's case illustrates the devastating personal effect of a divorce not wished for and the social and cultural pressure not to admit the pain. More important, her dual response to the divorce, in ordinary social interactions on the one hand and in poetry on the other, and the reactions of members of her community to these divergent expressions reveal something critical about the *ghinnāwa*'s role in social life.

One day this woman of about forty told me about her divorce. The event she described had occurred a year before I arrived in the camp where she had spent the twenty years of her married life. She said:

My youngest daughter was nursing in my arms when he left me. I was sick and tired. "The man" came up to me one afternoon as I sat by the oven. He said, "You're divorced." I said, "Thanks, that's just fine by me." He said, "You can go home to your relatives now." I answered, "And leave my daughters here to be servants to the other women? No. I'll stay here with my children." For a year and a half we did not speak to each other. Now we greet each other. I didn't want him. I don't want anything from him except to build me a house to live in with my son—a place where I can feel at home. I didn't care when he divorced me. I never liked him. He had taken another wife, but that didn't bother me. I never fought with her. Why should I? These things don't bother us.

This statement did not surprise me. Its tone of aggressive nonchalance was consistent with that expressed by other men and women when they talked about their marriages, even those uncomplicated by divorce or polygyny. As we saw in the last chapter, this type of emotional response to painful situations is characteristic.

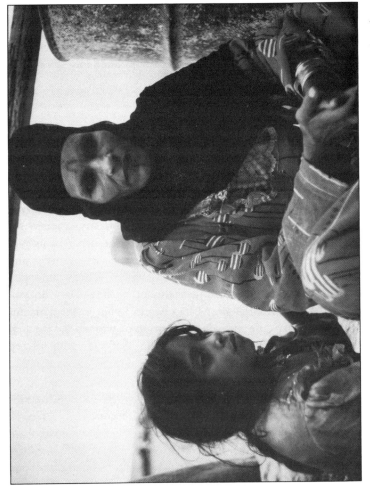

Mother and daughter

Yet, two days later, we were sitting with several other women in her household, chatting during a lull in the busy round of domestic activities, when conversation turned to the whereabouts of her ex-husband, who was away on a trip. Suddenly she recited a short poem:

> Memories stirred of the beloved
> should I release, I'm flooded by them . . .
>
> khaṭarhā sirīb ʿazīz
> kēf nashā nsīl bi . . .

I remembered the first time I had met Ṣafiyya. I had arrived with another young woman, an Egyptian university student, for my first visit to the camp. Ṣafiyya had asked if either of us was married. We both replied in the negative. She leaned over and advised us earnestly, "Don't ever get married. What would you want with marriage? Men are just sons of bitches. They do you no good." A few months after I had begun living in the community, I showed my tape recorder to a group of women for the first time. Some volunteered to sing, including Ṣafiyya, who offered this song:

> Oh eyes be strong
> you cherish people and then they're gone . . .
>
> yā nẓār dīrun ʿazm
> tghālī ʿarab wyfārgū . . .

There was no doubt in the minds of all who subsequently heard this song on tape that it referred to her ex-husband.

The incongruity between what Ṣafiyya said in ordinary language and what she expressed in poetry is striking. Her ordinary statements alternated between denials of concern about her loss and her husband's rejection and expressions of bitterness and anger. Yet both of her poems convey the impression of sadness.

The tears connoted by images of flooding and the reference to eyes are indices of sadness and suffering. The warnings to herself about the consequences of letting go and the exhortation to her eyes to be strong suggest the vigilance and effort required to control this sadness.

The reactions of other women in the community, including her co-wives, to her statements, both poetic and nonpoetic, give valuable clues to the functions of *ghinnāwa*s. The taped song elicited both the nervous joking of people embarrassed by a display of immodesty and the sympathetic noises of people who cared, understood her situation, and were moved by her recitation. She had recited the other poem in the presence of a number of women, including her co-wives, who said nothing. When I asked her what the poem meant, one co-wife joked, "Go ask 'the man' when he comes home." Ṣafiyya begged me not to.

A few months after my conversation with her, Ṣafiyya's husband decided to take her back. She suddenly began to dress nicely, wearing *kuḥl* in her eyes, and she suggested that her older children sleep with their grandmother, not in her room. She joked that she was waiting for her *nugūṭ* (wedding gifts). Her blatant pleasure at the remarriage scandalized everyone. People gossiped and teased her. Her outraged mother-in-law exclaimed, "She wants him, she wants him! Come on, her son is already a man!" It was not as if no one had suspected her feelings—these women knew perfectly well from her poems how attached she was to the man. As long as she expressed these feelings in *ghinnāwa*s, they had sympathized; but when she expressed them openly, outside of poetry, they began to criticize.

A number of observations about the role of poetry in matters of the heart can be drawn from this case. Sentiments of attachment to a loved one that violate the moral code, which for women centers on sexual modesty, find expression in poetry. For the most part, these poetic revelations are contradicted by public protestations of indifference and denials of attachment congruent with the cultural ideology about sexual love. When individuals slip and convey messages in the inappropriate medium, sharp criticism alerts them to their transgression, thus reinforcing the system.

The same pattern of divergent discourses on love is apparent in the responses of another woman, whose husband took a second wife. Like divorce, polygyny can be a source of anguish for Bedouin women, but concern over loss of the husband's affection is similarly considered culturally inappropriate and personally immodest.

Polygyny among Awlad 'Ali is on the increase thanks to the influx of wealth from smuggling, the skyrocketing value of their traditional lands along the Mediterranean coast, and other economic developments. I gathered from discussions with the older members of the community that in former generations, rather than put up with a co-wife, women were more likely to divorce their husbands or make life so difficult that their husbands would be dissuaded from remarrying. Now other women scold and mollify first wives with such statements as, "Are you the only one this has ever happened to? These days it is to be expected. It happens to everyone." Women joke that only the poor have their husbands to themselves because these men cannot afford second wives. In the community I lived in, over a third of the men married longer than two years had more than one wife. The correlation between wealth and polygyny is clear; only one of these men was not from the wealthy core families.

Reactions to a husband's second or third marriage vary. In some cases, especially when the senior wife has been consulted or has approved or even chosen the new wife, things go smoothly. People could always point to examples of households in which co-wives were "like sisters." My community had several such pairs of cooperative co-wives who rarely fought and appeared to be close and inseparable companions. In many other cases, however, women meet the news of their husband's decision to take a second wife with less equanimity, and relations between co-wives are often strained or volatile.

In addition to social pressure against displaying negative responses to the prospect of sharing a husband, internal pressures for comportment in terms of sexual modesty determine many women's public responses in this trying situation. The concern to convey indifference to the loss of the husband's affections under-lay the response of one woman whose husband was about to take another wife. One day he accused her of having stolen a ten-pound note that was missing from his pocket (he later found the note in another pocket). She was hurt by the false accusation and angry, but rather than going home to her kin in anger, as she might have done under ordinary circumstances, she forced herself to stay. She worried that people would misconstrue her motives and assume that she had left because of the husband's upcoming marriage, not the false accusation. In households where polygyny is already a fact, women often take the offensive, seizing on viola-tions of their rights to validate displeasure. An unhappy wife can always find some infraction on which to hang her complaints, because polygyny is clearly regulated in Bedouin society; the re-quirement that a husband treat his wives equally, from following a strict nightly rotation to bringing each identical gifts, right down to every bar of soap, opens vast possibilities for grievances.

And yet, if women feel compelled in mundane social interac-tions to mask overt signs of jealousy or feelings of betrayal—indicators of affection toward and attachment to their husbands—they can and do express those sentiments in poetry. The following case illustrates the relationship between poetic and ordinary state-ments about the loss of a husband's affections, focusing specifi-cally on the portrayal of indifference in ordinary discourse, rather than its alternative, anger.

In our first conversation after she heard the news that her hus-band of sixteen years was going to take a second wife, Mabrūka, Rashīd's wife and mother of his six children, complained that her husband never bought her nice things for her room. She denied, however, that the upcoming marriage bothered her. She asserted, "Let him get married, I don't care. But he should buy me nice things. He's worthless, he always was. A real man asks after his family, sees to it that they have everything they need."

As the wedding arrangements proceeded, problems arose. In the last chapter I described Mabrūka's angry response on discovering that the gifts her husband had offered her were not equivalent to the ones he had brought the bride, and her subsequent rejection of the gifts. I also presented some of the sad poems she recited, poems that carried messages of attachment to her husband and a sense of abandonment.

Mabrūka did not attend the wedding or help with the preparations for it, as do many senior wives. When her sister arrived at the wedding and found her missing, she went to talk to her. Mabrūka calmly insisted that her help was sorely needed at the wedding of some neighbors being celebrated concurrently and that was why she hadn't gone.

When her husband spent several days more than the customary week-long honeymoon with his new bride, Mabrūka protested that she did not care. She added that she had no intention of visiting the new bride's household to welcome her, nor did she wish any visitors. A woman in her household reported that she had said, "Let him stay there." I happened to be visiting her when her husband returned for the first time in the ten days since the wedding. He came with goods from the market; she was quiet, only muttering under her breath about what he had failed to buy. He took his gun to go hunting, and as he walked away, she commented to me, "It's been ages [literally, years] since we saw him." I asked sympathetically if she missed him. She replied abruptly, "No way. Do you think he is dear to me? I don't even ask about him. He can come and go as he pleases."

Moments later she recited a few poems. One suggested her consternation over the events of the recent past, brought up by his sudden appearance; another conveys a sense of betrayal:

> They always left me
> stuffed with false promises . . .
>
> dīmā khallō l-'agl
> 'āmrāt bimwā'īdhum . . .

In the course of this interchange Mabrūka's mother-in-law and a close woman-friend joined us. They spontaneously added to her poems, voicing what they assumed she was experiencing. These same women had previously scolded her, or teased her, for her angry reactions, but through poetry they consoled her by showing their empathic concern. For them, the poetic discourse served as a medium in which they could recognize the legitimacy of attachment to a husband. The themes common to all the poems these women recited were those of sadness, suffering, and despair. Among the poems was one that referred explicitly to polygyny, the rich man being a euphemism for a married man.

> My tears rushed down like a flood on a hill
> flowing over the match of the rich man . . .
>
> ḥdiran kēf sēl il-'ilu
> dmū'ī 'ale ṣōb il-ghanī . . .

Another one, sung by the friend, evoked a despair so powerful it could drive someone to abandon human society and to roam outdoors like an animal.

> Despair of them, dear one, made you
> a stray who wanders between watering places . . .
>
> khallāk yāshum yā l-'ēn
> dhulīl tdūrī 'al l-ignī . . .

As time passed, Mabrūka seemed to adjust. She still sometimes complained of illness, fevers, and bad teeth; then she had a miscarriage. She was also put in a difficult position when Fāyga ran away. But she rarely talked about her husband. She continued to recite poetry, though. The poems a few months after the marriage reflect sadness mingled with philosophical resignation to reality, as in the following:

Patience is my mourning for the loved one
and your job, oh eye, is to cry . . .

'azāy fī 'azīz iṣ-ṣabr
wintī 'alēk yā 'ēn il-bkā . . .

Another alludes to the effort it takes to control her concern:

Patience is better than thinking
if only you can manage it, oh self . . .

iṣ-ṣabr khēr min it-tafkīr
'alēh kān yā 'ēn tagdarī . . .

These cases confirm the strong link between poetry and matters
of love, romantic or conjugal, and justify us in designating the
ghinnāwa as a discourse of love. This discourse seems to be opposed to the mundane discourse of ordinary language structured
by overt social values and honor-linked personal ideals. Individuals whose ordinary actions and statements conform to the modesty code, who take pains to present themselves as moral and
worthy of respect, use poetry to comment on their personal fortunes and tribulations in love and to express sentiments that violate the canons of modesty. Poems are vehicles for the expression
of attachments to sweethearts or spouses that, if communicated in
everyday social interaction, would damage reputations and jeopardize claims to respectability and, at the individual level, would
ordinarily undermine self-image and self-presentation. In the final
chapter I turn to the questions raised by this observation: that
contradictory discourses on love coexist, just as do the divergent
discourses of honor and vulnerability explored in chapter 6.

IDEOLOGY AND
THE POLITICS OF SENTIMENT

Why do individuals in Bedouin society appear able to express through poetry the sentiments of weakness that violate the honor code and the sentiments of romantic love that violate the modesty code without incurring the opprobrium of the community or losing the self-esteem derived from embodying the moral ideals of their society? What is the significance of having two culturally constituted and sanctioned discourses available to individuals to express their interpersonal experiences? Analysis of the social contexts in which poetic recitations occur, as well as the special qualities of poetic language and form, will suggest some of the answers to the first question; uncovering the cultural meaning of the poetic discourse and its link to the social and political system will explain the rest. Only after proposing answers to these questions are we in a position to assess what the disjunction in Bedouin discourses implies about the relationship between a society's official ideology and individual experience and to grasp why Awlad 'Ali glorify the poetic discourse that violates the ideology of honor and modesty.

The Social Contexts of Discourse

One key to the puzzle of why individuals can express certain sentiments in one medium and not in another is the social contexts in
which the two discourses come into play. Except at ritual occasions,
individuals share poems only with close friends, social peers, or
lovers. Men share them with close kinsmen of the same generation
or with lower-status men; they do not sing before senior agnates or
patrons. Women recite poems to close kinswomen, women with
whom they share a household, or neighbors, and because their
world is less stratified, the range of categories of women with whom
they share poems is greater.

One is most likely to share poetry with those individuals from
whom one does not *taḥashsham*. As I argued earlier, *ḥasham* refers
both to a state of embarrassment or shame and to the corresponding acts of modesty or deference. *Ḥasham* as the experience of
shame arises in interpersonal interactions between social unequals
or strangers; it is conceptualized in the idiom of exposure and
manifests itself through a language of formality, self-effacement,
and the cloaking of the "natural" weaknesses or sources of dependency, which includes anything having to do with bodily needs,
sexuality, and so forth. *Ḥasham* in this sense is the correlate of
social distance, being both a response to that distance and a means
of maintaining it.

Poetry is the discourse of intimacy. Sharing poems, like exposing natural weaknesses, marks the absence of *ḥasham* between
individuals. Poetry indexes social distinctions by following the
lines of social cleavage. It usually does not cross the boundaries
created by differential power and status, including those associated
with gender. The firmest barrier is between men and women.
Women are careful not to let men hear them sing, and they claim
to be extremely embarrassed (*yitḥashshamū*) if heard.[1] Women
were even reluctant to share their poems with me until I assured
them I would never reveal the poems to any men. Men, too, can

be shy about having women hear their songs. A man I knew well volunteered to sing some of his own compositions for me but insisted that I lend him my tape recorder so he could tape them privately. But this modesty about poetry does not apply just to male-female interactions. Young men do not sing in the presence of their elders either, and in former times senior men did not attend certain of the wedding festivities, in particular those in which the young men sang, an avoidance that Peters (1965) reports among the Cyrenaican Bedouins as well.

The only exception to this barrier merely proves the rule. As described earlier, the exchange of poetry between men and women is not only acceptable but also mandatory in the special circumstances of courtship and romance. In romance, the gap between the sexes is deliberately breached and intimacy declared through this sharing of poetry. Here poetry indexes intimacy between those most distant in normal circumstances.

At the same time, sharing poetry enhances the closeness between intimates, differentiating it clearly from the social distance of nonintimates. It does so by giving this closeness the substance of secrets. In contrast to the masking and formality of the discourse of social distance, the discourse of poetry is one of self-exposure and familiarity; the sentiments of helpless vulnerability, weakness, and passion expressed in it violate the codes of honor and modesty. Insofar as the poems through which these sentiments are revealed are private and confidential, they are like secrets: secrets function to exclude those who do not share them and to closely bind those who do. Thus, categories of equals gain cohesion and divisions between nonequals are intensified, reinforcing the structures of Bedouin society.

Ordinary discourse is public, not secret. It is intended for general audiences composed of any number of categories of individuals with varying types of relationships to the self. The public world is the arena in which self-presentation is judged. As Goffman (1971, 185) puts it, this is where the individual "goes about constrained to sustain a viable image of himself in the eyes of others." Routine interpersonal encounters have also been described as "dramas of social censorship involved in the maintenance of the public order" in which people conceal "from public attention facts about themselves (including their emotional reactions and intentions) which they experience as too dangerous to disclose" (LeVine 1982a, 297). Insofar as *hasham* can be understood as deference to those who represent the social order, it is not surprising that if ideals are flouted, as they are in poems, it will not be in the presence of the people from whom individuals *tahashsham*.

For Awlad 'Ali, the discourses of honor and modesty belong in this public arena of everyday, ordinary-language interactions. In this sphere individuals strive to portray themselves as conforming to general personal ideals: they seek to appear potent, independent, and self-controlled, and they deny their sexuality, a source of both dependency and defiance of the social order. The only sentiments appropriate to this image are anger, attribution of blame, and denial of concern.

Other analysts have emphasized the social dimension of the honor discourse in Arab societies but have failed to note that it is bound by social context. Abou-Zeid (1966, 258) argues that, for Awlad 'Ali, honor is related to conformity to prevailing social norms as well as to the realization of social ideals. Bourdieu (1979, 111) notes, "The sense of honour is enacted in front of other people. *Nif* [point of honour] is above all that which leads a man to defend, at all costs, a certain self-image intended for others." And Eickelman (1976, 138), speaking of propriety (*theshsham*), says, "The locus of propriety is not so much the inner moral consciousness of a person as his public comportment with respect to those with whom he has regular face-to-face relations." None of these analysts, however, considers discourses outside the public realm.

We might be tempted to conclude from the context-bound nature of the discourses that Awlad 'Ali individuals experience a split between public and private that corresponds to self-presentation in terms of cultural ideals on the one hand versus revelation of "inner reality" on the other. Given our own cultural assumptions about the "real self" as expressed in spontaneous impulse versus a more institutionally oriented view that considers the self "real" only when it is expressing social ideals (cf. Turner 1976), we might want to interpret the honorable and modest self-presentations in the public sphere as structured masks worn for social approval, and the poetic discourse of weakness and romantic love as simple reflections of personal experience, of real feelings shown to friends.

There are two problems with this interpretation. First, it assumes a Goffmanesque alienation of social actors from the cultural ideals of their society. Recognizing that everyday expressions are guided by the honor code set by official ideology, we might, with Goffman, take the cynical attitude that these displays of honor and modesty are just rational acts of self-presentation, that

> in their capacity as performers, individuals will be concerned with maintaining the impression that they are living up to the many standards by which they and their products are judged. . . . But, *qua* performers, individuals are concerned not with the moral issue of realizing these standards, but with the amoral issue of engineering a convincing impression that these standards are being realized. (Goffman 1959, 251)

But this purely dramaturgical view misconstrues and devalues the meaning of social conformity in Bedouin society and underestimates the motivational power of the desire to be moral or good. Individuals in Awlad 'Ali society perceive the moral standards less as norms than as values; therefore, it is a matter of self-respect and pride that the individual achieve the standards, not an obligation.[2] There exists no source of self-definition or evaluation other than the standard. Moral virtue also justifies standing in the community. Belonging is essential because there is no life outside the group, no alternative social group other than the community of agnates into which one is born or, in some cases, another community to which one attaches, composed nevertheless of other Bedouins. Thus, respectability achieved through embodiment of the code's virtues is isomorphic with self-respect. This fusion of self-regard and the respect of others makes meaningless Goffman's distinction between realizing moral standards and giving the impression of realizing them. For individuals in Awlad 'Ali society, conformity to the code of honor and embodying the cultural ideals set by that code for the individual are not empty acts of impression management but the stuff of morality. This is the great strength of the ideology of honor and modesty as a means for perpetuating a system of power relations: by framing ideals as values, in moral terms, it guarantees that individuals will desire to do what perpetuates the system, thus obviating the need for overt violence or force.

Protective Veils of Form

Granting the authenticity of the discourse of everyday life means that nonpoetic public expressions cannot be dismissed as mere social masks hiding spontaneous inner feelings. But a second criticism of this formulation emerges from a consideration of the form and character of the "private" discourse. Neither *ghinnāwa*s nor the ritualized mourning laments associated with them could be characterized as original, spontaneous expressions of sentiment. Individuals reach for ready-made forms to give voice to those personal sentiments that seem to violate the cultural ideals; thus, their poetry, so intimate and expressive, is in fact culturally constituted—a highly conventional and formulaic idiom—and "crying" (*bkā*) is even more fixed. If anything, this discourse is, in form and content, more thoroughly circumscribed by tradition and more rigidly structured than is the discourse of everyday life. It would be hard to label one as *less* cultural than the other, just as neither could be labeled *less* social than the other.

Before taking up the significance of this cultural constraint of sentiments, I want to show how the cultural character and rigid form of poetry afford a certain amount of protection for the individual in expressing the "deviant" sentiments of dishonor and immodesty. Poetry cloaks statements in the veils of formula, convention, and tradition, thus suiting it to the task of carrying messages about the self that contravene the official cultural ideals. As noted, the *ghinnāwa* is a highly formulaic and stylized verbal genre. Formula renders content impersonal or nonindividual, allowing people to dissociate themselves from the sentiments they express, if revealed to the wrong audience, by claiming that "it was just a song."[3] Inherently ambiguous, formulaic poems protect the anonymity of the poet, of the addressee, and of the subject. Pronouns appear in the plural even when only one person is being referred to, and gender is rarely marked. No names are ever included, assuring that only those already intimates of the person reciting will know the true significance and referent of the poem.

Formulaic style also marks utterances as extraordinary and sets them apart. Even more than the situational markers of social context to which they are tied, formal linguistic markers clue people not to apply ordinary standards to what is conveyed in this medium. That the same individuals responded differently, depending upon the mode of expression—poetry or ordinary actions—to Rashīd's longings for his bride and Ṣafiyya's for her husband indicates the association of content and form. These individuals exempted the poetic statements from the same standards of honor and modesty they applied so rigorously to mundane discourse. They sympathized with the sentiments expressed in poetry but condemned the same ones when expressed nonpoetically.

Most important, formulaic language, or rather the communication of sentiment in poetry, allows individuals to frame their experiences as similar to those of others and perhaps to assert the universality of their experiences. This identification with others grants their personal expressions a semblance of social conformity despite their obvious violation of the moral code. Especially because *ghinnāwa*s are associated with traditional romances and the tragic tales of love, every time individuals recite poems they evoke this grand and mythical world; by putting their personal experiences in poetry, individuals implicitly liken themselves to the much-admired tragic heroes and heroines of lore. They recast their own personal experiences in a grandiose and culturally valued form, thus lifting their experiences out of the realm of ordinary life, where they would be taken as signs of immodesty or individual defiance of senior kinsmen and the system they represent.

At the same time, *ghinnāwa*s call up a world of tradition, since the tales with which they are associated are alleged to be true stories from the distant past, and many poems have long, although not always preserved, histories. The link to tradition is also found in people's association of singing with the past, which most look back on as a golden age. In short, through association with the traditional Bedouin world, the sentiments that violate the cultural ideals of honor and modesty gain social legitimacy and seem less dangerous: poems, as part of a great cultural tradition, cannot represent rebellions against the values of society. Presented in such a conventional and formulaic idiom, the messages of personal violations of the code can hardly be perceived as idiosyncratic.[4] Thus in various ways the form of the discourse shapes its capacity to carry certain types of messages. Poetry as a form provides a modest way of communicating immodest sentiments of attachment and an honorable way of communicating the sentiments of dependency.

The Meaning of Poetry

Still, the temptation to interpret individuals' poetic statements as revelations, if veiled and indirect, of experience lingers. So does the suspicion that the discrepancy between what people say in the two media suggests hypocrisy. The analysis of how the sentiments of anger and indifference are appropriate to the ideals of the moral codes of honor and of modesty showed that sentiments have cultural meaning, that various sentiments are valued differently, and that sentiments can be used to symbolize something about the person expressing them. There is no reason to presume that the sentiments of the poetic discourse are any less meaningful in cultural terms or that their expression does not contribute to the creation of an image, if contrapuntal, of self. Like any communication, poetry is not merely expressive but also persuasive.[5]

Just as people's actions and words in everyday social interactions are always directed partly toward others, so their poetic productions are directed toward an audience. Although people do sing when alone, they usually recite poems in the presence of other people or mark them for absent addressees by vocatives such as "oh beloved" (*yā 'alam*). Poetry is not, any more than is the public discourse of honor, a simple reflection of the experiences and sentiments (however shaped by cultural conventions and constructions) of the person reciting. Even if the links between sentiment, on the one hand, and cultural values and the motivational power of the desire for respect and respectability through conformity to the moral code, on the other, are most evident in the ordinary statements made in public, this does not mean that poetic statements are not motivated. The question is, motivated by what? Toward what ends? The answers are complex.

I have already considered some of the functions of poetry. First, because poetic discourse indexes social intimacy, reciting poems to particular individuals communicates, and even creates, closeness. Poetry recitation is thus a strategy for bridging social distance, seen most clearly in its use in courtship. Second, by framing personal experience in poetic terms, individuals protect themselves in two ways from the criticism that accompanies violations of the moral code: in expressing personal sentiments about life experiences in the shared terms of a highly conventional and traditional form of oral lyric poetry, individuals proclaim their similarity to others and assert the universality of their experiences; and by reciting love poetry from romances, they cast their own personal experiences in culturally valued terms.

Attention to the rhetoric of poetry suggests something else about the motivations of poetic recitations. Although it is hard to generalize, because *ghinnāwa*s vary so much in content, it can be argued that the goal of poetic presentations is to move people and thus get them to act toward one in a particular way. One of the ways this is done is through projecting an image of self by describing certain types of sentiments. Whereas the expressions of ordinary discourse are meant to win respect and respectability for the individual, achieved through conformity to Bedouin society's officially espoused values of independence, the goals of poetic presentations are twofold: to win sympathy and to get help. In poetry, the rendering of experience in terms evocative of childhood wins sympathy and disarms moral criticism.

Awlad 'Ali themselves argue that reciting poetry moves people and brings about changes in their actions or attitudes. The dual aspect of persuasion is reflected in people's comments on the efficacy of poetry.[6] Poetry's purpose of transforming attitudes, of moving people emotionally, is evident in statements such as "good poetry makes you cry." Poetry's ability to affect acts is suggested by impressive accounts of times when just hearing a poem recited by someone wronged induced the hearer to change a course of action. The model for this type of change is the love story in which a woman already mounted on her wedding camel en route to her husband's community dismounts and runs off with an admirer who sings her a *ghinnāwa*. The power of poetry to bring about desired changes is alluded to in a haunting poem I heard:

> I've lost their tracks, the loved ones
> perhaps my singing will bring them . . .
>
> dhahabit gēshun l-awlāf
> kannība zinīnī yjībhun . . .

The efficacy of poetry has to do with its idiom. Poetry is associated with weakness, vulnerability, helpless dependency, and intimacy; it is a kind of self-exposure before intimates. In Bedouin society, these experiences and states of being are all closely linked with childhood, as Awlad 'Ali consider children to be by nature helpless and dependent. The unsocialized child, who does not yet have *'agl,* is free to cry in pain, to express fear, and to seek help, without criticism. Children live in a world of intimacy, held, coddled, and adored by anyone they encounter in their households and communities. Distinctions of age or gender have little meaning for them, the men showing them just as much affection as do women and older children.

By invoking in their poetry experiences associated with childhood, drawing an analogy between themselves and young children, individuals metaphorically assume an identity and imply a quality of relationship calculated to elicit a certain type of response in others. The rhetoric of poetry is, "I am like a child. Please treat me as you would a child, and judge me by the standards applied to children." This appeal is made directly to the poems' audiences, the intimates usually within the singer's community, and "magically" to the absent persons who caused the pain or are the objects of desire, to whom the poems are implicitly addressed.[7]

This appeal first of all frames the social relationship between singer and audience, actual or potential, as one of the mutuality and complementarity characteristic of relations within the family, rather than of the antagonism and jockeying for position of independent figures. The poet seeks to evoke in his or her audience the sentiments of tender care that a dependent child inspires in its caretakers. Many poems explicitly request help or care, invoking other relationships between the helpless and powerful; for example, some appeal for medical treatment (treat me, heal my wound), and some supplicate God. At the minimum, poetic confessions of weakness seek to disarm those more powerful individuals perceived as inflicting pain or attacking the poet. A critical element in the Bedouin model of family relations, extended to relations between unequals, is the obligation of the strong to care for the weak, or at least to refrain from asserting dominance over them.

The analogy with children also serves to absolve individuals of responsibility for the statements they make in poetic form. Awlad 'Ali consider children innocent and moral. They believe, with other Muslims, that those who die in childhood automatically go to heaven. Socialization to independence, self-mastery, and recognition of one's place in the hierarchy begins in earnest only after the child is about five and intensifies as he or she grows, reaching its peak in early adolescence. Socialization involves learning the discourse of honor; growing up, the responsibility to conform to the values of the honor code. Thus, when individuals liken themselves to children, they compel others to suspend the ordinary terms for judging moral worth, thereby undercutting criticism that might otherwise greet the poetic revelations of sentiments that violate moral conventions, particularly those applying to sexuality. The childhood idiom suggests that poetic statements are amoral, not immoral.

Poetry, however, is never a lone discourse. For the individual and his or her intimates, what is said in poetry and what is said in ordinary language always exist side by side: their interplay is essential to their meaning. The two juxtaposed discourses can be seen as commenting on each other, just as the secret comments on the manifest world (Simmel 1950, 330). Ironically, poetic discourse seems to comment on the ordinary discourse of everyday life in ways that ultimately enhance the meaning of the latter and the honor of the person reciting. One might, then, consider poetry and the expression of feeling it represents as integral to honor.

The poetic revelations of weakness and attachment to others give dimension to the tough independence affected in ordinary social interactions in at least three ways. First, by admitting the existence of an attitude toward others and a range of sentiments that lie outside the confines of the system of honor, individuals demonstrate that their conformity to the code in everyday actions is voluntary. This voluntary aspect is crucial both to honor, which is above all about autonomy, and to modesty. As Riesman argues for Fulani society, where men openly flout official morality in their continual quest for women,

> this defiance enhances the value of the individual, both for his own sake and as a member of society. By acting against the moral code the individual is demonstrating that he is a free being and that his actions are not automatically determined by social rules and social pressures. But if the individual is free to disobey, then he is free to obey too and the value of his adherence to the society is thereby enhanced. (1971, 611)

By acting aggressively and proudly in ordinary life while at the same time revealing feelings of vulnerability, people show that they are choosing to act in accordance with the moral code. This factor is even more important to modesty. As I argued in chapters 3 and 4, Bedouins see coercion as stripping acts of their meaning. Like that of dependents such as young men, women's submission is demeaning to them and worthless to their superiors unless perceived as freely given. By acting modestly with social superiors while expressing immodest feelings to intimates, they show that they are choosing to recognize those with more authority as well as the social system that gives these people their authority.

The expression of sentiments in poetry gives meaning to the discourse of everyday life in a second way. By channeling such powerful sentiments into a rigid and conventional medium and delimited social contexts, individuals demonstrate a measure of self-mastery and control that contributes to honor. Those who feel deeply but lose control, like the tragic characters who die of broken hearts or go mad from grief, are held in awe but not considered social beings; along with the loss of self-mastery, they have lost their honor and forfeited their positions as members of society. The social standing of those who express their responses to losses or other difficult personal situations in forms other than poetry confirms this interpretation. Mad people, idiots, and children all express their experiences in an unstructured way. They reveal things in inappropriate social contexts and are too explicit. People in all three categories are also considered outside society in some sense—they are not fully social beings or proper members of society. This status results not so much because they are dependent, ineffectual, or not in control of their appetites, but rather because they lack *'agl,* which in this context manifests itself as an inability to distinguish social contexts and to use appropriate cultural forms to express their sentiments. Those who express strong sentiments of attachment and vulnerability in the culturally approved way can still claim to embody the cultural ideals.

Third, by exposing this other side of experience, individuals impress on others that their conformity to the code and attainment of the cultural ideals of personhood are neither shallow nor easy. Bourdieu argues that in the Kabyle system of honor, the person who is particularly exposed to outrage but who nevertheless manages to secure respect is especially meritorious. He also argues that honor is only meaningful for the man who has "things worth defending" (1979, 119). Following this logic, it might be suggested that the greatest respect is accorded the person who, despite struggles with powerful vulnerabilities and passions, is a proper member of Awlad 'Ali society, a person with honor. One Bedouin man told me that there were three common causes of insanity, all having to do with loss: when someone dear dies, when you are rich and suddenly lose everything, and when you cannot have the one you love. These are the very things people sing about, which suggests that poetry is taken as a sign of powerful feeling creatively managed. Poetry may be so cherished by the Bedouins precisely because it allows people to express, and their intimates to appreciate, the profundity of that which must be overcome to conform to society's values.

Expressing feelings of vulnerability and love in poetry may thus give meaning to the strength and independence individuals

Women preparing ewes for milking

display in their everyday lives. Poems win for those who recite them admiration along with sympathy.

The Politics of Sentiment

It is clear that individuals are shielded from the consequences of making statements and expressing sentiments that contravene the moral system if they do so in poetry. By sharing these "immoral" sentiments only with intimates and veiling them in impersonal traditional formulas, they even demonstrate that they have a certain control, which actually enhances their moral standing. But if we turn from how individuals use poems to the poetry itself as a cultural discourse, as a set of rule-bound statements that represent a vision of reality, an even more intriguing set of questions presents itself. If the disjunction between the messages carried by the two discourses occurs not just on the individual level but on the cultural level as well, and if ordinary discourse is that generated in accordance with the values that support the dominant social and political system, then is poetry the discourse of antistructure? If poetry is associated with opposition to the system, why is it not condemned or repressed? Why is it glorified?

The *ghinnāwa*'s antistructural character is evident not just in the type of sentiments regularly carried by it but in its associations as well. Its closest association is with the traditional Bedouin romance. Poems are always included in love tales that celebrate the often tragic course of romance, a force usually condemned as threatening to the social system. Thwarted love, especially between a man and woman from different tribes, is the theme of the most poignant Bedouin love stories, which are recounted as true tales of the distant past.[8] In a few, cousins fall in love but are prevented from marrying by the girl's wealthy father who does not wish to let her marry his poor brother's son; from what I could gather, those stories usually ended happily with the young nephew triumphing. More commonly, the sweethearts are unrelated, and their love is thwarted by the girl's cousin, as in the following archetypal love story:

> Once upon a time there was a boy and a girl who were in love with each other. The girl's father's brother's son heard about this and was furious. He swore she would never marry the boy and claimed her [*masakhā*] for himself.
>
> Now, the girl and the boy used to meet secretly to talk at the tent of an old lady, a neighbor of theirs. One day, the boy announced that he was leaving on a journey. He was going to the oasis of Siwa to get dates. He promised that after he returned, he would marry the girl. He said to her:
>
> > Happiness in my absence is a failing
> > and grief between us the sign of love . . .
> >
> > zahā fī ghiyābī naqṣ
> > wil-ḥizn bēnnā mārat ghalā . . .
>
> With that he set off with a caravan of camels. He was away for a long time. On his way back, only two days from home, he fell ill and died. He had instructed his companion earlier, "If I die on the way, please carry my body home so my family can bury me." So his companion loaded his corpse on a camel and journeyed the rest of the way home.
>
> When his family heard what had happened, they wailed and cried. Meanwhile, the girl had seen the camels returning to his camp but wondered, "Why don't I hear trilling and the firing of rifles [signs of celebration]?" She ran to find out, and when she did, she wailed and cried with his kinswomen.
>
> Her cousin discovered that she had gone to her lover's camp and followed her. He ran in and grabbed her from among the mourners and started beating her. She tried to run away, but he chased her, beating her until she fell dead, right on the fresh grave of her sweetheart.
>
> Her cousin was enraged. He swore at her, "Even in death you're a slut!" He demanded that they not bury her near the boy, so they carried her about a kilometer away and buried her.

After a while, a palm tree sprang from the head of the boy's grave, and a tree sprang from the head of the girl's. The trees grew and grew until their fronds crossed high in the sky. The cousin grew angry when he saw this, thinking, "She still can't keep away from him, even in death?" So he went to find a woodcutter to cut down the trees.

As the woodcutter was trying to chop down the tree that grew over her grave, the axe flew out of his hand and into his eye, blinding him. He went home and fell ill. In his sleep a vision of the boy came to him and said:

> May God cut you down, oh woodcutter
> you cut the rope as they were filling [at the well] . . .

> allah yigṭaʿak yā najjār
> gāṭiʿ dlī fī mlāhum . . .

Then he parted with the words:

> Love must bring forth fruits
> which join each other in their sky . . .

> l-asbid min ghalā ynabbit athmār
> yitʿālagun fī smāhum . . .

This story has several remarkable features. It celebrates the desires of individuals against the demands of the system, as codified in the first cousin's right to his father's brother's daughter—the cousin seeks to enforce the system as the girl and her lover refuse to accept it. The heroine is both defiant and a "slut," hence lacking in modesty; her tragic end may hold a lesson for Awlad ʿAli about the ultimate power of the system. At the same time, however, she and her sweetheart are heroic, and their defiance ends in a victory of sorts. People who listen to such tales admire the behavior of lovers and do not condemn it as immoral, and they appreciate the poetry that expresses the lovers' feelings.

Poetry is associated with antistructure in ways other than this explicit link to romance and sexuality. People perceive poetry as un-Islamic and poetic recitation as impious, just as "crying" at funerals is considered wrong from a religious point of view (and so is not done by women who have been on the pilgrimage to Mecca). The fact that the very word "to sing" (*ghannī*) cannot be said in mixed-sex company suggests its antistructural quality. Another indication is that people say they *taḥashsham* or are embarrassed/ashamed/modest about singing in front of nonintimates, especially elders. Elders, too, avoid settings such as weddings and sheep shearings where, at least in the past, *ghinnāwa*s were publicly sung. Even the rhetoric of poetry gives it an antistructural flavor, as if poetry were the language of the unsocialized child as opposed to the ordinary discourse of adult conformity. The final and most persuasive link is in who sings or recites *ghinnāwa*s. Although older men occasionally recite them, *ghinnāwa*s are most closely associated with youths and women, the disadvantaged dependents who least embody the ideals of Bedouin society and have least to gain in the system as structured. Poetry is, in so many ways, the discourse of opposition to the system and of defiance of those who represent it: it is antistructure just as it is antimorality.

The existence of dissident or subversive discourses is probably not unusual. What may be peculiar to Awlad 'Ali is that their discourse of rebellion is both culturally elaborated and sanctioned. Although poetry refers to personal life, it is not individual, spontaneous, idiosyncratic, or unofficial but public, conventional, and formulaic—a highly developed art. More important, this poetic discourse of defiance is not condemned, or even just tolerated, as well it might be given all the constraints of time and place and form that bind it. Poetry is a privileged discourse in Awlad 'Ali society. Like other Arabs, and perhaps like many oral cultures, the Bedouins cherish poetry and other verbal arts. Everyone listens attentively whenever poems are recited or sung. People memorize poems, repeat them, and are moved by them. For Awlad 'Ali, poetry represents what is best in their culture, what they consider distinctively Bedouin. Poetry is associated with the glorious past, when Awlad 'Ali lived without Egyptian government interference, migrating freely, herding sheep, riding horses, and being brave and tough.

People are thrilled by poetry. They are drawn to *ghinnāwa*s, and at the same time they consider them risqué, against religion, and slightly improper—as befits something antistructural. This ambivalence about poetry is significant, and it makes sense only in terms of the cultural meaning of opposition. Because ordinary discourse is informed by the values of honor and modesty, the moral correlates of the ideology that upholds the Awlad 'Ali social and political system, we would expect the antistructural poetic discourse, with its contradictory messages, to be informed by an opposing set of values. This is not the case. Poetry as a discourse of defiance of the system symbolizes freedom—the ultimate value of the system and the essential entailment of the honor code.

As a declaration of autonomy, of freedom from domination by the system, poetry is cherished, even though it carries subversive messages and is associated with those denied autonomy in Awlad 'Ali society. People admire poetry in the same way they secretly admire youths' or women's refusals to submit to tyranny or to accept domination by the system or its representatives. In the story quoted in chapter 7 (p. 211), the Haj mentioned that his father had asked to hear the poems he had sung to the woman he was wooing, a sign of approval and admiration. The Haj's father also indicated that he was proud of his son for having defied the system and the woman's cousins. In the tragic romance recounted above, the heroine, although accused by her cousin of being a "slut," was admired for her defiance. As I argued in chapter 3, docility in women, as in men, is unattractive. I remember being shocked to find out, after hearing so much about the value of *hasham,* that the women in my community considered one young girl the most outstanding in the camp: she was tough and difficult, always yelling back at her mother, refusing to do what she was told, and bossing her brothers around, and she was first in her class at school (and one of its few girls). Her mother admitted proudly that she herself had been difficult (*wa'ra*) when young.

This girl's willful defiance, which emphatically did not apply in the sexual sense, as she was extremely proper, even hostile, toward males, was even grudgingly admired by her sometimes-exasperated father.

I argue that the ambivalence about poetry, like the ambivalence about defiance on the part of those for whom modesty is supposed to be the path to honor, may reflect a fundamental tension in the organization of Bedouin social and political life. The ambivalence may derive from an uneasy recognition that the system of hierarchy within the lineage and the family in fact violates the basic tenets of the political system based on segmenting genealogy. All those who analyze the politics of Arab tribal societies, including Caton (1984), Cole (1975), Evans-Pritchard (1949), Lancaster (1981), Meeker (1979), and Peters (1967), stress the importance of autonomy and equality as the theoretical principles on which the political system is predicated and which it is designed to maximize. These are the principles Awlad 'Ali stress in their descriptions of their own system of political organization. The values of personhood implied by the honor code are appropriate to a life in which men must be willing to fight to defend themselves or, if Meeker is right, must find appealing a potentially violent life of adventure made possible by mounted pastoral nomadism.

Yet, if we turn from external affairs between men or groups of men to internal affairs within the camp and family—from the official view of politics to the arena not usually represented in the language of power—the problem becomes clear. In this "domestic" context, the system puts control over resources and power over dependents in the hands of elder male agnates, creating an internal domination that contravenes the paramount ideals. As I have shown, this hierarchical domination is justified through the elaboration of a moral code that rationalizes the privilege of elders and dignifies the deference of dependents. The contradiction is tempered by attributing to relations of inequality the qualities of mutuality implied by the familial idiom, and by focusing on the "goodness" associated with voluntary modesty. But the contradiction is never fully resolved, because it cannot be. Poetry expresses this problem. A discourse of defiance mostly by those slighted in the system, it is exalted because a refusal to be dominated is key to Bedouin political life, and it is avoided by elders because it threatens to expose the illegitimacy of their authority.

I began this study with the proposition that it was important to look at the poetry of personal life rather than the better-known and more commonly studied poetry of the men's world of heroism, violence, and tribal politics. Personal poetry has led us back to politics. However, it has led us to an expanded vision of politics, to include not just the system by which external relations are ordered but also the system that organizes internal relations of domination—two systems at odds. Poetry has such an important place in Awlad 'Ali culture because it reflects this collision.

It is even tempting to speculate on the connection between the demise of poetry—or, more accurately, its increasing confinement to the private world of intimates and its gradual disappearance from public ceremonial occasions—to changes in Awlad 'Ali social and political structure. As noted in chapter 2, sedentarization, an increasing involvement in the market economy, and the extension of private ownership to all sorts of resources have led both to more stable inequities in the distribution of wealth and a correspondingly more rigid social hierarchy and to a growing disparity in the positions of men and women. This institutionalization of social inequality, when combined with the increasing restriction of the political autonomy of local groups and individuals by central governmental authorities in the Western Desert, may undermine the bases for the ideology of honor that corresponded to and continued to make possible a different sort of system. If poetry was the symbol of defiance, valued because domination was not acceptable, might not the withering of poetry be related in some way to these new circumstances? Younger Bedouins listen to Egyptian radio and are becoming familiar with Egyptian popular culture; they tend not to know how to compose or recite poetry, a fact the older generations deplore. There are fewer and fewer ceremonial occasions at which traditional poetry is sung. But just as wealthy men maintain camel herds obsolete in the age of trucks, and many men lovingly burnish their shotguns though they rarely use them except to hunt the occasional wild bird, Bedouins still cling to both the ideology of honor and poetry as symbols of their noble past. It remains to be seen for how long.

Ideology and Experience

Whatever the restrictions on social contexts appropriate to the two discourses, however apt the poetic form for the content it carries, whatever the motivations of communications, and whatever the cultural meaning of the two discourses, the fact remains that the Awlad 'Ali Bedouins have at least two culturally elaborated discourses about the self and personal sentiments. The relationship of these discourses to individual experience, a topic set aside as I considered their cultural meanings, must now be taken up.

There is little doubt that the ideology of honor is the dominant or official ideology of Bedouin culture. In the last two chapters I showed how individuals' responses to situations in their personal lives took shape in terms of this ideology, as mediated through morality. The sentiments individuals expressed in the discourse of everyday life were those that best represented the highest values in this moral system: aggressive autonomy and denial of vulnerability or longing. But the coexistence in people's poetic expressions of a set of contrary sentiments raises questions about the extent to which the dominant ideology determines or ordinary behavior reflects individual experience.

Anthropologists commonly assume that describing the ideology or the culture is equivalent to describing the behavior and experience of members of society. Even Bourdieu, perhaps the most sophisticated theorist working on the ethnography of the Middle East, sometimes takes a position granting official ideology a totalitarian role in structuring experience. For instance:

> Official language, particularly the system of concepts by means of which the members of a given group provide themselves with a representation of their social relations (e.g., the lineage model or the vocabulary of honour), sanctions and imposes what it states, tacitly laying down the dividing line between the thinkable and the unthinkable. (1977, 21)

Although we can never know the exact relationship between experience and its articulation, we can assume that there is some congruence and that an examination of cultural discourses tells us something about individual experience. The existence of two Bedouin discourses leads us to conclude that the dominant ideology of honor does not set the limits on the "thinkable and the unthinkable," or perhaps the "feelable and unfeelable." Nor do descriptions of the moral discourse of honor exhaust Awlad 'Ali experience.

Does poetry represent another set of values and ideals of personhood that inform individual experiences? As we saw above, the sentiments carried by the poetic discourse of defiance take much of their meaning from their opposition to the sentiments of ordinary life. In a similar way, poetry could be said to stand for the freedom to experience that which is outside the official system. What are we to make of these experiences of vulnerability and deep attachment that poetry communicates?

One possibility is that these are natural experiences that fall outside of "culture," in the sense of that which is shaped by the dominant ideology. This position entails the assumption that by giving human existence a distinct form, any culture must necessarily sacrifice or exclude much. Thinking in hydraulic terms, one might propose that what is excluded in forming a given cultural system erupts, if not in ordinary public discourse, then somewhere else—in the Bedouin case, in poetry. This "eruption" idea would imply that official ideology not only cannot wholly determine the experiences of individuals living in a particular society but also cannot encompass the range of their experiences.

The link already discussed between the sentiments and images of poetry and those appropriate to childhood as Bedouins conceive it might be taken as evidence that the experiences conveyed in poetry represent not just *extra*cultural eruptions, but also vestiges of *pre*cultural experience. The child is, after all, not yet socialized into the culture and is not yet motivated to conform to its values. This association with childhood might even lead us to wonder what sorts of longings for intimacy and deeply buried vulnerabilities exist in people socialized early into autonomy.

The problem with these interpretations is that they do not take into account the specific form in which such experiences are articulated, namely, a genre of traditional formulaic poetry. The experiences conveyed in poetry are no more spontaneous or acultural than the ones of ordinary discourse. They may not fit with the experiences sanctioned by the dominant ideology, but neither are they idiosyncratic, private, and unofficial. Sentiments disallowed in the honor system are more than allowed to surface here; they are given a distinctively Bedouin cultural form and sanctified, shaped and bound by the limited range of themes and metaphors of the poetic genre. These sentiments are also glorified and sanctioned by the forms in which they are articulated. Linguistic marking, both in form and performance, draws attention to them and grants them a special status. The hyperbole in the poetic expression of sentiments may also highlight the importance of the message.[9]

The contours of the poetic discourse, like those of the discourse of personal morality, are culturally given. Awlad 'Ali individuals are born into a society in which they hear and learn to recite *ghinnāwa*s, providing them with a rich vocabulary for articulating certain sentiments. How much poetry actually shapes their experiences in intimate life is impossible to know, but it seems likely that the poetic conventions would lead them to experience recurrent situations in similar ways. For example, love stories might set a tone and provide a model for interpreting or framing events in people's romantic lives. Many of the poems individuals recite apropos of their own difficulties in love come from particular love stories. By drawing poems from these grand tales of passion to express their own sentiments, individuals, in defining their situations in a particular way both for themselves and for others, might be molding their lives to the culturally shared imagery of old stories. By alluding to the stories through the use of *ghinnāwa*s, people might be framing their wishes and situations as part of a familiar tragic and universal type. Does this affect how they experience them?

Rather than positing one monolithic cultural ideology that determines experience, it is probably fair to say that there are at least two ideologies in Bedouin culture, each providing models of and for different types of experiences.[10] The danger of this formulation is that it still suggests an overly rigid cultural conditioning that risks reducing human beings to automatons. I want to suggest instead that these discourses are not templates, but rather languages that people can use to express themselves. In enabling people to express experiences, these discourses may enable them to feel those experiences. But the fact remains that it is people who make the statements.

Here I think the fact that poetry is art is relevant. Although I cannot take up the formidable questions of the role of art in society or of the relationship between art and individual experience,[11] I want to make two points. First, as an art, poetry allows for a certain creativity. The canons may be confining and the metaphors and formulas of the *ghinnāwa* limited, but they are not imprisoning. New combinations are always possible, to give voice and perhaps life to new sentiments that go beyond what has already been said and felt. In that sense, poetry may be not just a symbol of the individual's freedom to defy culture's power to define and delimit experience, but also a tool to be used in that defiance.

Second, taking a cue from Bateson (1972), I will speculate on another function of poetry. In an article on Balinese art, Bateson boldly argues for a view of art (including poetry) as a corrective to a too-limited and ultimately destructive understanding of the world as provided by ordinary consciousness. He sees art as having "a positive function in maintaining . . . 'wisdom,'" which in his terminology is the recognition of "interlocking circuits," in contrast to the short-term goal-oriented views that make everyday life efficient (1972, 147). Setting aside his grandiose perspective and his cybernetic vocabulary, I would offer the related proposition that Awlad 'Ali's poetry of self and sentiment be viewed as their corrective to an obsession with morality and an overzealous adherence to the ideology of honor. Taken to an extreme, this ideology, which maintains the social and political system, would foster defensive and belligerent attitudes and make nearly impossible many forms of human intimacy. Poetry reminds people of another way of being and encourages, as it reflects, another side of experience. Its message may be sanctified by the ritualized formality of its carrier.[12] This vision is kept alive by those who benefit least from the system that the honor ideology maintains. And maybe the vision is cherished because people sense that the costs of this system, in the limits it places on human experience, are just too high.

APPENDIX:
FORMULAS AND THEMES
OF THE *GHINNĀWA*

The Awlad 'Ali *ghinnāwa* is a form of traditional oral poetry. Scholars of oral literature and Arab poetry would no doubt find a thorough analysis of this genre and greater attention to the textual interesting. What follows is a brief and preliminary discussion of the use of formulas and the range of themes in the *ghinnāwa* that will do little more than hint at the rich field awaiting analysis.

Bedouin individuals either draw poems from a cultural repertoire or compose them extemporaneously, playing with familiar themes, phrases, and structures. I thus characterize the poetic discourse as formulaic, but I mean something less rigid than the use of actual formulas, which Lord and Parry have shown to be key elements of the composition and recitation of traditional epic poetry (see Lord 1971). Since rhyme is absent and meter need not be sustained for any length, and because there is little pressure to compose rapidly during performance, complex formulas may be less essential in this genre. However, images, phrases, and themes recur. The *ghinnāwa* even has a specialized vocabulary, its most common and characteristic terms being ones rarely heard in ordinary speech. Some of these terms are so ubiquitous that they must be viewed as conventions or simple formulas.

Awlad 'Ali do not seem overly concerned with distinguishing between original poems and those heard and repeated, a feature characteristic of oral poetry (Lord 1971, 101). The answers I got to questions of authorship were not reliable. Often, just after someone had told me a poem was theirs I would hear it from someone else. Several people told me that "in the olden days" everyone could compose poems but that since few could now do so, most people merely repeated poems by rote. Even so, certain individuals are recognized as particularly gifted and interested in poetry. These individuals do compose original poems, remembering the date and occasion of the composition. For example, one man recited a poem to me that he said he had composed eight years earlier about a married woman whom he had loved.

Only under a few special circumstances do people self-consciously quote or repeat the poems of others. The first is in recounting well-known Bedouin love stories or romances, in which the dialogue between lovers is nearly always in poetry of the *ghinnāwa* form. The second is when they relate true-life events that involved the exchange of poetry. In both these cases, the poems are prefaced by the phrase "she said . . ." or "he said . . ."

In any case, the line between original poems and poems in the repertoire is extremely thin. In individual recitations, whether at formal occasions such as weddings or in the course of ordinary conversations, people tend to recombine formulaic elements creatively or to elaborate on familiar themes within traditional constraints to create their own songs, as can be seen by comparing poems.

THE USE OF FORMULAS

The simplest variations in poems depend on the composer's ability to substitute words and phrases to change the meaning only slightly. The following two poems, recited by different people over a year apart, illustrate this:

> Oh eyes be strong
> you cherish people and then they're gone . . .

yā anẓār dīrun 'azm
tghālī 'arab wyfārgū . . .

It's your fate, oh eye
you cherish people and then they're gone . . .

maktūb yā l-'ēn 'alēk
tghālī 'arab wyfārgū . . .

Similarly, substituting phrases or hemistiches can produce slight changes in meaning, as in the following two poems, the first recorded by Falls in 1906, the second by me in 1979:

Tears won't bring your sweetheart
endure your malady patiently . . .

dami' mā yjīb habīb
'ala dāk yā 'ēn uṣubrī . . .

Tears won't bring your sweetheart
pay no mind and be quiet . . .

dami' mā yjīb habīb
blā bāl yā 'ēn isiktī . . .

Alternatively, a poem's framework or mode of construction might be retained while the content shifts. This can be seen in the following two poems, the first recorded by me, the second by Qādirbūh (1977, 144), which are built around the idea of before and after:

Today they moved to distant camps
who before just a shout would bring . . .

il-yōm bā'adū bid-dār
illī gabl 'āyta tjībhum . . .

They patiently endured for years
what before they could not have borne a day . . .

ṣbirun yā 'azīz snīn
illī gabl yōm ykēdhun . . .

Many poems are variations on a theme and play with a common metaphor. The following two are selected from scores revolving around the theme of the wounds of love:

> The wounds, oh beloved, of your love
> heal some days then open again . . .

> jrūḥ yā 'azīz ghalāk
> yabran ayām wynāwidh ukhra . . .

> My wounds were just about healed
> and today oh my torment, they tore open . . .

> jrūḥī gabl biryanāt
> wil-yōm yā 'adhābī naggadhan . . .

Although these particular examples were not described as such, they would most likely be considered what Awlad 'Ali refer to as "sister songs." One of the important forms of exchange involves answering one person's poem with its sister, that is, another poem that plays on the same theme or picks up a key image, word, or metaphor. When one woman recited the poem that follows and was answered by another woman, people pointed this out to me as an example of sister songs.

> Take the night an hour at a time
> sleepless until they draw near . . .

> khudhī l-lēl bis-sā'āt
> smūr nīn yā 'ēn yagrabaw . . .

> Your sleeplessness in deepest night
> is torment but you can bear it . . .

> smūrik 'agāb il-lēl
> 'adhāb ghēr yā 'ēn tiḥimlī . . .

Shearing songs are sometimes called sister songs, too. The annual spring sheep shearing was once a festive occasion undertaken by young men from the camps, not the specialists who now travel from camp to camp. The *ghinnāwa*s of shearing (*jallāma*) differ from others in their allusions and symbolism, all tied to imagery of sheep and goats. For example, in shearing songs the words for the beloved, *'alam* and *'azīz* (see chapter 5), are replaced by the words for sheep (*ghanam*) and goats (*mi'īz*), which rhyme with them. Other words are replaced by ones that refer to such things as wolves, milk, and butter, which have much to do with sheepherding. The true meaning of the poems usually has to do with love, and their sister songs, which must be known to fully appreciate these shearing songs, are explicit.

Perhaps even more common than responding with sister songs to the *ghinnāwa*s of others is answering with a retort or repartee. This is the form romantic dialogues usually take, and I heard a number of such poetic conversations about various subjects. The following exchange from a love story illustrates the nature of "response" (*radd*) poems. The man said:

> Shame on you, oh beloved
> to forget me when you are eternally in my thoughts . . .
>
> 'ēb yā 'azīz 'alēk
> tinsīnī wnā dōm fākrik . . .

to which the girl might answer in any of various ways, including:

> Fear not for your love
> it's pressed between my eyelash and eye . . .
>
> ghalāk lā tkhāf 'alēh
> madsūs bēn 'ēnī whidbha . . .

or its sister song:

Fear not for your love
you'll find it even after two long years away . . .

ghalāk lā tkhāf 'alēh
ḥattā in ghibit 'āmēn tajidu . . .

Qādirbūh (1977), Al-Ghannāy (1968), and Jibrīl (1973) all give numerous examples of love stories, told as true stories, that involve such exchanges. Most intriguing is the fact that the first two authors relate stories in which some of the poems exchanged are nearly identical, although the stories themselves are not (Qādirbūh 1977, 132–33; Al-Ghannāy 1968, 8), suggesting that not only do individuals play with formulas in their spontaneous poetizing, but even in storytelling people vary the originals in standard ways and are not terribly concerned with reproducing the poems word for word.

Sister songs and response poems are the two culturally elaborated forms of poetic wordplay, but individuals sometimes spontaneously play with poems for humorous or serious effects. By substituting incongruous words, people can make statements, often ironic, about situations. In these cases, as with the shearing songs, the meaning depends on the prior familiarity of reciter and listener with the original. For example, one day a woman was teasing her husband's client's wife. A large sheep herd had been brought nearby to be fattened for market, and the young client, responsible for caring for them, was forced to spend his nights outdoors with the sheep, not at home with his wife. The woman sang:

Fdhūla is the verdure of the eye
evening he spends with me and sleeps out in the open . . .

Fdhūla rabī' l-'ēn
yamsā ma'āy wybāt fil-khalā . . .

Fdhūla is the affectionate diminutive of the man's name, suggesting that the singer was expressing the wife's sentiments in the poem. The wife responded to the teasing with mock anger, acting offended that she should be suspected of caring about her husband's absence at night and, by implication, sexuality, which threatened her image as modest. Yet what made the poem so humorous was that it called up a more serious poem that followed the same form:

> The heart, oh you far away
> in the evening is with me and sleeps where you are . . .

> il-galb yā bi'īd id-dār
> yamsā ma'āy wybāt 'indak . . .

Other poems depend for their effect and meaning on strange twists given familiar poems. In one case, by changing just one word an old woman fundamentally altered the meaning of a poem and highlighted a comment she wanted to make on a current situation. She sympathetically recited the following poem to her daughter-in-law, whose husband had just married another wife:

> Thirty ships of true love
> loaded with love's dues went off course . . .

> thlāthīn markab ṣōb
> wāsgāt gānūn khaṭaw . . .

As I later discovered, this poem was a transformation of the "correct" or more traditional one, which was most likely known to the other listeners:

> Thirty ships of true love
> loaded with love's dues and affection . . .

> thlāthīn markab ṣōb
> wāsgāt gānūn wghalā . . .

I translate *gānūn,* which literally means law, as "love's dues" because I think this better conveys the sense of the term in this poem. Informants glossed the term *gānūn* in this case as *wājbāt,* or duties. By changing just the last word from "affection" to "mistake" (which I translated as "off course" in keeping with the seafaring imagery of the poem), she poignantly highlighted the injustice of her daughter-in-law's situation. Instead of getting the affection due her after so many years of marriage, she had lost all.

THEMES

Although I would argue that typologies based on topics or key words tell us little, since the meaning of the poems derives primarily from their social contexts and uses, a look at common themes may give some sense of the arenas in which the *ghinnāwa,* as distinct from other genres of oral poetry, comes into play.

A limited number of rough categories based on central themes or metaphors emerge even from a quick scan of the corpus of poems I collected. Undue weight should not be given to this particular set, since it does not represent the fruits of systematic sampling but only of listening and recording poems that came up spontaneously or were volunteered. The categories might not be quite the same as those that would emerge from an analysis of other collections, although Jibrīl's (1973, 71) list of "poetic pillars" on which *ghinnāwa*s are built is close to mine. It is interesting to speculate about changes over time, however. For instance, Falls (1908) does not have a single poem about "despair" (*yās*), which I found to be one of the most elaborated themes, although some differences might also be attributed to gender, since most of the poems in my collection are women's, and I suspect he has few, if any, not recited by men.

Most of the four hundred and fifty poems I collected fall into a number of overlapping categories based on theme or key image, and many of the poems combine elements. Nearly all the poems have to do with powerful sentiments arising in interpersonal relationships. In many cases, it is clear that the reference is to love relationships between men and women; more often the poems are ambiguous in reference and are used to describe sentiments that arise in all sorts of close relationships, including those between kin, friends, mothers, and children.

With the exception of wedding *ghinnāwa*s, which express sentiments of happiness, pride, well-wishing, welcome, and family rivalry, poems expressing positive sentiments are not common. Among the most numerous and haunting are the poems about despair, usually the result of loss in love or inability to have the loved one. This sentiment is endowed with qualities of an independent entity whose character and devastating effects on the poet are explored in images as violent as the following:

> I built, when despair was away,
> castles it knocked down when it came . . .
>
> banēt fī ghiyāb il-yās
> gṣūr wēn mā jā hadhun . . .

Despair can also be described in images drawn from nature. In the following poem, the imagery is more consistent in Arabic than in English because the opening of a well is called an "eye."

> Blinded by the sandstorm of despair
> the wells of love were plugged . . .
>
> 'amāhum 'ajāj il-yās
> byār il-ghalā nīn in-'amun . . .

In the following poem, despair is vaguely anthropomorphized:

> I wonder, is despair
> a phantom or my companion for life . . .
>
> z'ama yā l-yās iz-zōl
> willā rafīg dīmā lkhāṭrī . . .

Sometimes intermingled with poems of despair are those about separations, moving away, long distances—experiences probably all too frequent in the lives of a nomadic people. The sentiments are those of the difficulty of parting, the longing for those far away, the sense of emptiness after loved ones have gone, and the misery of having no news. This theme may be overrepresented in my corpus, because people with whom I lived sang many to me as I prepared to depart for a break in the middle of fieldwork and later for my return home. They also sang for me, empathizing with the state they presumed I must be in, being so far from home and my own loved ones.

In *ghinnāwa*s, sadness, whatever its cause, is customarily conveyed through imagery of tears (*dmū‘*) and weeping (*bkā*), likened variously to cloudbursts, floods, rivulets, mirages, or described through its effects on the eyes, tangling eyelashes and causing blindness. A number of examples of this type were presented above.

Another set of poems of suffering draws on imagery of bodily ills. Withering of the body, wasting away, dizziness, headaches, and unspecified pain are some of the poetic symptoms of painful emotional experiences. Often it is not just a matter of illness, but of wounds of love, festering, healing, requiring medication, or incurable. Most of these images are familiar from the lyrics of Arab love poetry, from the pre-Islamic ode to the Andalusian *muwashshaḥ* (Compton 1976, 60), to parts of which the *ghinnāwa* has been likened (Jibrīl 1973, 114).

Helpless suffering and sadness are by no means the only sentiments that find expression in poems. There are defiant poems of anger and a sense of betrayal. People rebuke and insult others through poetry, although rarely to their faces. Much of the imagery in this type is drawn from tribal hearings where injustices can be brought up, grievances aired, claims settled, and appeals for rights made.

The Bedouins may conceive of the *‘agl* as based in the heart, but they think of it as also profoundly connected to thoughts and memories and, ultimately, to worries. Many poems warn of the dangers of excessive worry and thought. Thinking and remembering are often linked in poetry to assorted maladies, especially anxiety, insomnia, restlessness, and confusion. They even lead to premature aging, as the following poem suggests:

> You go grey in the prime of youth
> if your mind troubles you, dear one . . .
>
> tshīb winit fī masbāg
> il-'agl lū shākīk yā 'alam . . .

The last major category is that defined by philosophical or religious themes, including, but not restricted to, songs sung by the descendants of saintly lineages of Mrābṭīn at their festivals (*mūlid*s). To comfort themselves or others in adversity, individuals often recite poems that play on themes of God's power to change things or of the immutability of fate, destiny (*naṣīb*), what has been "written" (*maktūb*), and one's divinely decreed lot in life (*gism*). Misfortune is also attributed to luck (*bakht*), which is considered to be ultimately God-given. Patience (*ṣabr*), one of the great religious virtues, is enjoined as a response to difficult situations. These poems betray the importance of the Islamic faith in the lives of Awlad 'Ali.

NOTES

1. A more accurate spelling would be Awlād 'Alī, but I have followed the standard spelling used by ethnographers to designate this group.

2. I found it necessary to leave periodically for Cairo and Alexandria. I also took one long break when I returned to the United States for two months in the summer of 1979.

3. It became apparent to me long after I had been living with the family that my arrival had been the main impetus for their move to the new house. They had decided that the old house was too small to accommodate me comfortably. The new house, significantly larger and more elegant than the simple structure they had all lived in for years, had been built on the other side of the road from the core community to establish claim to the land on which it stood. Those who moved into the new house were quite lonely at first, and I felt responsible for having disrupted this family's life and for having separated the women from their companions. As time passed, however, the women felt that the loss of companions was amply compensated by the increase in status and comfort; they developed closer ties to a different set of households.

4. The actual ties binding those in a residential community are not so simple, as is apparent from the composition both of the community I lived in, which was not limited to those bound by agnation, and of the camp described by Peters (1965). See chap. 2, n.23.

5. In the cases of Paul Riesman (1977) and Vincent Crapanzano (1980b), the results of self-reflection and careful attention to the encounter between themselves and their informants are enlightening. The insight and understanding arise from the fact that neither investigator dwells excessively on himself. Manda Cesara's *Reflections of a Woman Anthropologist* (1982) is an example of what can happen when the balance shifts.

6. For a discussion of the conventions of ethnographic writing, see Crapanzano (1977) and Marcus and Cushman (1982).

7. A classic example of the consequences of an American woman's insensitivity to social communication patterns and standards of morality in Egypt can be found in Vivian Gornick's *In Search of Ali Mahmoud* (1973).

8. Mourning rituals are discussed in chapters 3 and 6.

9. Both Makhlouf (1979) for Yemen, and Rogers (1975) for southern France also note the advantages of women's social invisibility in the company of men for gaining access to information.

10. For elaboration of the notion that men were excluded from the women's world, see Abu-Lughod (1985a); for a vivid description of a sex-segregated community in Iraq, see Fernea (1965).

11. The *s* at the end is not part of the Arabic; I have added it to form the plural as in the English rather than using the Arabic plural. Smart (1967) transcribes the word as *ghannāwa*.

12. Not just in form but in function too, haiku and other forms of traditional Japanese poetry share much with the Bedouin *ghinnāwa*. Note, for example, the resemblance of the exchange of poetry as a mode of secret communication between lovers in Lady Murasaki Shikibu's eleventh-century novel, *The Tale of Genji,* to the Bedouins' exchange of poetry in courting, as described in chapters 5 and 8. Perhaps the major difference is that the *ghinnāwa* is an oral, not a written, form, so the calligraphy that is so important to the Japanese poetic tradition is irrelevant in this case.

13. Some German travelers and Orientalists had collected examples of Awlad 'Ali poetry in the late nineteenth and early twentieth centuries. Some of these collections are riddled with errors. In the 1960s, J. R. Smart made a study of Awlad 'Ali songs and poetry but published little of his work. Like the German scholars to whom he constantly refers, he is not an ethnographer and did not live with the Bedouins. He conducted his study in a few months, during which time he traveled extensively (Smart 1966, 203), and it is thus unlikely that he had much opportunity to hear the poems and songs in their normal performance contexts. In some cases, he seems uncertain about the occasions on which such genres of poems or songs are properly performed. There is also a small body of literature in Arabic on Libyan folk poetry that provided examples, exegeses, and typologies, but again, little contextual material. These sources will be discussed in chapter 5 and in the Appendix.

14. Sowayan (1985) seems to be an important exception. I regret that his book appeared after I completed my manuscript and that I was therefore unable to incorporate its arguments. For a sensible survey of the field of oral literature, see Finnegan (1977).

15. Here I use the term *discourse* in its narrow linguistic sense, as a

formalized type of communication (see, for example, Labov 1972). Otherwise I will use it in a broader sense, as explained in chap. 1, n.23 (below).

16. Neither study was available until I returned from the field.

17. See Asad (1973) for an intelligent discussion of anthropology and colonialism.

18. Caton (1984, 430) notes that Yemeni tribesmen think it manly to chant poetry and that for a man to sing poetry in public would be a disgrace. Women sing poetry. This distinction does not hold for Awlad 'Ali, although singing poetry is considered shameful and inappropriate in social contexts other than those of intimacy and weddings. See chapters 5 and 8.

19. Caton hints, in his discussion of chanting versus singing, that this valuation is true for the Yemenis. Qādirbūh (1977, 137–39) also cites in a footnote the disdain some Libyan Bedouin men had for certain poems he collected, which the men said were women's poems. The relationship between poetry and women and youths will be discussed in chapter 8. For an interesting theory about the Dinka's association of youths with songs, see Deng (1972, 1973).

20. Lancaster (1981, 68) notes Rwala Bedouin women's poetic talents but unfortunately does not analyze their poetry. Boesen's (1979/80) study of Pashtun women's plaintive poetry and T. B. Joseph's (1980) study of Moroccan Berber women's wedding poems are exceptions to the general dearth of research in this area.

21. The same can be said of Geertz's (1976) emphasis on agonistic communication and poetic exchanges in Morocco and Sowayan's (1985) focus on men's poetry and politics.

22. It is also possible that Awlad 'Ali place greater emphasis on personal than on heroic poetry, perhaps related to their lesser concern with political adventure under conditions of relative peace and a semisedentary existence based on a combination of pastoralism and agriculture. Meeker (1979, 193–208) suggests just these sorts of differences between the Cyrenaican Bedouin of North Africa (to whom Awlad 'Ali are kin) and the pure pastoral nomads of northern Arabia in the early part of this century. My hypothesis about the changing role of poetry (chapter 8) supports this interpretation.

23. My use of the term *discourse* to refer to the actions and words of everyday life as shaped by the dominant ideology of honor, although broader than the usage common in sociolinguistics, is consistent with the more current usage that follows Foucault (1972, 1980) and literary critics of various sorts. See p. 186 and chap. 6, n.2 for a more precise definition.

24. I use the term *ideology* broadly (see Bourdieu 1977) to refer to what many anthropologists might prefer to call culture. I do not mean the term in the Marxist sense of mystification. Rather, ideology is the stuff of definitions of the world, that which allows people to understand and act. Its relationship to social and political systems must be determined in each historical and ethnographic instance.

25. I do not discuss the concept of shame that usually tags along with honor because, as I will argue, modesty is the more important concept to pair with honor, being of the same order but applicable to women and the weak. See chapters 3 and 4 and chap. 3, n.10.

26. See chap. 3, n.2, for references to the literature on "honor and shame" in Mediterranean societies.

CHAPTER TWO

1. The Libyan Desert is one name for the vast desert dissected by the Egyptian-Libyan border. For the most part, I will refer to the Egyptian side by the term the Egyptians prefer: the Western Desert.

2. The word the Bedouins use is *nawāshif*. Classified among the dry foods are cereals, dates, and milk products. Vegetables are not considered dry. It would be interesting to explore their food classification system further.

3. Although I have used the word *spring* to refer to a season, the Bedouins do not use it that way. For them, *rabī'*, the word usually translated as "spring," is not a season but a state of pasture. When there has been sufficient rain in the months of October through January, shrubs and grasses thrive in the desert. When the desert is green, they say there is "spring"; in bad years when there is little rain, the desert is not green and there is no "spring."

4. These changes, of course, are happening to Bedouins throughout the Middle East. For other cases in Jordan, Syria, and Saudi Arabia, see Abu Jaber et al. (1978); Chatty (1976, 1978); Ibrahim and Cole (1978); Katakura (1977); and Lancaster (1981).

5. Citing a report by those who landed with Napoleon in 1798 that the Awlad 'Ali were at war with the Hanādī tribes of Egypt near Alexandria, Obermeyer (1968, 7) takes issue with Evans-Pritchard's (1949) statement that the expulsion took place well after 1800. Most likely, certain segments were forced out of their territories in Cyrenaica through a process of "slow, continuous, and cumulative minor alterations which are

even today part of the Bedouin system of territorial relations" (Behnke 1980, 162). The rest were driven out in a major battle at the end of the century in which the Ḥarābīs enlisted the aid of the Turks and Arabs from Tripoli (Evans-Pritchard 1949, 50; Johnson 1973, 32; Obermeyer 1968, 5).

6. The Mrābṭīn claim no genealogical connection to the Saʿādi tribes, nor any overarching genealogical links among themselves, although they are divided into groups called tribes. There are two categories of Mrābiṭ tribes: those who formerly paid tribute and those who were pious or holy figures (*mrābṭīn bil-brka*). Generally considered socially and politically inferior, those who have not lost their reputations for piety are held in awe. They used to serve as peacemakers and continue to be healers. There is much confusion about their origins and their social position, suggesting a need for a careful study of these groups. Peters (1977) discusses the relationship between the free tribes and clients of various sorts, but his research concerns an earlier period in Libya, where the situation seems to have been different. Behnke (1980) considers a more recent period. I consider some aspects of the relationship between the Mrābṭīn and the Saʿādi in chapter 3, but there is much about their social and religious roles that I could not include here.

7. Total population estimates range between 120,000 and 170,000. These are no doubt inaccurate, since census figures for the Western Desert do not distinguish Bedouins from non-Bedouin migrants to the urban centers, Marsa Matruh in particular, and the reclaimed lands of Mariut. Moreover, figures specifically for Awlad ʿAli do not indicate whether Mrābiṭ tribes are included.

8. Sources for the history of Awlad ʿAli during this period include Baer (1969); von Dumreicher (1931); Falls (1913); Murray (1935); Obermeyer (1968); and Stein (1981).

9. In 1940 the British told the nomads to flee the Italian advance in the west and prepared refugee camps near ʿAmriyya in the east for them. Axis armies marched into the Western Desert in 1940, and by 1942 Rommel had advanced his headquarters to Marsa Matruh. After the German defeat at Alamein in November 1942, the Bedouins returned to their lands to find much lost (Obermeyer 1968, 16–17; Bujra 1973, 144). The older Bedouins I spoke with remembered the war, the crowded camps, the bombing, the parachutes, the airplanes. As we passed the cemetery in Alamein, one man recalled terrible scenes after the battles, when the bodies of young men lay everywhere. One legacy of the war is the widespread presence of land mines, which explode, maiming and killing Bedouins every year.

10. For a discussion of the projects undertaken and their effects, see Bujra (1973) and Stein (1981).

11. Christians—Europeans or Coptic Egyptians—do not constitute a vivid reference point for self-definition, since contact with them has been minimal; for most Bedouins, they are little more than a rumor. In any case, their religion, however little understood, is distasteful, and the European languages are alien. Christians are on the edge of the Bedouin world, necessary to the distinction between Muslim and non-Muslim, a radical but almost abstract distinction that is seldom relevant in daily life.

12. The Bedouin dialect is closely related to the Eastern Libyan dialect and differs from Cairene and rural Egyptian in vocabulary, pronunciation, and some elements of grammar. Awlad 'Ali clothing is also distinct from that of either urban Egyptians, whom the Bedouins describe as *lābis affandī* (dressed as effendis or bureaucrats, i.e., in Western clothing and bareheaded); peasants (*flūḥ*); or Upper Egyptians (*ṣa'ayda*), who wear the flowing bell-sleeved gallabiya and some form of cap or turban, in the case of men, and the smocked, unbelted robes and either a black headcovering or kerchief, in the case of women. Bedouin dress differs in important ways and is thought of as more "modest" and thus in keeping with the decorum prescribed by the Koran. The Bedouins set great store by headcoverings, and their robes cover their arms to the wrists and their bodies to the ankles. Men wear on their heads a *ṣmāda,* a headcover similar to that worn in other parts of the Arab world but here often wrapped as a turban; this has replaced the traditional small red felt cap called a *shanna.* Under the robe, called a *thōb,* with shirt-tailored collar, sleeves, and breastpocket, all men wear *sirwāl,* baggy pants that narrow at the ankles. For formal or ceremonial occasions, no man is caught without his *jard,* a large white woolen blanket knotted at the shoulder and draped like a toga. Women wear their hair in numerous small braids tied together in a topknot, which they cover with a black cloth called a *ṭarḥa* that is wrapped and knotted in such a way that it covers the hair, neck, and shoulders and can be pulled over the face to serve as a veil. Their dresses are long-sleeved, ankle-length, and gathered at the waist. No woman ever goes without a belt, the most common type being a woven red wool sash about sixteen inches wide and six feet long, which is folded in half along the width, wrapped several times around the waist, and fastened with a large safety pin. Women tuck into its folds an amazing array of small objects—bars of soap, lemons, jewelry, money, spices—whatever they wish to carry with them or keep away from others. The symbolism of the black veil and the red belt, the keys to femininity, is explored in chapter 4.

13. Since there is an official adoption procedure for both individuals

and whole tribal segments, the genealogical links are certainly not always those of blood. This fact accounts for some of the heterogeneity of racial types among Awlad 'Ali. It is clear from the complaints of the British that this adoption procedure was widespread during the first decades of the twentieth century. For example, Jennings-Bramly, the Frontiers District Officer stationed in Burg el-Arab, proposed in a memorandum (London 1926) to the Minister of War dated September 24, 1926, to increase the number of men who could be conscripted by weeding out the peasants who had gotten themselves adopted, often through payments, into Bedouin tribes to avoid conscription. He condemned this "nefarious practice" and estimated that up to one-third of every tribe consisted of adopted peasants (certainly an exaggeration). Apropos of this topic, I was told a story, perhaps apocryphal, about Jennings-Bramly's attempt to rectify the situation. As I was being tested on the names of parts of the Bedouin tent, my teacher laughed and claimed that I was going to be a true Bedouin. He related that "Bramlī," a clever man familiar with the Bedouins, had set up a test to separate the true Bedouins from the peasants claiming tribal status: he called each man into a traditional Bedouin tent and asked him to name the parts. My teacher commented with pride that only a true Bedouin could answer correctly.

14. The meaning of the complex concept of *ḥasham* will be explored in chapters 3 and 4.

15. For a masterful elucidation of the issues involved in analyzing this model of political relations based on the segmenting genealogy, see Meeker (1979, 11–15, 183–208).

16. The role of the segmentary model as an ideology in social life has again been brought into question in the recent work of Moroccanists such as Eickelman (1976) and H. Geertz (1979), who argue that the segmentary model obscures the realities of Moroccan economic, political, and social life and propose, respectively, a diffuse concept of "closeness" (*qarāba*) and a notion of shifting dyadic ties as more accurate models. I tend to agree with Combs-Schilling (1981) that this may be a false dichotomy and that both models are ideologies available to individuals and operative on different organizational levels.

17. If Awlad 'Ali use the kinship idiom to describe or organize political relations, it is because this idiom provides such a powerful metaphor for close social relationships and carries so much in the way of sentiment. It makes political alliance and order seem "natural" rather than arbitrary. Yet Peters reminds us not to assume that this model of social relationships espoused by the Bedouins is an accurate reflection of the way their society operates. He argues that the segmentary lineage system must be

seen as a folk model "which enables them, without making absurd demands on their credulity, to understand their field of social relationships, and to give particular relationships their *raison d'être*." But, he continues, "it would be a serious error to mistake such a folk model for sociological analysis" (1967, 270). I would add that when the kinship idiom is taken out of the domestic or interpersonal realm and given ideological primacy in such culturally valued arenas as political and economic relations, its legitimacy is enhanced and its original power to inform interpersonal relations reinforced.

18. The term Awlad 'Ali use for bonds of agnation or common patrilineal descent is translated as "group feeling" by Rosenthal in his translation of Ibn Khaldun's *Muqaddimah* (1958) and as "social solidarity" by Issawi (1950). It is intriguing that Ibn Khaldun's fourteenth-century comments on "group feeling" strike many of the same notes my discussion of Awlad 'Ali conceptions of social life does. For example, in a section entitled, "Group feeling results only from (blood) relationship or something corresponding to it," he argues that well-known ties of blood, combined with close contact, lead to the greatest solidarity because kinship creates natural bonds of affection and identification (for example, leading a person to experience shame when a relative is treated unjustly). The closer the kinship tie, the greater the group feeling. Ibn Khaldun adds, however, that the same sentiment can develop regarding neighbors, allies, or clients when close contact characteristic of kin ties develops among them (1958, 264–65).

19. Bourdieu describes the same process of "reading" kinship relations in different ways, depending on the social context. He notes that the official (male) reading recognizes links through men, whereas the heretical (female) reading notes the more direct links through women (1977, 41–42).

20. McCabe (1983) presents data from a Lebanese village suggesting that there is less sexual desire in marriages between close cousins, specifically paternal parallel cousins who have had intimate childhood association. She argues that this corroborates A. Wolf's (1970) argument (based on the analysis of marital histories for two types of marriage in Taiwan, adopted daughter-in-law marriage and marriage between strangers) that childhood familiarity suppresses sexual desire.

21. Early explanations of the Arab preference for patrilateral parallel-cousin marriage argued that it served to keep property within the family, a position criticized by Murphy and Kasdan (1959) and Keyser (1974). The literature on preferential patrilateral parallel-cousin marriage is vast.

Bourdieu (1977, 32–33) presents a summary of the positions, and Eickelman (1981, 129–31) presents not only a summary but also a relatively complete list of articles on the subject.

22. The emotional pain caused by this relationship's impermanence is evident in a proverb my host recited regarding my stay with his family: Forbid living together because of parting (*harram l-'ishra bisabab il-fargā*).

23. Bourdieu recognizes the bonds forged by common property in his comment that "the genealogical relationship is never strong enough on its own to provide a complete determination of the relationship between the individuals which it unites, and it has such predictive value only when it goes with the shared interests, produced by the common possession of a material and symbolic patrimony, which entails collective vulnerability as well as collective property" (1977, 39–40). As Peters (1965, 1967) demonstrates for the Cyrenaican camel-herding Bedouins, however, residence, common property, and kinship are not coterminous in practice. The Awlad 'Ali are no exception. At the core of the camp I lived in were the adult sons of two men and their various dependents, including wives, children, and clients. Attached to them were poor families belonging to two branches of the same tribe. Peters provides good comparative material from late-1940s Cyrenaica, where he estimates that the level of coresidence of agnates was as high as 80 percent (1967, 262), but he shows in his analysis of the links between members of a particular camp that a number of other types of bonds, especially those through women, determined the actual composition of the camp (Peters 1965). Beware of the discrepancy between Peters's diagram and his verbal description—corrections can be found in J. Davis (1977, 234–35).

24. For a fascinating comparison of the Turkish and Arab constructions of joint honor, see Meeker (1976). See also chapter 4 for an elucidation of the logic of honor killing.

25. A man or a group of brothers arrive with a sheep or a goat, unless they are too poor or distantly related, in which case they substitute ten Egyptian pounds for the sheep. For women, the money gift is essential. In addition, women may bring other sorts of things, such as candy, biscuits, or fruit beverage syrup (*sharbāt*), but these are optional. At circumcision celebrations, women give money to the mother and grandmother of the circumcised boy; at homecomings, they give to the wife or wives and mother of the man, and occasionally to his sisters. At weddings, the mother, grandmother, and sisters of the groom, and the bride the following morning, all receive *nugūt* (wedding gifts) from the groom's side of the family. The bride's relatives give money to her

mother, grandmother, and perhaps an older sister. These money-gifts are generally quite small (ranging from ten piasters to an Egyptian pound, or approximately U.S. $1.45), but given women's minimal access to cash, even such small amounts can be difficult to come by. The amount given at any event depends on previous exchanges, just as the men's sacrifices are returns on previous gifts. (The only exception to this rule is the gift presented to the new bride by her husband's kinswomen and neighbors, which intitiates her into the exchange network of the community and marks the establishment of relationships between her and these women. Her first outing will be to return the gift at the appropriate occasion.) Women take note of the amount they receive and try to increase it slightly when they return the gift. For practical reasons the escalation usually stops at one pound. Men generally do not increase the number of sheep, but they may try to improve on the original gift by giving a higher-quality animal.

26. The concern about sexuality is the main impediment to girls' education. Until five years ago, the only schools in the vicinity of my community were in the towns, about four kilometers away. No one would consider sending a daughter that far. When a local school was established within sight of the community, some of the girls attended, but most soon dropped out, complaining of the discipline and corporal punishment by urban teachers. They faced no opposition at home for their truancy. Only one girl in the community had continued to the fifth grade. Her father permitted her to continue over the objections of his brothers, who thought she was getting too old to be mixing freely with boys from outside the community. Women with daughters in school complained that school made the girls disobedient and lazy. The mutterings of the one girl who was in the fifth grade did hint that education may indeed have important effects on Bedouin lifestyles. In frustration at the heavy burden of chores she was expected to carry, she sometimes cursed "this rotten Bedouin way of life" and expressed a wish to marry someone educated and live a genteel life in a town or city. At the same time, however, she was fiercely prejudiced against foreigners, Christians, and even Egyptians and staunchly defended Bedouin values, particularly those of modesty and proper comportment. In the urban areas, where schools are more accessible and education more respected, attendance by girls is higher. Still, according to Stein's figures on the status of education in the Western Desert in 1976, girls constituted no more than 29 percent of the school population (1981, 39). It is not clear whether his figures include the non-Bedouin populations, especially in Marsa Matruh; if so, the figures would be inflated.

CHAPTER THREE

1. The persuasive functions of analogy and metaphor have been explored by Burke (1969) for propaganda and by Tambiah (1968) for magic.

2. The literature is quite extensive. The volume edited by Peristiany (1966) remains a classic. References to some major theoretical positions are to be found at the end of chapter 4. J. Davis (1977) and Gilmore (1982) summarize some of the diverse materials in their recent reviews of Mediterranean anthropology. On the Christian side, Campbell (1964) provides some of the most thorough ethnographic description, while Blok (1981), Brandes (1980), Gilmore (1980), Herzfeld (1980), and Pitt-Rivers (1977) each make significant arguments. Meeker (1976) and Bourdieu (1966, 1977, 1979) present the most stimulating discussions of honor on the Islamic side of the Mediterranean. For a more traditional approach to the honor code in the Islamic world, see Abou-Zeid (1966) on Awlad 'Ali. Most recently, Wikan (1984) has made the important point, which my own analysis certainly confirms, that the concepts of honor and shame should not be seen as binary opposites. Herzfeld (1984) warns of the dangers of reifying the Mediterranean culture area.

3. This matter of the moral worth of Mrābṭin is complicated by the facts that certain tribes are associated with religious piety and that most saints and healers come from Mrābiṭ tribes. Awlad 'Ali associate Islam with morality, sometimes even noting how their ideas about honor are against Islamic principles.

4. I have chosen to refer to the recent version of this paper, which first appeared in Peristiany (1966), because the translation is better and the author has made a few modifications.

5. Lancaster (1981, 67) describes the same stoicism in the face of physical pain as characteristic of the Rwala Bedouins.

6. There do seem to be differences in usage for the word *'agl*, however. Eickelman interprets it for the Moroccan case in terms similar to those I use for the Bedouin instance. He argues that "reason is the capacity to discern realistically existing, if ephemeral, patterns of dominance and deference in the social order and to act appropriately" (1976, 141). He notes that "reason grows in a person with his ability to perceive the social order and to discipline himself to act effectively within it" (1976, 138). Anderson (1982, 405) argues that for the Pakhtun in Afghanistan, *'agl* is "sense" or "reason" and "is manifest as cooperation and composure and is acquired by learning in society, most especially in public worship." A

systematic comparison of local beliefs about *'agl* in societies across the Muslim world would make an interesting study.

7. According to Dwyer (1978), Moroccans hold similar beliefs. She notes, "Given the uncertain origins of male responsibility, it is not surprising that most men are said to reach their quota of *'aqel* (intelligence, responsibility) relatively late in life. Its flowering is believed to begin at the earliest at age forty, when a context that is maximally conducive to the development of responsibility tends to take place" (1978, 101).

8. See Mohsen (1975, 39) for more on the *'awāgil* of the Western Desert.

9. For a good description of the procedure followed by women who "throw themselves" on the mercy of a religious figure or tribal leader in order to obtain a divorce, see Mohsen (1967, 163–65). Such a woman is said to be *rāmya*.

10. For instance, it is tempting to translate *ḥasham* simply as "shame," thereby placing our discussion of the Awlad 'Ali squarely in the middle of a familiar anthropological discourse on honor and shame. As will become clear, however, to do so would necessitate interpreting the concept as the opposite of what it is. For Awlad 'Ali, modesty and shame are forms of honor. Dishonor is another matter.

11. S. Davis (1983, 156–57) notes similar uses of the term in Morocco.

12. For elaboration of these ideas on sexual segregation, see Abu-Lughod (1985a).

CHAPTER FOUR

1. Females are disadvantaged in this social system, being prevented from gaining that which facilitates achieving honor. Although they retain their own tribal identities and affect their children's status to some degree (Abou-Zeid 1966, 257), they cannot pass on their affiliation. They thus become somewhat peripheral to the patriline and consequently to the genealogy through which some aspects of honor pass. Economically, women are nearly always dependents. They can own property and are entitled, according to Islamic law, to half as much of an inheritance as each brother. In practice, women rarely own productive property, either land or animals, and they give up their share of the inheritance to their brothers on the assumption that they can return to their natal homes if need be and that their brothers will always be willing to care for them and support them. For more on the relationship between brothers and

sisters, and the continued dependence of women on their brothers in married life, see Granqvist (1935) and Rosenfeld (1960). Economic dependence limits women's capacity for independent action as well as their ability to act generously and to gain dependents. In other words, it limits their *gadr,* or power, a key element of honor.

2. It is interesting to compare this version with a short folktale collected by Dwyer (1978, 45) in Taroudannt, Morocco, which describes how Adam and Eve looked for each other every day, but when Adam finally found Eve, she denied having ever looked for him.

3. I never saw this ritual performed, but I found references to the same type of doll in Granqvist (1935, 84). She notes that in their wedding ceremonies, the Palestinian villagers used an effigy of the bride that was also called a *zirrāfa.* R. Joseph (n.d.) mentions the use of a similar doll in the "bride of the rain" ceremony in a Moroccan Berber community.

4. Fischer (1978, 204–5) compares Muslim, Zoroastrian, and Jewish beliefs and rituals surrounding menstrual pollution.

5. For more on the meaning of right and left among the Arabs, see Chelhod (1973).

6. The fact that women are rarely identified socially as mothers may also be related to the compromising nature of a social state that is so closely tied to sexuality and sexual acts. Unlike most other parts of the Arab world, the use of teknonyms is rare in the Western Desert; it is not a sign of respect to call anyone "mother of so-and-so." Bedouins use first names in address, first name often followed by either father's first name or tribal affiliation in reference. Even more telling, when people related to a young person through his mother (i.e., maternal relatives) wish to refer to him or identify him by these maternal links, they call him "So-and-so, his father is so-and-so" in which the mother's name is substituted for the father's. Paternity is a social fact given emphasis in a social system organized around notions of patrilineal descent; it is not closely associated with the natural acts of sex.

7. The sartorial marking of the transition is far more dramatic among the more traditional Rashāyda Bedouins of eastern Sudan (see Young 1982).

8. I leave this word untranslated because I was never able to find out what it meant. The word usually means "scissors" and, given that the woman later commands it to cut out the tongues of Muḥammad būh Sulṭān's slaves, it seems plausible to consider it some kind of animated scissors.

9. This static equation recalls Ortner's (1974) seminal argument that the universal devaluation of females is based on their closer symbolic

association with "nature," as opposed to "culture," with which men are more closely associated. My argument, like many of those sparked by her piece (see, for example, MacCormack and Strathern 1982), suggests that the simple version of the formulation does not hold up cross-culturally.

10. Granqvist (1935, 161) notes a similar belief among Palestinian villagers of the late 1920s. She reports that villagers believe an unclean woman can harm others, quoting an informant as saying, "If anyone has bad eyes, and an unclean woman looks steadily at this person, it is not good."

11. A patrilateral parallel cousin may assert his claim to marry his first cousin, even if she or her father wishes a different match. It often happens that marriages arranged by the father or brother are prevented at the last minute by the intervention of the father's brother's son. Some cases, like one that occurred while I was in the field, are quite dramatic: all the wedding guests were gathered, when suddenly the bride's cousin, accompanied by his weapon-brandishing supporters, rode up in a truck and carried away the bride. Cousins usually assert their rights long before the wedding and are rewarded either by a monetary compensation or by the breakdown of negotiations between the kin of the prospective bride and groom.

12. My argument follows the same lines as Bourdieu's. He too views parallel-cousin marriage as a "refusal to recognize the relationship of affinity for what it is" and writes that this type of marriage is "most perfectly consistent with the mythico-ritual representation of the sexual division of labor" (1977, 44).

13. However, the opposite message—that she should forget her family—is sometimes carried in ditties sung to the bride, as in the following wedding song:

> If he puts his arms around you
> forget your father who raised you
>
> kān 'alēk liffā bīdēh
> būk illī rabbāk insēh

14. For more on divorce among Awlad 'Ali, see chap. 7, n.4.

15. To simplify matters for the reader, I have treated the word as if it were English, adding an *s* to imply that it is a verb in the third person, rather than using the third person singular feminine Arabic form.

16. The same dynamic can be seen at work in matters of vengeance. A homicide is an attack on the victim's group that reveals it to be vulnerable: in the eyes of others, the group is weak. Avenging the homicide is a way of reasserting power and strength, of wiping out the shame of having been attacked. The matter of honor killings is complex. Although

killing the woman is, in principle, the only way of restoring honor, in fact it seems to happen very rarely. I heard only two stories about brothers who had killed their sisters for sexual misconduct, and both incidents had happened fifteen years earlier. I heard many more hushed stories of women whose families moved to distant areas or who were married off to distant strangers who had not heard of the scandals or to cousins willing to cover up for the family. The ideals of honor and the realities of family closeness and humanity are in conflict in such cases. See also Antoun (1968).

17. Three anthropologists besides Anderson have written insightful pieces on veiling that recognize its multiple uses and meanings in Muslim contexts (Abu-Zahra 1978; Fischer 1978; Makhlouf 1979). They recognize the association of veiling with morality but do not reduce it to simplistic terms of sexuality or Islam. In general, the work on veiling done by anthropologists specializing in India and Pakistan is more sophisticated, perhaps because they are forced to look at social factors rather than religious ones, since only some of the groups that veil in India are Muslim. Jeffery (1979) shows how veiling and seclusion, because of their association with Islam and piety, are used to enhance the authenticity of Muslim shrine-keepers in Delhi. Sharma (1978, 1980) describes a situation in North India, where Hindu women veil but for a different set of people— only affines—from those for whom Bedouin women veil. She makes an interesting argument about the functions of this type of veiling in a situation of village exogamy. There are also a number of excellent articles gathered in a collection edited by Papanek and Minault (1982).

18. This precedence of generation over age was obvious in an interchange I overheard between a man and his maternal uncle's young wife. She veiled for him, and he told her not to, arguing, "How can I call you *khālti* [my maternal aunt] if you veil for me?"

19. This behavior may account for Kennett's (1925) misleading observation that Awlad 'Ali women did not veil. I noticed that when a foreigner (British) came to visit our household when the men were absent, the women not only greeted him unveiled but also stared unabashedly.

20. Even circumstance can be used to justify an unorthodox approach to veiling. When I noticed that one young woman (about twenty-one years old, with one infant) who had married her paternal and maternal first cousin and thus lived in the same camp in which she had grown up did not veil for her father, I asked why. Several adolescent cousins of hers explained that when she had first married, she had begun to veil for her father. But then once when she fell ill, her father offered to drive her to the doctor in town, and riding in the back of his pickup truck, the wind

blew her veil from her face. She then decided not to bother veiling for him anymore.

CHAPTER FIVE

1. See the Appendix for background on the exchange of poems and linguistic play in Awlad 'Ali *ghinnāwa* composition and performance.

2. For a wonderfully thorough and sensitive discussion of the many ways texts derive their meanings from a variety of contexts, see Becker (1979).

3. Most of the types of poems and songs, including the *barrāka, majrūda,* and *ṭagg* recorded by Smart (1966, 1967), Hartmann (1899), and Falls (1908, 1913), are no longer sung regularly, at least by the Bedouins with whom I lived. Cassette tapes of these songs, many smuggled from Libya, are extremely popular, and I became familiar with them through this medium. Most of these genres were associated with wedding festivities, which have changed dramatically in the past few decades. In the past, weddings and circumcision ceremonies were celebrated for up to seven days. The main activities were singing and poetry recitations, mostly by the young men. The major wedding performance was the *ṣaff,* in which the young men formed a semicircle and clapped and sang while a young woman, usually a sister or cousin of the groom, danced completely veiled in their midst (for descriptions, see 'Abd al-Ḥamīd 1969, 136–40; Mason 1975; and Qādirbūh 1977, 114). The men's songs extolled the dancer's beauty, detailing parts of her face and body. Most of the women over thirty remembered this well. At the weddings I attended, however, women only danced for each other. Another genre of wedding song was associated with fetching the bride, who in the past was carried in a litter (*karmūd*) on camelback but now is brought in a car or truck. Smart (1966, 207) correctly presumes that the genre called the *barrāka,* an example of which he translates and analyzes, is associated with this part of wedding rituals.

4. In his general discussion of Bedouin poetry, Smart confirms that "the distinction between the two [poems and songs] has never been clearly set out" (1966, 202) and admits that his rough classification of the Western Desert's corpus of poetry into two categories—poems (spoken or recited) and songs (chanted or sung)—is based on nothing more than how he personally heard the pieces performed (1967, 246).

5. Smart (1967, 247–48) also notes that the term *gōl* "seems to be the only general term for poetry and song."

6. Smart (1966, 206) says the *ghinnāwa* was the only type of song he heard women sing. Women actually sing another type of long song and occasionally recite bits of spoken poetry, which they recognize as men's poetry. At one wedding, a group of old women huddled in a circle and began to perform some of the songs traditionally sung by men at weddings. Under normal circumstances they would not have performed these songs (not even the men do anymore), but they did so to assert their Bedouin identity in reaction to the Egyptian peasant songs the bride's retinue was singing. Although *ghinnāwa*s can be sung by men or women, Qādirbūh (1977, 137–39) makes reference in a footnote to an intriguing incident when some men reacted disdainfully to a number of poems he had collected, which they referred to as women's poems. Qādirbūh deplores their sexism. I did not detect this distinction in the community where I did my fieldwork, and I heard women repeat poems they heard men recite. This issue of gender and poetry requires further investigation.

7. The *ghinnāwa* sounds totally different when recited and when sung, making the determination of meter both difficult and in some ways irrelevant. Smart (1967, 250) argues that Awlad 'Ali songs, including the *ghinnāwa,* are composed on an accentual basis, and Al-Ghannāy (1968) classifies the meter as *al-muqtaḍḥib.* From the examples presented in this book, it will be clear that there is quite a bit of variety in the rhythm of the poems, but, even so, this rhythm is only relevant to the poetry when recited; when sung, the sense of meter is completely lost.

8. People with especially good voices tend to repeat the words more often, since this gives them a chance to play with the melody and to stretch out the song. Qādirbūh's (1977, 122) suggestion that the difference in length depends on whether songs are sung in the city, where they are easy to hear, or in the desert, where people must project their voices and repeat words in order to be heard at great distances, seems highly conjectural. Ron Jenkins (personal communication) has suggested the more intriguing but unverifiable possibility that the form of singing enacts the halting revelation and holding back of sentiment that the poems themselves represent in Bedouin social life.

9. For a critical examination of the utility of the concept of formula, see Finnegan (1976).

10. Qādirbūh (1977) estimates that these songs make up 60 percent of eastern Libyan oral literature, although this figure seems quite arbitrary.

Al-Ghannāy (1968, 7) says they are the most loved, something I can confirm for Awlad 'Ali.

11. I translate the term variously, depending on the poem. When the meaning depends specifically on the imagery of eyes, I translate it literally; at other times, I translate it as "self."

12. I was interested to see that Falls (1908) translates *khāṭr* as the German *Gemüt,* a word with no real English equivalent that is usually translated poorly as "soul" (Steven Caton, personal communication).

13. *'Azīz* is a standard Arabic term meaning, among other things, scarce, dear, or beloved. The origin of *'alam* is ambiguous. The most likely derivation is the word meaning something prominent or highly visible by virtue of being at an elevated point. By extension, when applied to people, it means someone exalted or important, i.e., a loved one. There may be some truth to Qādirbūh's (1977, 125) hypothesis that the use of the word for this genre stems from the idea that poetry expresses prominent, even the highest, social values of Bedouin society. This possibility will be considered in the final chapter.

14. The competitive aspect of poetic composition was central to the institution of the *mijlās,* in which young men congregated at the tent of a talented unmarried woman to exchange poems with her. It is said that the reward of the young man whose poem best answered hers was the right to marry her. Although the Bedouins with whom I lived had heard of this institution, described in Jibrīl (1973, 66), none reported witnessing it. I suspect that if it ever existed, it was in the distant past. Of the other occasions for singing *ghinnāwa*s that seem to have disappeared, only sheep shearings (discussed in the Appendix) were mentioned to me. Qādirbūh (1977, 108) mentions grain threshings, and tattooing.

15. In the less distant past, and more recently further west than I did my research, the exchange of *ghinnāwa*s at weddings was common. According to informants, the young men forming the semicircle in front of the camp not only sang or chanted the longer types of poetry, primarily to the dancer (*ḥajjāla*), but also individually directed *ghinnāwa*s to girls or women of whom they were enamored. The women and girls, all gathered in a tent nearby, could hear all that the men sang, and individual women responded with songs.

16. For a sophisticated analysis of the relationship between weddings and circumcisions and the concern with sexuality in Moroccan circumcision rituals, see Crapanzano (1980a).

17. To give the flavor of the genre of wedding *ghinnāwa*s, I will present a few examples, which the reader can compare with the more common *ghinnāwa*s unassociated with wedding ceremonies. At one wedding, on the

way to pick up a bride from her father's house, the groom's father's brother's daughter sang numerous songs, including the following:

> We're used to the house of the high
> we won't descend to the low . . .
>
> mwālfīn dār l-'ilū
> niḥnā fil-luwṭā mā ninizlū . . .

By this she complimented her own family as high in status and morality and implied a compliment to the bride's family, which must have been of equal status, since it was considered suitable for providing a marriage partner. In another song, she expressed her pride in her cousin by likening him to a falcon bringing home his prey (the bride). I was unable to identify the type of bird called *trushūn*, so I have translated it as sparrow because people explained that it was a very small bird. It may, however, be an owl. The important point is that it is a lowly bird, opposed to the great falcon.

> A falcon, not a sparrow
> he lifted his hood and brought his prey . . .
>
> ṭēr ḥurr mō trushūn
> jallā kmāmtu jāb ṣēdu . . .

The bride's kinswomen sing to her on the night before the wedding and as they accompany her to her husband's house. Many of their songs, like the following, express sentiments of sadness at her departure:

> The house and the neighbors suffered
> over her departure, eye of the gazelle . . .
>
> shkā l-bēt wij-jīrān
> 'alē mashīthā 'ēn l-arilī . . .

Their sense of loss suggests the worth of the girl they are giving away. In the following *ghinnāwa*, the bride's kin indicate their lack of interest in the bride-price, implying that the groom's family is the one that has gained:

> Loser is the one with the money
> winners are those who took the loved one . . .
>
> khasrān ṣāḥb il-mālāt
> wkāsib illī wākhdhu l-'alam . . .

These samples by no means represent the full range of sentiments expressed in wedding poems. In addition to the formulaic and predictable expressions of joy or happiness, specific points are made pertaining to the individuals involved or to the particular marriage. For instance, at a man's second wedding his first wife's kin are likely to recall the virtues of their kinswoman and implore his consideration.

There is a genre of rhyming wedding ditty known as the *shittāwa* that accompanies the *ghinnāwa*s but is sung by unmarried girls rather than married women. Although I did not find the *shittāwa*s to be related to the *ghinnāwa*s with which they were interspersed during the wedding festivities, this may be due to the decay of a tradition. Qādirbūh (1977, 144), based on his Libyan material, describes the two as always linked thematically, while Jibrīl (1973, 92) adds that men sing both types of song as the dancer dances before them at weddings. Since women no longer dance in front of men at weddings but instead perform for each other, it is not surprising that they have taken over the songs that accompany the dancing and that they might have lost the original structure of the thematic links.

18. Because of differences in performance context and content, I classify these wedding and circumcision *ghinnāwa*s as separate from those recited in everyday life. Awlad 'Ali do not make a lexical distinction between them, but they can readily identify their appropriate contexts. Analysis of these wedding poems will be undertaken in another study.

19. Qādirbūh (1977, 116) likens *ghinnāwa*s to proverbs, yet it must be remembered that the Bedouins do have proverbs (*amthāl*), which they clearly distinguish from poems. He argues that, like proverbs, *ghinnāwa*s have stories that go with them but that they can still be understood even after the stories have been lost. I would argue that the similarity lies more in the social functions of the genres. Both genres are marked linguistic forms, set apart from ordinary conversation but included within it, that individuals use in social interactions to make statements about particular current situations through cultural formulas that refer to the past. Although proverbs are more didactic, and poems more expressive, both are rhetorical, intended to persuade or to define situations for action, as Burke (1969) would say. This point will be discussed in the final chapter. For an innovative analysis of the use of proverbs, see Seitel (1977).

CHAPTER SIX

1. Both Becker (1979) and Irvine (1979) argue that the issue of formality and informality is far more complex than Bloch's (1975) argument about the distinction between ritual and ordinary speech would indicate.

By noting that degree of formality and informality can vary both in speech acts and in the social contexts of these acts, both authors draw our attention to the possibility that everyday speech can be formal and formulaic, just as ritual speech or formal discourses might be informal and relatively spontaneous. This possibility is significant for this study because it means that the two discourses can be considered equivalent and thus can be compared.

2. In Foucault's terminology, these discourses might be termed more precisely "discursive formations," but he himself notes and defends the ambiguity of his use of the word *discourse* (1972, 80). In his later work (1980) he notes that discourses are linked to power. See also Said (1978).

3. This translation and some of the others that follow differ slightly from interpretations I have published elsewhere.

4. I have translated *al-ghanī* (literally, "the rich man") as "married man" because it is a common poetic euphemism for a polygynously married man (not surprising, as generally it is the wealthy men who take more than one wife).

5. In this poem I have translated the Arabic word *khāṭr* as "soul." See chapter 5 for an explanation and a warning not to apply any metaphysical connotations to it.

6. Evidence that this phrase is formulaic comes from the following report by Charles Doughty concerning the Arabian Bedouins (quoted in Meeker 1979, 28): "All [Bedouin] talk is one manner of Arabic, but every tribe has a use, *loghra,* and neighbours are ever chiders of their neighbours' tongue. 'The speech of them,' they will say, 'is somewhat "awry," *awaj.*' "

7. For a comprehensive discussion of feuding and vengeance, see Black-Michaud (1975) and Peters (1951, 1967).

8. These symptoms bear a close resemblance to the affective and behavioral responses reported in studies of bereavement. Marris (1974, 26) calls attention to the following symptoms: "physical distress and worse health; an inability to surrender the past—expressed for instance, by brooding over memories, sensing the presence of the dead, clinging to possessions, being unable to comprehend the loss, feelings of unreality; withdrawal into apathy." A cross-cultural survey of reactions to death based on data from the Human Relations Area Files (Rosenblatt et al. 1976, 6) notes that in addition to strong emotions, death provokes changes in patterns of behavior including "loss of appetite and consequent weight loss, disruption of work activities, loss of interest in things ordinarily interesting, a decrease in sociability, disrupted sleep and disturbing dreams."

CHAPTER SEVEN

1. Jibrīl (1973, 76), who defines the genre known in Libya as *ṣōb khalīl* by length, meter, and topic, says that all of these poems deal with some aspect of love or feelings toward the loved one. He goes too far, although there is little doubt that the *ghinnāwa* is more closely associated with love than with any other theme. Many of the examples presented in chapter 5 were love poems, and some of the cases described in chapter 6 concerned loss in love. Other examples can be found in the Appendix.

2. Because of relations of respect between father and son, sons would never sing in front of their fathers. The interest the Haj's father showed in his son's poems indicates his secret admiration for his son. Why he might have such an admiration will be explored in the final chapter.

3. It is customary to take the bride on a formal visit (called the *zawra*) to her family's house fifteen days after the wedding and to bring along some sheep for sacrifice and also perhaps tea, sugar, and flour. In this case, the groom's family had already taken her to see her brother and mother, with whom she had lived before her marriage. Then they had paid a visit to her uncles, prominent men with whom this family wished to be associated. They paid her father a special visit because he lived separate from her mother, whom he had divorced years earlier, and her brothers. (The father was last on the list because he lived furthest away.) In most cases, only one *zawra* would have sufficed, but the groom's family took advantage of the complicated residence pattern (ideally, the girl's father and uncles would have all been in one camp) to display their generosity.

4. Divorce is a complicated matter among the Awlad 'Ali. According to Islamic law, a man can repudiate his wife by pronouncing the formula "I divorce you" three times consecutively. This, for the Bedouins, constitutes a "final" divorce, or what I have called an official divorce. The Bedouins also usually require that the husband write this formula on a piece of paper for the divorce to be recognized. After this type of divorce a husband cannot take his wife back without remarrying her formally, which he cannot do unless she marries and divorces someone else in the interim; he must also pay bride-wealth again. There are, however, nonfinal divorces, which are much more common. If the husband only says the formula once, he may take his wife back if she agrees. Many of the couples in my community had at one time been estranged in this way. In some cases, the wife returned to her family for periods ranging from two days to nine months; in other cases, she remained in

the camp. Usually the husband had to give her a gift of some jewelry or money when he decided to take her back.

CHAPTER EIGHT

1. This modesty about *ghinnāwa*s even applies to wedding songs, as I discovered during a bridal procession when the wife of the man driving the car we rode in confessed her embarrassment about singing in front of her husband. This was the first time she had done so, even though they had been married nearly twenty years.

2. Turner (1976, 1008–9) argues that the difference between values and norms "is principally in the eye of the beholder. . . . The object (value) and the rule (norm) are two constructions the individual can place on the same phenomenon. Which construction is foremost in his experience makes important differences in his relationship to social structure." He goes on to argue that different conceptions of the self—in his model, self-as-impulse and self-as-institution—correspond to different experiences of these phenomena.

3. The use of a formulaic medium to express sentiments that threaten self-image may serve the individuals reciting poems as a psychological distancing mechanism, just as the identification with the experiences of others implied by the use of well-known poems to express sentiments may be psychologically reassuring in times of crisis.

4. For this reason I find Boesen's (1979/80, 238) analysis of a genre of Pashtun women's love songs (called *landai*) a bit weak. She argues that women's infidelities and the love songs that glorify them are "the individual's personal revolt against a system which denies her the right of disposing of her own body and choosing her own fate." Yet she also notes that "the 'revolt' of women does not challenge the Pashtun social code of honour as such." It seems to me that she has not considered the possibility that the messages of the love songs are somehow also part of the code, or at least culturally accepted, which indeed they must be if they are a well-known genre.

5. For a seminal discussion of the performative or illocutionary function of language, see Austin (1975).

6. Burke (1969, 50) notes this dual definition of rhetoric as that which changes attitude and/or action: "Thus the notion of persuasion to *attitude* would permit the application of rhetorical terms to purely *poetic* structures; the study of lyrical devices might be classed under the head of

rhetoric, when these devices are considered for their power to induce or communicate states of mind to readers, even though the kinds of assent evoked have no overt, practical outcome."

7. In many cases, the person to whom the poem is addressed may indeed eventually hear it from someone else, but in most cases I suspect this does not happen. To follow the path of particular *ghinnāwa*s through the community would make a fascinating study. For an interesting discussion of the possible functions of communications to absent addressees, such as magic spells, greeting cards, and love songs, see Rosenberg (n.d.).

8. These stories are part of a genre that differs from two other types of folktale both in its tragic aspect and in its incorporation of *ghinnāwa*s. Although I collected only a few, I know there were many more.

9. I am grateful to Robert A. LeVine for drawing my attention to this point.

10. This, of course, is Geertz's felicitous phrase (1973b, 123).

11. The issue of the relationship between art and individual experience is complex and well worth exploring. Some anthropologists who have written recently on this issue are Friedrich (1979), with regard to poetic language in particular, and Geertz (1976).

12. See Rappaport (1971) for an intriguing argument about the relationship between ritual and the sanctity of messages.

BIBLIOGRAPHY

'Abd al-Ḥamīd, 'Awāṭif. 1969. "Al-usra al-badawiyya al-mutawaṭṭina fī marsa maṭrūḥ" (The sedentarized Bedouin family in Marsa Matruh). Master's thesis, Alexandria University, Egypt.

Abou-Zeid, Ahmed M. 1959. "The Sedentarization of Nomads in the Western Desert of Egypt." *UNESCO International Social Science Journal* 11:550–58.

———. 1966. "Honour and Shame Among the Bedouins of Egypt." In *Honour and Shame,* ed. J. G. Peristiany, 243–59. Chicago: University of Chicago Press.

———. 1979. "New Towns and Rural Development in Egypt." *Africa* 49:283–90.

Abu Jaber, Kamel, Fawzi Gharaibeh, Saleh Khasawneh, and Allan Hill. 1978. *The Bedouins of Jordan: A People in Transition.* Amman, Jordan: Royal Scientific Society Press.

Abu Jaber, Kamel, and Fawzi Gharaibeh. 1981. "Bedouin Settlement: Organizational, Legal, and Administrative Structure in Jordan." In *The Future of Pastoral Peoples,* ed. John Galaty, Dan Aronson, Philip Carl Salzman, and Amy Chouinard, 294–301. Ottawa: International Development Research Center.

Abu-Lughod, Lila. 1985a. "A Community of Secrets: The Separate World of Bedouin Women." *Signs: Journal of Women in Culture and Society* 10:637–57.

———. 1985b. "Honor and the Sentiments of Loss in a Bedouin Society." *American Ethnologist* 12:245–61.

Abu-Zahra, Nadia. 1970. "On the Modesty of Women in Arab Muslim Villages: A Reply." *American Anthropologist* 72:1079–87.

———. 1974. "Material Power, Honour, Friendship, and the Etiquette of Visiting." *Anthropological Quarterly* 47:120–38.

———. 1978. "Baraka, Material Power, Honour, and Women in Tunisia." *Revue d'histoire maghrébine* 10–11:5–24.

Altorki, Soraya. 1973. "Religion and Social Organization of Elite Families in Urban Saudi Arabia." Ph.D. diss., University of California, Berkeley.

Anderson, Jon. 1982. "Social Structure and the Veil: Comportment and the Composition of Interaction in Afghanistan." *Anthropos* 77:397–420.

Antoun, Richard T. 1968. "On the Modesty of Women in Arab Muslim Villages: A Study in the Accommodation of Traditions." *American Anthropologist* 70:671–97.

Asad, Talal, ed. 1973. *Anthropology and the Colonial Encounter.* New York: Ithaca Press.

Austin, John L. 1975. *How to Do Things with Words.* Cambridge, Mass.: Harvard University Press.

Awad, Mohamed. 1954. "The Assimilation of Nomads in Egypt." *Geographical Review* 44:240–52.

Baer, Gabriel. 1969. *Studies in the Social History of Modern Egypt.* Chicago: University of Chicago Press.

Bateson, Gregory. 1972. "Style, Grace, and Information in Primitive Art." In *Steps to an Ecology of Mind,* 128–52. New York: Ballantine Books.

Beauvoir, Simone de. 1953. *The Second Sex.* New York: Knopf.

Beck, Lois, and Nikki Keddie, eds. 1978. *Women in the Muslim World.* Cambridge, Mass.: Harvard University Press.

Becker, A. L. 1979. "Text-Building, Epistemology, and Aesthetics in Javanese Shadow Theatre." In *The Imagination of Reality,* ed. A. L. Becker and Aram Yengoyan, 211–43. Norwood, N.J.: Ablex.

Behnke, Roy. 1980. *The Herders of Cyrenaica.* Urbana: University of Illinois Press.

Black-Michaud, J. 1975. *Cohesive Force: Feud in the Mediterranean and the Middle East.* New York: St. Martin's Press.

Bloch, Maurice. 1975. "Introduction." In *Political Language and Oratory in Traditional Society,* ed. Maurice Bloch, 1–28. London: Academic Press.

Blok, Anton. 1981. "Rams and Billy-Goats: A Key to the Mediterranean Code of Honour." *Man,* n.s. 16:427–40.

Boesen, Inger W. 1979/80. "Women, Honour and Love: Some Aspects of the Pashtun Woman's Life in Eastern Afghanistan." *Folk* 21–22: 229–39.

Bourdieu, Pierre. 1966. "The Sentiment of Honour in Kabyle Society." In *Honour and Shame,* ed. J. G. Peristiany, 191–241. Chicago: University of Chicago Press.

———. 1977. *Outline of a Theory of Practice.* Cambridge: Cambridge University Press.

———. 1979. "The Sense of Honour." Chap. 2 in *Algeria 1960.* Cambridge: Cambridge University Press.

Brandes, Stanley. 1980. *Metaphors of Masculinity: Sex and Status in Andalusian Folklore.* Philadelphia: University of Pennsylvania Press.

Briggs, Jean. 1970. *Never in Anger.* Cambridge, Mass.: Harvard University Press.

Bujra, Abdalla S. 1967. *A Preliminary Analysis of the Bedouin Community in Marsa Matruh Town.* Cairo: Social Research Center at the American University in Cairo.

———. 1973. "The Social Implications of Developmental Policies: A Case Study from Egypt." In *The Desert and the Sown: Nomads in the Wider Society,* ed. by Cynthia Nelson, 143–57. Berkeley: Institute of International Studies, University of California.

Burke, Kenneth. 1969. *A Rhetoric of Motives.* Berkeley and Los Angeles: University of California Press.

Campbell, John K. 1964. *Honour, Family, and Patronage.* Oxford: Oxford University Press.

Caton, Steven. 1984. "Tribal Poetry as Political Rhetoric from Khawlān Aṭ-Ṭiyāl, Yemen Arab Republic." Ph.D. diss., University of Chicago.

Cesara, Manda [pseud.]. 1982. *Reflections of a Woman Anthropologist: No Hiding Place.* London: Academic Press.

Chatty, Dawn. 1976. "From Camel to Truck: A Study of Pastoral Adaptation." *Folk* 18:114–28.

———. 1978. "Changing Sex Roles in a Bedouin Society in Syria and Lebanon." In *Women in the Muslim World,* ed. Lois Beck and Nikki Keddie, 399–415. Cambridge, Mass.: Harvard University Press.

Chelhod, Joseph. 1973. "A Contribution to the Problem of the Pre-eminence of the Right, Based on Arabic Evidence." In *Right and Left: Essays on Dual Symbolic Classification,* ed. Rodney Needham, 239–62. Chicago: University of Chicago Press.

Cole, Donald P. 1975. *Nomads of the Nomads: The Al-Murrah Bedouin of the Empty Quarter.* Chicago: Aldine.

Collier, Jane. 1974. "Women in Politics." In *Women, Culture, and Society,* ed. Michelle Z. Rosaldo and Louise Lamphere, 89–96. Stanford, Calif.: Stanford University Press.

Comaroff, John, ed. 1980. *The Meaning of Marriage Payments.* London: Academic Press.

Combs-Schilling, M. Elaine. 1981. "The Segmentary Model Versus Dyadic Ties: The False Dichotomy." *MERA Forum* 5(3):15–18.

Compton, Linda Fish. 1976. *Andalusian Lyrical Poetry and Old Spanish Love Songs: The Muwashshah and Its Kharja.* New York: New York University Press.

Crapanzano, Vincent. 1977. "On the Writing of Ethnography." *Dialectical Anthropology* 2:69–73.

———. 1980a. *Rite of Return: Circumcision in Morocco.* Vol. 9, *The Psychoanalytic Study of Society,* ed. Warner Muensterberger and L. Bryce Boyer. New York: Library of Psychological Anthropology.

———. 1980b. *Tuhami: Portrait of a Moroccan.* Chicago: University of Chicago Press.

Cromer, Earl of. 1908. *Modern Egypt.* Vol. 2. New York: Macmillan.

Davis, John. 1977. *People of the Mediterranean: An Essay in Comparative Social Anthropology.* London: Routledge & Kegan Paul.

Davis, Susan. 1983. *Patience and Power: Women's Lives in a Moroccan Village.* Cambridge, Mass.: Schenkman.

Deng, Francis Mading. 1972. *The Dinka of the Sudan.* New York: Holt, Rinehart & Winston.

———. 1973. *The Dinka and Their Songs.* Oxford: Clarendon Press.

Denich, Bette S. 1974. "Sex and Power in the Balkans." In *Woman, Culture, and Society,* ed. Michelle Z. Rosaldo and Louise Lamphere, 243–62. Stanford, Calif.: Stanford University Press.

Dumreicher, Andre von. 1931. *Trackers and Smugglers in the Deserts of Egypt.* London: Methuen.

Durrell, Lawrence. 1957. *Justine.* New York: Dutton.

Dwyer, Daisy H. 1978. *Images and Self-Images: Male and Female in Morocco.* New York: Columbia University Press.

Eickelman, Dale. 1976. *Moroccan Islam: Tradition and Society in a Pilgrimage Center.* Austin: University of Texas Press.

———. 1981. *The Middle East: An Anthropological Approach.* Englewood Cliffs, N.J.: Prentice-Hall.

Elshtain, Jean. 1981. *Public Man, Private Woman: Women in Social and Political Thought.* Princeton, N.J.: Princeton University Press.

Evans-Pritchard, E. E. 1949. *The Sanusi of Cyrenaica.* Oxford: Clarendon Press.

Falls, J. C. Ewald. 1908. *Beduinen-Lieder der libyschen Wüste.* Cairo: Verlag F. Diemer, Finck & Baylaender.

———. 1913. *Three Years in the Libyan Desert: Travels, Discoveries, and Excavations of the Menas Expedition.* London: T. Fisher Unwin.

Fernea, Elizabeth. 1965. *Guests of the Sheik: An Ethnography of an Iraqi Village*. Garden City, N.Y.: Doubleday.

Finnegan, Ruth. 1976. "What Is Oral Literature Anyway? Comments in the Light of Some African and Other Comparative Material." In *Oral Literature and the Formula*, ed. Benjamin A. Stolz and Richard S. Shannon III, 127–66. Ann Arbor: Center for the Coordination of Ancient and Modern Studies, University of Michigan.

———. 1977. *Oral Poetry: Its Nature, Significance, and Social Context*. Cambridge: Cambridge University Press.

Fischer, Michael M. J. 1978. "On Changing the Concept and Position of Persian Women." In *Women in the Muslim World*, ed. Lois Beck and Nikki Keddie, 189–215. Cambridge, Mass.: Harvard University Press.

Foucault, Michel. 1972. *The Archaeology of Knowledge*. New York: Pantheon Books.

———. 1980. *Power/Knowledge*. Ed. Colin Gordon. New York: Pantheon Books.

Friedrich, Paul. 1977. "Sanity and the Myth of Honor." *Ethos* 5:281–305.

———. 1979. "Poetic Language and the Imagination." Chap. 13 in *Language, Context, and the Imagination*. Stanford, Calif.: Stanford University Press.

Galaty, John, Dan Aronson, Philip Carl Salzman, and Amy Chouinard, eds. 1981. *The Future of Pastoral People. Proceedings of a Conference Held in Nairobi, Kenya, 4–8 August 1980*. Ottawa: International Development Research Center.

Geertz, Clifford. 1973a. "Person, Time, and Conduct in Bali." Chap. 14 in *The Interpretation of Cultures*. New York: Basic Books.

———. 1973b. "Religion as a Cultural System." Chap. 4 in *The Interpretation of Cultures*. New York: Basic Books.

———. 1976. "Art as a Cultural System." *Modern Language Notes* 91:1473–99.

Geertz, Clifford, Hildred Geertz, and Lawrence Rosen. 1979. *Meaning and Order in Moroccan Society*. Cambridge: Cambridge University Press.

Geertz, Hildred. 1979. "The Meanings of Family Ties." In *Meaning and Order in Moroccan Society*, by Clifford Geertz, Hildred Geertz, and Lawrence Rosen, 315–91. Cambridge: Cambridge University Press.

Gellner, Ernest, and John Waterbury, eds. 1977. *Patrons and Clients in Mediterranean Societies*. London: Duckworth.

Al-Ghannāy, 'Abd Rabbuhu. 1968. *Dirāsāt fil-adab al-shaʿbī* (Studies of popular culture). Benghazi, Libya: Maktabat al-andalus.

Gilmore, David. 1980. *The People of the Plain: Class and Community in Lower Andalusia.* New York: Columbia University Press.

———. 1982. "Anthropology of the Mediterranean Area." *Annual Review of Anthropology* 11:175–205.

Goffman, Erving. 1959. *The Presentation of Self in Everyday Life.* New York: Anchor Doubleday.

———. 1971. *Relations in Public.* New York: Basic Books.

Goody, Jack. 1976. *Production and Reproduction.* Cambridge: Cambridge University Press.

Gornick, Vivian. 1973. *In Search of Ali Mahmoud: An American Woman in Egypt.* New York: Saturday Review Press.

Granqvist, Hilma. 1931/35. *Marriage Conditions in a Palestinian Village.* Vols. 1 and 2. Helsinki: Sodorstrom.

Hartmann, Martin. 1899. *Lieder der libyschen Wüste.* Abh.f.d. Kunde des Morgenlandes 11,3. Leipzig: Brockhaus.

Herzfeld, Michael. 1980. "Honour and Shame: Problems in the Comparative Analysis of Moral Systems." *Man,* n.s. 15:339–51.

———. 1984. "The Horns of the Mediterraneanist Dilemma." *American Ethnologist* 11: 439–54.

Huntington, Richard, and Peter Metcalf. 1979. *Celebrations of Death: The Anthropology of Mortuary Ritual.* Cambridge: Cambridge University Press.

Ibn Khaldun. 1958. *The "Muqaddimah": An Introduction to History.* Vol. 1. Trans. Franz Rosenthal. London: Routledge & Kegan Paul.

Ibrahim, Saad E., and Donald P. Cole. 1978. *Saudi Arabian Bedouin.* Cairo Papers in Social Science, Vol. 1, no. 5. Cairo: American University in Cairo.

Irvine, Judith. 1979. "Formality and Informality in Communicative Events." *American Anthropologist* 81:773–90.

Issawi, Charles. 1950. *An Arab Philosophy of History: Selections from the Prolegomena of Ibn Khaldun of Tunis (1332–1406).* London: John Murray.

Jeffery, Patricia. 1979. *Frogs in a Well: Indian Women in Purdah.* London: Zed Press.

Jibril, Salāḥ al-Dīn Muḥammad. 1973. *Tajrīdat ḥabīb maʿ kitāb khalīl wa qaṣāʾid ghazaliyya* (The battles of Habib with the Book of Khalil and poems of courtship). Benghazi, Libya: Maktab qurīna lil-nashr wal-tawzīʿ.

Johnson, Douglas L. 1973. *Jabal al-Akhdar, Cyrenaica: An Historical Geography of Settlement and Livelihood.* University of Chicago Department of Geography, Research Paper no. 148. Chicago: University of Chicago.

Joseph, Roger. N.d. "The Semiotics of Reciprocity: A Moroccan Interpretation." Unpublished manuscript.

Joseph, Terri Brint. 1980. "Poetry as a Strategy of Power: The Case of Riffian Berber Women." *Signs: Journal of Women in Culture and Society* 5:418–34.

Katakura, Motoko. 1977. *Bedouin Village: A Study of a Saudi Arabian People in Transition*. Tokyo: University of Tokyo Press.

Kennett, Austin. 1925. *Bedouin Justice*. Cambridge: Cambridge University Press.

Keyser, James. 1974. "The Middle Eastern Case: Is There a Marriage Rule?" *Ethnology* 13:293–309.

Labov, William. 1972. "Rules for Ritual Insults." Chap. 8 in *Language in the Inner City*. Philadelphia: University of Pennsylvania Press.

Lancaster, William. 1981. *The Rwala Bedouin Today*. Cambridge: Cambridge University Press.

Leach, Edmund, ed. 1967. *The Structural Study of Myth and Totemism*. London: Tavistock.

Lévi-Strauss, Claude. 1967. "The Story of Asdiwal." In *The Structural Study of Myth and Totemism*, ed. Edmund Leach, 1–47. London: Tavistock.

LeVine, Robert A. 1982a. "Gusii Funerals: Meanings of Life and Death in an African Community." *Ethos* 10:26–65.

———. 1982b. *Culture, Behavior, and Personality*. 2d ed. New York: Aldine.

Lichtenstadter, Ilse. 1976. *Introduction to Classical Arabic Literature*. New York: Schocken Books.

London. Public Record Office. 1926. Lt. W. Jennings-Bramly to Minister of War. FO 141/514.

Lord, Albert B. 1971. *The Singer of Tales*. New York: Atheneum.

Lutz, Catherine. 1982. "The Domain of Emotion Words on Ifaluk." *American Ethnologist* 9:113–28.

McCabe, Justine. 1983. "FBD Marriage: Further Support for the Westermarck Hypothesis of the Incest Taboo?" *American Anthropologist* 85:50–69.

MacCormack, Carol P., and Marilyn Strathern, eds. 1980. *Nature, Culture, and Gender*. Cambridge: Cambridge University Press.

Makhlouf, Carla. 1979. *Changing Veils: Women and Modernisation in North Yemen*. London: Croom Helm.

Marcus, George, and Dick Cushman. 1982. "Ethnographies as Texts." *Annual Review of Anthropology* 11:25–69.

Marris, Peter. 1974. *Loss and Change*. New York: Pantheon Books.

Mason, John P. 1975. "Sex and Symbol in the Treatment of Women: The Wedding Rite in a Libyan Oasis Community." *American Ethnologist* 2:649–61.

Maṭar, 'Abd al-'Azīz. 1966. "Khaṣā'is al-lahja al-badawiyya fī iqlīm sāḥil maryūṭ" (Peculiarities of the Bedouin dialect in the region of coastal Mariut). *Majallat majma' al-lugha al-'arabiyya* 20:99–105.

Maybury-Lewis, David. 1967. *Akwe-Shavante Society*. Oxford: Clarendon Press.

Meeker, Michael. 1976. "Meaning and Society in the Near East: Examples from the Black Sea Turks and the Levantine Arabs." *International Journal of Middle East Studies* 7:243–70, 383–422.

———. 1979. *Literature and Violence in North Arabia*. Cambridge: Cambridge University Press.

Mernissi, Fatima. 1975. *Beyond the Veil: Male-Female Dynamics in a Modern Muslim Society*. Cambridge, Mass.: Schenkman.

Mills, Margaret. 1978. "Oral Narrative in Afghanistan: The Individual in Transition." Ph.D. diss., Harvard University.

Mohsen, Safia Kassem. 1967. "Legal Status of Women Among the Awlad 'Ali." *Anthropological Quarterly* 40:153–66.

———. 1975. *Conflict and Law Among Awlad 'Ali of the Western Desert*. Cairo: National Center for Social and Criminological Research.

Murasaki, Shikibu. 1976. *The Tale of Genji*. Trans. Edward G. Seidensticker. New York: Knopf.

Murphy, Robert, and Leonard Kasdan. 1959. "The Structure of Parallel Cousin Marriage." *American Anthropologist* 61:17–29.

Murray, George W. 1935. *Sons of Ishmael: A Study of the Egyptian Bedouin*. London: Routledge.

Musil, Alois. 1928. *The Manners and Customs of the Rwala Bedouins*. New York: American Geographical Society.

Needham, Rodney, ed. 1973. *Right and Left: Essays on Dual Symbolic Classification*. Chicago: University of Chicago Press.

Nelson, Cynthia, ed. 1973. *The Desert and the Sown: Nomads in the Wider Society*. Berkeley: Institute of International Studies, University of California.

Nimkoff, Meyer F. 1965. *Comparative Family Systems*. Boston: Houghton Mifflin.

Obermeyer, Gerald J. 1968. "Structure and Authority in a Bedouin Tribe: The 'Aishaibat of the Western Desert of Egypt." Ph.D. diss., Indiana University.

Ortner, Sherry. 1974. "Is Female to Male as Nature Is to Culture?" In

Woman, Culture, and Society, ed. Michelle Z. Rosaldo and Louise Lamphere, 67–87. Stanford, Calif.: Stanford University Press.

———. 1976. "The Virgin and the State." *Michigan Discussions in Anthropology* 2:1–16.

Paige, Karen Eriksen. 1983. "Adolescence, Maturation, and Psychosocial Ritual." NIMH Final Report, Grant # RO1 MH 31516.

Papanek, Hanna, and Gail Minault, eds. 1982. *Separate Worlds: Studies of Purdah in South Asia.* Columbia, Mo.: South Asia Books.

Peristiany, Jean G., ed. 1966. *Honour and Shame: The Values of Mediterranean Society.* Chicago: University of Chicago Press.

Peters, Emrys L. 1951. "The Sociology of the Bedouin of Cyrenaica." Diss., Lincoln College, Oxford.

———. 1960. "The Proliferation of Segments in the Lineage of the Bedouin of Cyrenaica." *Journal of the Royal Anthropological Institute of Great Britain* 90:29–53.

———. 1965. "Aspects of the Family Among the Bedouin of Cyrenaica." In *Comparative Family Systems,* ed. M. F. Nimkoff, 121–46. Boston: Houghton Mifflin.

———. 1967. "Some Structural Aspects of the Feud Among the Camel-Herding Bedouin of Cyrenaica." *Africa* 37:261–82.

———. 1977. "Patronage in Cyrenaica." In *Patrons and Clients in Mediterranean Societies,* ed. Ernest Gellner and John Waterbury, 275–90. London: Duckworth.

———. 1978. "The Status of Women in Four Middle East Communities." In *Women in the Muslim World,* ed. Lois Beck and Nikki Keddie, 311–50. Cambridge, Mass.: Harvard University Press.

———. 1980. "Aspects of Bedouin Bridewealth Among Camel Herders in Cyrenaica." In *The Meaning of Marriage Payments,* ed. John L. Comaroff, 125–60. London: Academic Press.

Pitt-Rivers, J. A. 1977. *The Fate of Shechem, or the Politics of Sex: Essays in the Anthropology of the Mediterranean.* Cambridge: Cambridge University Press.

Qādirbūh, 'Abd al-Salām Ibrāhīm. 1977. *Ughniyāt min bilādi: Dirāsa fil-ughniya al-sha'biyya* (Songs from my country: A study of folk songs). Benghazi, Libya: Al-shirka al-'āmma lil-nashr wal-tawzī' wal-i'lān.

Rabinow, Paul. 1977. *Reflections on Fieldwork in Morocco.* Berkeley and Los Angeles: University of California Press.

Rappaport, Roy. 1971. "Ritual, Sanctity, and Cybernetics." *American Anthropologist* 73:59–76.

Riesman, Paul. 1971. "Defying Official Morality: The Example of

Man's Quest for Woman Among the Fulani." *Cahiers d'études afri-caines* 11:602–13.

————. 1977. *Freedom in Fulani Social Life: An Introspective Ethnography.* Chicago: University of Chicago Press.

————. 1983. "On the Irrelevance of Child Rearing Practices for the Formation of Personality." *Culture, Medicine, and Psychiatry* 7:103–29.

Rogers, Susan Carol. 1975. "Female Forms of Power and the Myth of Male Dominance: A Model of Female/Male Interaction in a Peasant Society." *American Ethnologist* 2:727–56.

Rosaldo, Michelle Z. 1980. *Knowledge and Passion.* Cambridge: Cambridge University Press.

————. 1983. "The Shame of Headhunters and the Autonomy of Self." *Ethos* 11:135–51.

————. 1984. "Toward an Anthropology of Self and Feeling." In *Culture Theory*, ed. Richard Shweder and Robert A. LeVine, 137–57. Cambridge: Cambridge University Press.

Rosaldo, Michelle Z., and Louise Lamphere, eds. 1974. *Woman, Culture, and Society.* Stanford, Calif.: Stanford University Press.

Rosenberg, Daniel V. N.d. "Magical Language and the Language of Magic." Unpublished manuscript.

Rosenblatt, Paul C., R. Patricia Walsh, and Douglas A. Jackson. 1976. *Grief and Mourning in Cross-Cultural Perspective.* New Haven, Conn.: HRAF Press.

Rosenfeld, Henry. 1960. "On Determinants of the Status of Arab Village Women." *Man* 60:66–70.

Said, Edward. 1978. *Orientalism.* New York: Pantheon.

Salzman, Philip Carl. 1978. "Does Complementary Opposition Exist?" *American Anthropologist* 80:53–70.

Sapir, J. David, and J. Christopher Crocker, eds. 1977. *The Social Use of Metaphor: Essays on the Anthropology of Rhetoric.* Philadelphia: University of Pennsylvania Press.

Schneider, Jane. 1971. "Of Vigilance and Virgins." *Ethnology* 10:1–24.

Seitel, Peter. 1977. "Saying Haya Sayings: Two Categories of Proverb Use." In *The Social Use of Metaphor*, ed. J. David Sapir and J. Christopher Crocker, 75–99. Philadelphia: University of Pennsylvania Press.

Sharma, Ursula. 1978. "Women and Their Affines: The Veil as a Symbol of Separation." *Man*, n.s. 13:218–33.

————. 1980. *Women, Work, and Property in North-West India.* London: Tavistock.

Shweder, Richard, and Robert A. LeVine, eds. 1984. *Culture Theory.* Cambridge: Cambridge University Press.

Simmel, Georg. 1950. *The Sociology of Georg Simmel*. Ed. Kurt H. Wolff. Glencoe, Ill.: Free Press.

Smart, J. R. 1966. "A Contribution to the Study of Form in Egyptian Bedouin Poetry." *Journal of Semitic Studies* 11:202–16.

————. 1967. "A Bedouin Song from the Egyptian Western Desert." *Journal of Semitic Studies* 12:245–67.

Sowayan, Saad Abdullah. 1985. *Nabaṭi Poetry: The Oral Poetry of Arabia*. Berkeley and Los Angeles: University of California Press.

Stein, Lothar. 1981. "Contradictions Arising from the Process of Sedentarization Among the Aulad Ali Bedouins of Egypt." In *Contemporary Nomadic and Pastoral Peoples: Asia and the North,* ed. Philip Carl Salzman, 33–44. Studies in Third World Societies, no. 18. Williamsburg, Va.: Department of Anthropology, College of William and Mary.

Tambiah, Stanley. 1968. "The Magical Power of Words." *Man,* n.s. 3:175–209.

Tillion, Germaine. 1966. *Le harem et les cousins*. Paris: Editions du Seuil.

Turner, Ralph. 1976. "The Real Self: From Institution to Impulse." *American Journal of Sociology* 81:989–1016.

United Nations Research Institute for Social Development. N.d. "The Role of Perceptions, Attitudes and Values of People in Relation to Environmental and Developmental Measures and Programmes: Land Reclamation in Mariout, Egypt, Research Design." Typescript.

Wikan, Unni. 1984. "Shame and Honour: A Contestable Pair." *Man,* n.s. 19:635–52.

Wolf, Arthur. 1970. "Childhood Association and Sexual Attraction: A Further Test of the Westermarck Hypothesis." *American Anthropologist* 72:503–15.

Wolf, Margery. 1972. *Women and the Family in Rural Taiwan*. Stanford, Calif.: Stanford University Press.

Yalman, Nur. 1963. "On the Purity of Women in the Castes of Ceylon and Malabar." *Journal of the Royal Anthropological Institute* 93:25–59.

Young, William C. 1982. "Decorated Bedouin Clothing: The Cultural Logic of Abstract Designs." Paper presented at the 16th Annual Meeting of the Middle East Studies Association, Philadelphia.

Zwettler, Michael. 1976. "Classical Arabic Poetry Between Folk and Oral Tradition." *Journal of Asian and Oriental Studies* 96:198–212.

————. 1978. *The Oral Tradition of Classical Arabic Poetry*. Columbus: Ohio State University Press.

INDEX

'Abd al-Ḥamīd, 'Awāṭif, 77, 288n.3
Abou-Zeid, Ahmed M., 42–43, 53, 123, 236, 283n.2, 284n.1
Abu Jaber, Kamel, 276n.4
Abu-Lughod, Lila, 274n.10, 284n.12
Abu-Zahra, Nadia, 16, 107, 287n.17
'Afārīt. See Spirits
Affect. See Sentiment
'Agl: defined, 90–91; and hasham, 108; and honor, 93, 97; in other Muslim societies, 90, 283n.6; as poetic term for self, 181–82; in poetry, 270; and political skills, 91; and sentiment, 243, 246; and sexuality, 93, 134, 148, 162; and women, 108–9, 124, 134, 157, 165. See also Honor
Agriculture: and cash economy, 41–43, 70; crops and, 3, 8, 40, 276; division of labor in, 72–73; and poetry, 275n.22; seasons and, 126
Altorki, Soraya, 16, 22
Anderson, Jon, 159, 283n.6
Anger, 54, 101, 193–94; in discourse of honor, 209; in response to death, 197, 200, 205–6
Antoun, Richard T., 107, 161, 166, 286n.16
'Aṣabiyya, 51, 280n.18. See also Kinship
Asad, Talal, 275n.17
Aṣl: defined, 41; and hasham, 110; and honor, 45, 87–88, 90, 103; moral qualities associated with, 45–46; and women, 105, 123. See also Honor; Kinship

Austin, John L., 295n.5
Autonomy. See Honor: and autonomy
Awlad 'Ali: collective identity, 40, 43–48, 71, 74, 76–78, 103, 278n.11, 278n.12, 289n.6; geographic location, 2, 7, 39–41; history, 41–43, 44, 71, 276n.5, 277n.6, 277n.8, 277n.9; population, 277n.7; relations with Egyptian state, 25, 42–43, 71–72, 77, 79, 251–52, 254; views of Christians, 13, 18, 43, 278n.11, 282n.26; views of non-Bedouin Egyptians, 23, 43, 44–51, 56, 104, 163, 282n.26; views of non-Egyptian Arabs, 14

Baer, Gabriel, 277n.8
Bateson, Gregory, 259
Beauvoir, Simone de, 30
Becker, A. L., 288n.2, 292n.1
Behnke, Roy, 50, 276n.5, 277n.6
Bkā. See Laments, ritualized mourning
Black-Michaud, J., 293n.7
Bloch, Maurice, 292n.1
Blok, Anton, 283n.2
Boesen, Inger W., 275n.20, 295n.4
Bourdieu, Pierre, 56, 89–90, 97, 166, 205, 236, 246, 255–56, 276n.24, 280n.19, 280n.21, 281n.23, 283n.2, 286n.12
Brandes, Stanley, 283n.2
Briggs, Jean, 17

Labov, William, 274n.15
Laments, ritualized mourning, 21, 25, 67, 69, 197–200, 207, 238, 250–51
Lamphere, Louise, 30
Lancaster, William, 79, 253, 275n.20, 276n.4, 283n.5
Language: Bedouin dialect, 278n.12; formal versus informal, 292n.1; formulaic, 239–40; official, 256; rhetoric, 295n.6. *See also* Discourse; Poetry
Lévi-Strauss, Claude, 29
LeVine, Robert A., 32, 206, 236, 296n.9
Libya: Awlad 'Ali ties to, 42; dialect in, 278n.12; labor migration to, 100; oral literature in, 289n.10; patron-client relations in, 277n.6; poetry in, 183, 274n.13. *See also* Cyrenaica
Lineage. *See* Kinship: agnation; Politics: segmentary lineage model of
Lord, Albert B., 261
Loss: as poetic theme, 26, 187, 189, 194–95, 246, 269, 290n.17; responses to, 205–7, 293n.8. *See also* Death
Love: and kinship bonds, 81; as poetic theme, 26, 34, 172, 182–84, 187, 193, 208–9, 217–18, 221, 226–28, 231–32, 240, 242, 246, 248, 250, 265–69, 294n.1; in relation to honor, 148, 208; stories, 174, 183, 209, 211, 248–50, 258, 262, 265; as threat to agnatic authority, 211. *See also* Sexuality
Lutz, Catherine, 34

McCabe, Justine, 280n.20
MacCormack, Carol P., 285n.9
Magic, 53, 113, 115, 190
Makhlouf, Carla, 274n.9, 287n.17
Marcus, George, 273n.6
Mariut, 1, 7, 12, 277n.7

Marriage: and affinal relations, 66; age at, 222; and agnation, 53, 55–56, 58–59, 77; arrangement of, 66, 77, 149, 158, 209–11, 215–21, 230, 290n.17; and bride-price, 77, 93, 96, 149, 188, 216, 290n.17; clothing as symbol of, 17, 134; and honeymoons, 230; husband-wife relations in, 46–47, 57–58, 81, 89, 94–96, 101–3, 105, 109, 154–57, 222–24, 229–30; and love matches, 149, 210–11; and patron-client relations, 64; as threat to agnatic group, 145–48; and virilocal residence, 123, 149–50. *See also* Marriage, patrilateral parallel-cousin; Marriage, polygynous; Sexuality; Weddings
Marriage, patrilateral parallel-cousin: disadvantages of, 57–58, 210; as fusion of maternal and paternal ties, 59–60; in love stories, 248–49; male cousin's rights to, 211, 286n.11; and mother-daughter bonds, 123; among other Arab peoples, 280n.20, 280n.21; as reinforcer of agnatic bonds, 6, 56–58, 145, 148. *See also* Kinship: agnation; Marriage; Marriage, polygynous
Marriage, polygynous: and divorce, 223; and lack of 'agl, 93; men's reasons for desiring, 190, 215; recent increase in, 228; relations among co-wives, 57, 155, 188, 220, 229; and wealth, 71, 92, 228, 293n.4; women's views of, 94–95, 149, 193, 199, 217, 228–31. *See also* Marriage; Marriage, patrilateral parallel-cousin
Marris, Peter, 206, 293n.8
Mason, John P., 288n.3
Matruh, 7, 44, 77, 163, 277n.9, 282n.26
Maybury-Lewis, David, 9